FoodSutra

A Memoir of the Foods of India

Shalabh Prasad

First published 2020

Copyright © Shalabh Kumar Prasad
Photography Copyrights as stated for each photo in Photo Copyrights at the end of the book.

The right of Shalabh Kumar Prasad to be identified as the Author of the Work has been asserted by him in accordance with the Copyright, Design and Patents Act 1988.

All rights reserved. No part of this publication may be reproduced, stored in a retrieval system, or transmitted, in any form or by any means without the prior written permission of the publisher, nor be otherwise circulated in any form of binding or cover other than that in which it is published and without a similar condition being imposed on the subsequent purchaser.

Published by Shalabh Kumar Prasad
Website: www.foodsutrabook.com

ISBN
Hardback: 978-1-8380651-0-2
Paperback: 978-1-8380651-1-9
eBook: 978-1-8380651-2-6

In memory of my mother

Premlata Prasad

*who inspired a love of food
which has given me a lifetime of pleasure*

Contents

Introduction		vii
1	Bengal: *Machher Jhol and much more*	1
2	Bihar: *My home food*	16
3	Punjab and Delhi: *Familiar stalwarts of North Indian food*	36
4	Mughlai: *From the kitchens of Emperors and Nawabs*	60
5	Uttar Pradesh: *More North Indian food including a deconstruction of Chaat*	85
6	Tamil Nadu: *Idli, Dosa, Sambar and beyond*	107
7	Kerala: *God's own food*	128
8	Karnataka: *More Dosa and many lesser known gems*	146
9	Andhra Pradesh & Telangana: *Where gunpowder is food*	160
10	Mumbai: *Food that inspires Bollywood masala films*	174
11	Goa: *Konkan and Portuguese simmered together*	193
12	Maharashtra: *Spices add life to variety of food*	205
13	Gujarat: *Snacks are also food*	219
14	Rajasthan: *Highest percentage of vegetarians and the best known dish is 'Red Meat'*	233
15	Best of the Rest: *Some well known, others not so much*	248
References		267
Photo Copyrights		269
Index of Dishes		273
About the Author		291

Introduction

About twenty years ago, when I first moved to the UK, I'd often be told by colleagues and friends here that they loved Indian food. On being asked what specifically they meant by 'Indian food', I'd get a list of dishes common in the Indian curry houses of the country. The dishes in these restaurants are mostly from the north of India, with a very small number of dishes from other parts of the country and some Indian-style dishes found only in the UK. I'd often find myself getting into long explanations about Indian food being more than what you find in the curry houses. This was the beginning of my pontificating about Indian food. As a self-proclaimed foodie, who was born in and has travelled widely in India, I started with a reasonably good base of knowledge. Whatever gaps there were, I've attempted to fill over the years. This was not particularly difficult, as it mostly required trying out foods from different parts of the country at every opportunity. As a foodie, how difficult can that be?

My research also led me to read up what I could on the foods of India. There are many books with recipes of dishes from various parts of India and hundreds of recipe websites. Finding recipes for Indian dishes is now quite easy. Many can even be replicated at home! The authors of such recipes are not looking to present each dish in the context of the country's food. So you end up knowing how to make a version of the dish but not necessarily whether it is authentic, when to eat it, what is usually eaten with it and indeed where you would find it if you were looking for it in India. This is not just relevant for non-Indians. Most Indians also have only a limited knowledge about foods from other parts of the country, apart from some famous dishes from a few states which are known all over the country. I realised that there isn't really a book that gives you a comprehensive overview of the foods of India. This is where the idea for this book came from, growing from what had up until then been sub-conscious research.

As I was researching the dishes, I found myself remembering occasions when I've eaten a dish and stories that are associated in my mind with a dish, a specific meal or a state's cuisine. I've described the dishes as a memoir, adding these memories and stories associated with the foods wherever it seemed right. Just a compendium of foods of India would be useful as a reference, but perhaps would be a difficult read. Hopefully, the description of the dishes interwoven with my personal experiences and other stories makes this book a little bit more interesting.

Foods of India – Just a little bit of history

The title of the book has the phrase 'Foods of India'. This is deliberate. There are many regional cuisines in India. There are some pan-Indian themes in the country's regional cuisines, such as the use of a variety of spices, frying as the preferred way of cooking, lots of dishes with a spicy gravy, etc. But these linkages are not sufficient to brand and group the various types of cuisines into one broad category. For convenience, I've described the foods of individual administrative states of India. These states have generally been created on the basis of linguistic and cultural identities. That means there is some consistency in the cuisine of each state.

It is tempting to try and connect current foods of India with ancient traditions. But it is a stretch. As much as it may seem that everything in India is ancient and links up to the Vedic times, the foods and cooking traditions of India are of varying ages: a few ancient ones no doubt, but most are only (!) a few hundred years old and many of even more recent vintage. Tandoori chicken is likely very ancient: there is some archaeological evidence in the Indus Valley Civilisation sites, pre 1500 BCE, of tandoor-like structures used to cook meat. But its curry cousin Murgh Makhani or butter chicken was probably created post 1947.

Having said that, there are a couple of historic influences that are still strong and visible in the foods of India. Food and good eating practices are mentioned in a number of ancient Indian texts. The biggest influence on food was of Ayurveda (the ancient Indian philosophy of healthy living and medicine). Simplifying a long and complex treatise, foods were supposed to be of two types, hot and cold. Hot food increased body energy and was hence best for cooler times and vice versa for cold food. Within these two broad labels, food was supposed to have one or more of six tastes, called 'rasa' in Sanskrit: sweet, sour, salty, bitter, pungent and astringent. Each taste was directly associated with the effect it would have on the body. This led to selecting food not just for the direct taste and nutrition, but also the role that it played in long term health and even its impact on behaviour. One key principle was the necessity to have a balance of tastes to ensure that the body's balance was maintained by the food eaten. This meant that all the tastes had to be included in meals as far as practicable. This is one reason why individual dishes in India have so many ingredients, and meals typically have multiple dishes with different types of tastes. The practice can be seen in even a simple meal where pickles, chutneys, yoghurt, etc. are eaten as accompaniments to the main dishes.

The other significant ancient influence is from the religions which originated in India. Jainism from the very beginning preached a fairly rigid form of ahimsa or non-violence towards all animals. For lay followers, this was translated into a form of lacto-vegetarianism abjuring all meat, fish and root vegetables but not dairy products. Buddhism initially was not against meat eating. Buddha himself was supposed to have been a meat eater. However, when it spread later all over the country, the killing of animals was specifically discouraged. Ancient Indian texts associated with Hinduism, on the other hand, were ambivalent towards non-vegetarianism, both encouraging ahimsa and vegetarianism in some places but also accepting meat eating in others. Under the influence of Jainism and Buddhism, vegetarianism was adopted in the revival of Hinduism in the first millennium CE. A combined result of these influences is the high incidence of vegetarianism now found across the country. Estimates vary but between thirty to forty percent of the country identifies as vegetarian, probably the highest proportion of population of any country in the world. The rest of the population, while non-vegetarian by definition, also do not eat a lot of meat and fish. There are significant variations in vegetarianism across the country and a few surprises. Punjab, the land of tandoori chicken and widely believed to be full of non-vegetarians, has one of the highest proportions of vegetarians in the country, about two-thirds of the population. Although Tamil Nadu is generally believed to be mostly vegetarian, due to the fame of vegetarian south Indian dishes such as dosa, idli, uttapam, etc., in fact only a miniscule percentage of the population is fully vegetarian.

It is even more difficult to ascertain when the Hindu strictures against eating beef became widely prevalent. The ancient texts are as usual open to multiple interpretations. Respect for cows comes through in many of the texts, as cattle were integral to the lives of the ancient Indians. But there is also evidence of beef consumption. Most scholarly works suggest that the strictures against eating beef became a part of the Hindu faith only during the revival of the religion in the first millennium CE.

Among other historic but relatively more recent influences on the foods of India are two from the last 500 years.

The first was the conquest of large parts of the country by Muslims from Central Asia and the Middle East. The first major Muslim kingdom in India was established in Delhi in 1206 CE. The Muslim rule reached its apogee in the Mughal empire which was dominant across the sub-continent for about two hundred years from the sixteenth century. Many of the Muslim rulers looked west to the Middle East, to other Muslim kingdoms, for inspiration on religion, culture and food. The Indian Muslim kingdoms also acted as a source of employment for many immigrants from those regions. Eating good food was considered a symbol of nobility and good living. Thus, in the long period of Muslim rule over substantial parts of the sub-continent, a rich and luxurious cuisine developed for the upper classes. This cuisine was rich in meat and incorporated imported ingredients and cooking techniques from lands to the north west of India. Indian ingredients, especially spices, and cooking methods, merged with the imports to create one of the best examples of fusion cuisine that you will find anywhere in the world, the Mughlai cuisine. One quirky offshoot of Muslim rule was that, since Islam prohibited the eating of pork, the consumption of pork, in addition to beef, disappeared from most parts of the country.

The second more recent influence was through the opening of sea trade with Europe, brought about by the discovery of the trade route round the Cape of Good Hope by the Portuguese. Vasco da Gama completed his voyage to India in 1498 CE. This, as we know from history, eventually led to the colonisation of India by the British. From a food perspective, the bigger impact was the discovery and import of new foods from the New World (the Americas). Chilli, tomato and potato were introduced into Indian cuisine around the sixteenth and seventeenth century. It is sometimes difficult to believe that chilli, the defining ingredient of so many Indian dishes, became a part of Indian cooking only a few hundred years ago. Before that, the heat in the food came from black pepper and a locally grown spice called long pepper, which was considerably more difficult to cultivate than chilli. The ease of cultivating chilli led to its quick adoption and spread across India. While the British rule over the country did add some European dishes to the country's varied cuisine, the impact was not as substantial as say the impact of Middle East and Central Asian foods.

In India, as in most other countries, you will find differences in the food that is eaten at home and what you get in restaurants, smaller eateries and sold by street hawkers. Of course restaurant food needs to be richer and more luxurious than home food in order for people to pay a price for it. But restaurant food in India is not simply a richer and more elaborate version of home food. Many restaurants serve food that you will rarely find at home. This is especially true for food requiring special equipment or special ingredients or that's just too complicated to be cooked at home. Tandoori food, for example, is rarely made at home in India. This is because most homes don't have a tandoor, a special type of clay oven. Even in Punjab, considered the home of tandoori cooking, tandoors are not widely found at home, though villages may have communal tandoors. Tandoori food has therefore been the preserve of restaurants and specialist eateries.

Similarly, many dishes are so complicated to make that they are only cooked by professional chefs, trained either the modern way in cooking colleges or traditionally under older chefs in restaurants and specialist eateries.

Then there is a category of food dishes where the effort that goes into the cooking is high and is best done in large volumes. This is true for many of the dishes that fall under the label of street food. Many of these require multiple cooked parts to be assembled together. The effort is justified only when cooking large amounts in one go, something which makes sense for a specialist hawker or shop but not necessarily at home.

About the Book – What you will find in it and where

The book is organised by descriptions of dishes from the states of India. All the major states (and regional cuisines within them) have been covered. Other states which are small or have foods similar to the bigger states are covered together in the last chapter through their best known dishes.

In each chapter, the reader will find descriptions of many of the dishes to be found in the state's cuisine(s). These dishes may or may not have originated in the state. A good example is the Roshogolla (also known as Rasgulla or Rasagola). I've described this sweet dish in the first chapter on Bengal. Till recently, it was widely believed to have originated in Bengal. But, in a farcical political drama in the last few years, the government of Odisha laid claim to be the state of origin for the dish. The resolution was a stereotypical bureaucratic compromise, with official Geographical Indications for both the Bengali Roshogolla and Odisha Rasagola. I've tried to identify where a particular dish has originated only where it is indisputable, which is not often. Otherwise, more practically, I've focussed on describing each dish in the state where it's traditionally popular and widely available.

For each dish, I've provided a description, key ingredients and an overview of the cooking process. I've also, where I first describe a dish or ingredient with its name in the local Indian language, translated it into English where possible. Food names are of particular interest to me, especially ones which are not just a description of the main ingredients. For example, the story behind why a fish is called Bombay Duck. For many dishes, I've embellished the description with my personal experiences and any facts or anecdotes associated with the dish. A dish with a backstory has just a little bit of added allure to me. I've also in all cases always described dishes that go together, or are standard accompaniments, one after the other. After all, a description of Machher Jhol (Bengali fish curry) would be incomplete without Bhaat (boiled rice), Chhole (spicy chickpea) without Bhature (a type of flatbread), Puttu (steamed rice and coconut roll) without Kadala (brown chickpea curry) etc.

There are no recipes in this book, apart from a description of the main ingredients for each dish. With every dish, I've attempted to explain what makes it taste great or not (that happens sometimes even with Indian food!), but I've not listed all the dozen or more ingredients that go into each dish in exact proportions or the exact sequence of cooking steps. The focus is on what someone eating the dish may want to know. If you are a cook of Indian food, aspiring or otherwise, this book will be a start in terms of understanding the huge range of dishes, where they come from and how easy or complicated they are, but you will need other sources for recipes. For a start, I've listed my favourite sources of recipes at the end of the book.

When researching this book, I found practically every dish had multiple recipes on the internet or in recipe books. Some of these recipes have been handed down through generations in the kitchen, at home and by professional chefs. Others are based on hearsay and guesswork. The recipes are thus of varying accuracy. I won't claim to have tested multiple recipes for every dish, since the intent was never to make this into a recipe book. Having said that, compiling a book like this has become so much easier now than it would have been even 25 years ago. There is at least information available on every dish if you look for it. For most dishes, my descriptions are of the traditional ways of cooking, though where modern methods are widely prevalent, I've made a mention of those.

This is a compendium, not a novel: each chapter can be read by itself, though the later chapters often reference dishes or ingredients which have been described in earlier chapters.

The book covers a long list of dishes. It should serve as a useful guide and reference for anyone who loves Indian food. While there is little need for background information to enjoy Indian or any good food, the experience is usually enhanced with a little bit of knowledge. For all readers, in India and abroad, it should be a handy refresher on familiar Indian foods and revelatory about foods from other parts of the country, especially as part of learning more about Indian culture.

Happy reading and eating.

Map of India

1
Bengal

Machher Jhol and much more

I've chosen Bengali food as my starting point as it was the first Indian food different from home food that I experienced and have memories of. In the early 1970s, my father's job took us to Haldia, a newly established industrial town deep in the south of the West Bengal state. (I've shortened the name of the state to 'Bengal' hereafter). We lived in the public sector company's 'township', a term used for purpose-built residential areas where the company employees lived. It was not wholly a Bengali area. Most of its managers were transferred in from other company locations outside Bengal, but a substantial part of the workforce was from various locations in Bengal. The school that I went to had children not just from our township but also from other nearby areas. Hence there were lots of opportunities to taste Bengali food, at school through shared bites from lunch boxes of classmates, and at their homes on social occasions.

Not surprisingly the first thing I discovered about Bengali food was the importance of fish. Bengal is blessed with many rivers and ponds resulting from plentiful rainfall. Fresh water fish of many types are commonly available. At home, we also ate a lot of fish (more on that a little later) so I was already familiar with a few of the Bengali favourites, Rohu (also spelt Rehu or Rui), and Katla, both freshwater fish of the carp variety. In Haldia, I also first tasted the Ilish (or Hilsa) and Bhetki. Ilish, a type of herring which swims upstream of rivers to breed, is found extensively in the rivers and estuaries of Bengal and Bangladesh and is considered a delicacy.

My earliest memories of Bengali fish are of the dry fried and curried varieties. The dry form was one which Bengali school friends would sometimes have in their lunch boxes. This was not an everyday occurrence as eating fish in any form is messy and time-consuming, not best suited for lunches eaten in a hurry by schoolboys. So, when someone had fish in a lunch box it was clearly a treat. A few lucky classmates would get a small, delicious bite. It was never enough.

The **Bengali fish fry** is an intermediate step in making fish curry. At its simplest, fish pieces coated with turmeric, red chilli and salt are fried in mustard oil over high heat. Mustard oil is key to cooking fish the Bengali way and gives Bengali fish its distinctive taste. Typically, when the fish curry is being prepared, a couple of fried pieces will be kept aside for tasting. Since fried fish also keeps better than raw fish, back in the days when refrigerators were not ubiquitous (and the power supply was unreliable even for those who owned a fridge), it often made sense to fry fish for a couple of meals at one go. Thus, there was always a chance in a Bengali household that some fried fish would be stored or saved from a previous preparation and make its way to a child's lunch box.

The Bengali fish curry or **Machher Jhol** is a famous dish and emblematic of the Bengali cuisine. (I've spelt the first part of the dish with 'chh' to represent the Hindi/ Bengali alphabet which sounds like an exaggerated 'ch' sound). I had this dish practically every time I ate at any Bengali friend's home in Haldia. It is an everyday dish with many variants to the recipe. As long as the fish is first fried in mustard oil and then added to a watery curry, called jhol, the dish is called machher jhol. The jhol is made by frying onions, tomatoes, ginger and garlic with whole and powdered spices, with water added at an intermediate stage. The spices used are not complex. There is a whole spice combination called Panch Phoron which is used widely in Bengali dishes. This spice combination has equal quantities of five (panch means five) whole spice seeds: fenugreek, nigella, mustard, fennel and a Bengali speciality called radhuni. For the jhol, a small quantity of these spices are initially tempered in mustard oil with bay leaves before the onions are added. The other ingredients are then added and fried with a few standard powdered spices: coriander, cumin, red chilli and turmeric. Water is then added to complete the curry. The already fried fish is added towards the end of the preparation.

Potatoes are frequently added for thickening the fish curry and, I suspect, to add volume to the dish. Sometimes the fish curry has brinjal (aubergine or eggplant) either in addition to the potatoes or as a substitute. I am not a great fan of this practice. As a child, I'd find ways of spooning out the fish and the curry without the brinjal. While researching recipes for machher jhol, I've found the addition of brinjal is quite widely practised. I am not sure how this enhances this already tasty dish and I suspect it primarily serves the purpose of making the servings look bigger.

No description of the Bengali fish curry can be complete without also describing **Bhaat**, which is boiled rice, always served as an accompaniment to fish curry. Boiled rice is not a Bengali speciality. But a lot of rice is locally grown, as the abundant rainfall is very suitable for paddy cultivation, and rice is an integral part of Bengali cuisine. There are hundreds of different varieties of rice grown in Bengal and Bangladesh. One of the best-known varieties and quite widely available is the Gobindobhog rice. It gets its name from being a religious offering or 'bhog'. It is a short grain rice which gets sticky and aromatic on cooking. The government of India has given this rice a Geographical Indication; an official recognition that only this variety, grown in Bengal, can be called by this name. The Geographical Indication has been given for a number of regional food specialities, some well-deserved and necessary, some questionable and even farcical. We will come across a number of these in this book.

Bhaat has traditionally been the main cereal for both lunch and dinner in Bengal. When eaten with fish curry, some liquid curry is first mixed with a small portion of rice and a bit of fish is then added in, all using your fingers, to make a morsel of food. Bengalis are especially adept, through years of practice from childhood, at sorting the bones from the fish flesh with their fingers. Licking the curry off your fingers is part of the ritual of enjoying this food, though it is best done surreptitiously in public places. This habit of eating fish curry only with rice is deeply ingrained in me, as it is with most Bengalis. I am happy to eat most curries with Indian breads, but somehow can't make breads of any kind work with fish curry.

A special Bengali fish dish, not easily found outside Bengal, is called **Bhapa Maach**, which translates to 'steamed fish'. In the traditional version, this dish is made of fillets of Ilish fish. The dish has a paste made by blending mustard seeds, grated coconut, yoghurt, green chillies, turmeric, sugar and salt. The fish pieces are smothered in this paste, wrapped in banana leaves and steamed. This practice of steaming fish in banana leaves is not common but is found in other states of India as well. The process can be made easier by steaming the fish inside a covered pot in a steamer, as banana leaves are not exactly standard items in grocery stores. But there is mystery and adventure in wrapping the fish in banana leaves and hoping for the best when the leaves are unwrapped. The Bengali steamed fish is quite unique in the use of mustard in the paste. It may sound like an unlikely speciality, but the tastes of mustard and coconut combine beautifully and this is quite a sophisticated dish.

A full Bengali meal, lunch or dinner, has one feature which makes it stand out among Indian regional cuisines. The Bengali meal is eaten as a sequential multi-course meal, the *service à la russe*, as is common with European meals but very unusual in India. This is true even if the meal itself is served as a thali, on a plate with all the dishes served at once. I remember receiving lessons on eating by courses, Bengali style, from a school friend Bhaskar in our hostel in the last couple of years of my schooling. We were roommates and had most of our meals together. The school was in Patna, Bihar, so the meals were not Bengali. A typical meal would have bhaat, roti, daal and a couple of vegetable dishes. I'd mix the rice, daal and the vegetables into one messy mixture before eating. Bhaskar, on the other hand, would fastidiously divide out the rice into three or four portions, eating each portion with one of the side dishes. "You get to taste each dish better" was his impeccable logic. Being the last one to finish a meal was a small price to pay.

A full multi-course meal is generally only had during special occasions and festivals. A regular family Bengali meal will have at most two or three courses. The starter courses are one or two vegetable dishes. A not so well-known starter is a mixed vegetable dish called **Shukto**, made with karela (bitter gourd), potatoes, carrots, beans, drumsticks (a bean like vegetable found in India) and raw bananas, cooked in mustard oil with mustard and poppy seeds, spices, with curry made of milk and water. This dish is eaten with a small portion of rice and is very much an acquired taste. It is not an easy dish to cook right and my experience with this has been generally disappointing. That may be mostly due to the fact that I don't like karela, so don't take that as a final word on the dish.

A second course in a multi-course meal could be a leafy vegetable dish called **Shak** (similar to Saag) which is basically fried spinach. This is a simpler dish to cook and is more common in family meals. A further vegetable dish may be added to a multi-course meal. It could be one of a variety of vegetable dishes, each with a single vegetable as its main ingredient. Vegetable dishes are collectively referred to as **Torkari** in Bengali. Individual dishes are named by using the name of the vegetable as a prefix to the word torkari. The recipes for these dishes tend to vary by region and family preferences. In my experience, there is very little that differentiates these torkari dishes from similar vegetable dishes found across northern India and especially in the Gangetic plain.

Daal, a generic name for cooked lentil, is eaten as a separate course or, as is common in other parts of the country, along with rice and vegetables. Daal is not required when eating just jhol with bhaat, but it is common to have it in a multi-course meal or when having dry dishes with rice. All types of daals are cooked by boiling a portion of lentils with water and a bit of turmeric and salt. The proportion of water and the cooking time are absolutely key to getting daal cooked to the right consistency. All over India, daal is always enhanced with a Chhonk or Tarka, of which there are many different types; a common Bengali one is just cumin seeds, red chillies and bay leaves, fried in a little bit of hot ghee.

In the UK, where I live now, we get a packaged daal called Bengali Coconut Daal, in grocery stores. This is a special type of Bengali daal dish, called **Chholar Daal** in Bengal. The lentil used is chana daal which is de-husked and split chana or brown chickpea. This legume is so popular in Bengal that it was named Bengal Gram by the British and the name has stuck. North Indians may find the name of the dish misleading as chhola is the name for white chickpea there. In the packaged variant that I get here, the daal is pre-cooked and in a plastic pack. In a smaller pack measured portions of whole spices are provided to fry and add to the daal as chhonk. Not perfect, but a very convenient alternative when I need a quick comfort meal of bhaat and daal.

An unusual vegetable dish found in Bengal is **Mochar Ghonto**. This is a dish I discovered as an adult in Bengali restaurants, but it is quite popular in households. Mocha in Bengali is banana or plantain flowers. Ghonto is a label for a dry vegetable dish. The dish is as exotic as the name makes it sound. It is quite delicately spiced and has coconut added to complement the taste of the banana flowers. It is not an easy dish to make as the banana flowers need quite a lot of preparation. The banana flower grows from the end of a bunch of bananas and is large and purple. Its purple leaves enclose the thin, delicate florets which go into this dish. The leaves need to be removed to get to the florets. Each floret has a non-edible string-like stamen which needs to be removed gently by hand, a time-consuming and tedious process. Once this is done, the flowers may need to be soaked in water overnight before cooking. The flowers are first cooked by boiling in water with salt. The dish is then prepared by roasting some bay leaves and cumin seeds in oil, then adding the boiled flowers and fried potatoes with ginger, chillies and grated coconut. The unique taste of the dish justifies the effort, though in appearance in may look like just another vegetable dish.

Fish curry is typically the main course of the meal. It is sometimes replaced or, more likely, followed by a mutton or chicken dish. In restaurants serving Bengali food, you may find a dish called **Kosha Mangsho**. Mangsho is the Bengali word for meat, specifically mutton or goat meat. Kosha is similar to the Hindi 'bhuna'. So, this is a slow-cooked mutton dish with a thick, dark brown gravy. It is one of the dishes in Bengali cuisine which shows the influence of Mughlai cooking, both in ingredients and technique. Mutton pieces are first marinated for a few hours before the dish is cooked. The marinade is of yoghurt with a few spices. The dish is cooked in mustard oil in which a large quantity of onions are fried with a number of whole spices. This is the base of the thick gravy. Mutton, with the marinade, is added to the fried onion mix and then cooked over low heat till the meat is tender and soft and the gravy a deep dark brown colour. Kosha Mangsho is a rich and heavy dish, good enough to be the centre piece in an elaborate meal. It tends to be the main alternative to fish curry when the latter is, on rare occasions, omitted from a big Bengali meal.

A proper multi-course Bengali meal is always topped up with a sweet dish, either plain yoghurt or a delightful sweetened yoghurt dish called **Mishti Doi**. In this dish, milk is first sweetened and thickened while boiling, and then left to ferment in earthen ware pots. Jaggery is often used instead of sugar for sweetening and gives the dish a brown colour to distinguish it from plain yoghurt. This dish is quite widely available across India now, even available in packaged pots, and can be eaten both as a light dessert or as an indulgent snack. We will encounter jaggery many times in this book. Called 'gur' in north India, it is a traditional ingredient found all over the country. It is a type of sugar made by boiling sugar cane juice till it has thickened. The thickened liquid solidifies into a golden or brown coloured solid when cooled. It is sold in solid lumps and is an essential item in traditional Indian kitchens.

Apart from bhaat, Bengali meals sometimes also have Indian style breads made of wheat flour as accompaniments. North Indian style Chapati, Roti or Paratha are quite common. A local favourite is called **Luchi** or **Loochi**, which is very similar to Poori found in other states. Luchi, like poori, is circular and smaller than roti, at about 10 to 15 cm in diameter, and is prepared by deep frying circular pieces of rolled dough. Luchi is made from Maida, which is finely milled and refined wheat flour, while poori is usually made from Atta, wholemeal flour. The characteristic feature of both luchi and poori is that they puff up during frying and collapse like punctured balloons when pricked.

In my school days in Haldia, luchi was often paired with a potato dish called **Aloor Dum** in our lunch boxes. Variants of this dish are available all over north India. There are various ways of making this dish. It can be completely dry or with a thick gravy or a thin curry. The dry version is mostly cooked with just whole and powdered spices. The gravy and curried versions can have a base of onions and tomatoes or of yoghurt. There is lots of scope for improvisation to suit personal tastes, one reason for its popularity across regions. The consistent ingredient is potato, typically whole baby potatoes or chunky pieces of new potatoes boiled and fried with the rest of the ingredients. Luchi and aloor dum make for a hearty and comforting breakfast. But they are also good for a quick meal, hence the popularity in school lunch boxes.

In addition to fish curry, one of the first Bengali specialities I was introduced to in Haldia was a snack called **Jhaal Murhi** (or Muri) sold by a street vendor outside school. Jhaal means 'lots of chilli' and murhi is the name for puffed rice. This snack is usually sold only by street side vendors. It has an incredible number of ingredients for an apparently simple looking snack. Vegetables include chopped onions, cucumber, tomatoes and a very small quantity of boiled potatoes or chickpeas. Chopped green chillies, ginger and coriander are added along with a blend of many spices for flavouring. Peanuts and Sev (a deep fried, lacy savoury snack made from Bengal gram flour) may be added for crunchiness.

All the ingredients are mixed with a dash of mustard oil just before serving. This last bit is always a part of the pleasure of ordering jhaal murhi. You get to watch in eager anticipation as the vendor scoops out the pre-prepared ingredients from their respective jars into the mixing bowl, adds the mustard oil and then gives the mixture a vigorous shake before scooping it for you in a paper cone. The paper cone used to be made of recycled newspaper and would not strictly meet health and safety standards of the more sanitised world now, but somehow jhaal murhi in anything else just doesn't taste the same. The vendor that I first bought from in school didn't just shake the mixture but pretended to do magic to it, reciting chants and throwing spells, to make the snack tastier for the young school kids crowding around him. For the longest time, I believed that the reciting the magic spells during the mixing was the final ingredient in making jhaal murhi. Without the chants and the spells, the experience of eating jhaal murhi now feels somewhat incomplete.

Gol Gappa, or **Puchka** as it is called in Bengal, is the most common street food in Bengal, as it is all over northern and western India. This dish is pretty much the poster dish for Indian street food and my guess is that most of you would have eaten it at some point. It is called Paani Poori in Mumbai and most of west India, Gupchup in east UP and Bihar, Paani Patashey in some parts of north India and gol gappa everywhere else. I prefer the name gol gappa as it describes the dish most evocatively, Gol = 'round' and Gappa = 'eat in one go'.

If you will indulge me, let me dissect this dish to explain what makes it so special. The dish has three components. The first is a small poori, round and about 5 to 6 cm in diameter, puffed up and hollow, made by deep frying rolled and flattened dough of wheat or semolina. The preparation of the poori is hard work and probably the reason that it is rare to make gol gappa at home. The second component is a small quantity of boiled, salted and spiced potatoes or chickpeas or both with a topping of tangy chutney. A small hole is made on the top of the poori, and a very small quantity, about a teaspoon of the potatoes or chickpeas with chutney is spooned into the poori. The third component, and the heart and soul of the gol gappa, is spicy water which can be made in a number of different ways. The most common varieties use a base of either imli (tamarind) paste or pudina (mint) paste with a number of spices for a sour, tangy and sharp taste. In the Bengali variety, a tamarind base is much more common. The loaded poori is dipped into a container of the spicy water to fill it up and needs to be eaten at once and in one go. What results is an explosion of different tastes in the mouth, like a Diwali night full of firecrackers going off. It is difficult to stop at one, so most vendors will serve three to four pooris in one serving.

Eating gol gappa can be messy. The thin poori, loaded with water, can and often does break in the journey from bowl to mouth – the trick is to keep the bowl below the poori at all times. If the poori breaks, the water falls back into the bowl and can be happily drunk once all the pooris have been eaten. The bigger problem is when the poori cracks just before you are about to swallow it. So, while with experience most of us have learnt to hold the poori gingerly enough so that it does not crack, you find experienced eaters leaning with their heads forward at the point of swallowing the poori. Just in case it cracks, it is better to have the water falling on the ground than on your clothes. Of course, if the poori is too big for your mouth, which rarely happens with good street vendors but may happen with poori prepared by amateurs, it is best to abort the mission! This is not a dish you can bite into.

While a number of India street food staples such as Samosa, Chaat, Bhel Poori, etc. are widely available in Bengal, I'd like to describe a personal favourite, the **Kathi Roll**. This is a Kolkata speciality and serves as a light meal to be had on-the-go. In the original kathi roll, a paratha (shallow fried flatbread), with kathi or mutton seekh kebabs, onions, chillies, carrots and chutney, is rolled up and wrapped in paper. The mutton kebab can be substituted with chicken tikka or paneer tikka. In one variety, the paratha is cooked with egg slathered on it for an egg roll. Add the mutton kebab or chicken tikka to the stuffing, and you get the Egg Kathi Roll, the best kathi roll of all.

Like all street food, the kathi roll can be tricky to eat. The paper wrapping is crucial. As an aside, earlier the paper used to be recycled newspapers, definitely not healthy, but now you are more likely to find clean, white food grade paper. The wrapping covers about half of the roll and is tucked into one end. This helps prevent the stuffing from squeezing out when you start eating from the other end. You need to eat up to edge of the paper, then fold the paper down a bit, eat some more and so on till you get to the last mouthful. At that point, the paper can be discarded, and the roll finished off. It sounds straight-forward, but even with experience, some of the stuffing will squeeze out. Eating street food is difficult without getting your hands dirty.

After eating a kathi roll, most Bengalis will pop into a sweet shop. Bengali sweets are famous across the country. It is common to find sweet shops outside Bengal branding themselves 'Bengali Sweet House' as a badge of good provenance and an obvious marketing tactic.

Roshogolla, called Rasgulla across northern India, is the best-known Bengali sweet. It is spelt and pronounced in many different ways. I've used the spelling for its typical Bengali pronunciation. It is a sweet dish which is also eaten as a snack. Whenever I've been to Bengal, I've seen people walk into a sweet shop at any time of day, buy a couple of roshogolla, eat them there and then and continue on their business. It is definitely not just a dessert. The dish itself is not complicated. It is made from chhena, a type of cheese made from milk. The best chhena is white in colour and the roshogolla gets its colour from there. Roshogolla are small balls of chhena cooked in a sugar syrup till the balls become light and spongy. The dish is always served with a bit of sugar syrup.

For the longest time, Bengal was believed to be the birthplace of the roshogolla. In a somewhat farcical turn of events, the government of the state of Odisha (previously spelt as Orissa) claimed roshogolla had originated there. I am not sure how such a claim could be verified or even if it is worth trying. The Bengal government tried to quell this by registering a Geographical Indication (GI) for the Bengali roshogolla. The Odisha government has in turn registered a GI, so we now have GIs for 'Banglar Rasogolla' from Bengal and 'Odisha Rasagola' from Odisha.

I went back to Kolkata, or Calcutta as it was in those days, for a couple of years as a post-graduate student in the late 1980s. (The city's name was changed in 2001 on the somewhat tenuous historic basis that there was a village called Kolkata where the city of Calcutta was established by the British. The real reason is that Bengalis pronounce Calcutta as Kolkata. The reason for the name change may just be mispronunciation masquerading as history!)

My college campus itself was some distance away from the city, but we made frequent trips to the city centre and I had the opportunity to rediscover some of the delights of Bengali cuisine. The college canteen itself had only a little Bengali food. But roshogolla was an integral part of all birthdays and other celebrations on campus. On 'Roshogolla Nights', the entire student population would be invited to celebrate an event, typically someone's birthday, with eat-as-many-as-you-can roshogolla as the only item on the menu. From there would emerge the 'Roshogolla King' of the college and generally, to no one's surprise, would be a Bengali.

A derivative dish from the roshogolla is **Rasmalai**, which is altogether more elaborate and luxurious. It is often the dessert that follows a rich and special Indian meal. While Bengali in origin, the dish is widely available. It is roshogolla served in 'malai' which is, in this case, sweet, thickened milk, flavoured with cardamom powder and chopped nuts. The thickened milk may be coloured either with saffron or food colour to a cream or light yellow shade. To differentiate the rasmalai from roshogolla, the roshogolla in rasmalai is often shaped into discs rather than spheres. The malai of the dish offers chefs opportunities for experimentation. So an innovative take on the rasmalai in a restaurant menu is often the first sign of a chef trying to break through.

The sweet dish that you cannot miss in Bengali sweet shops is **Shondesh** or **Sandesh**. It is common to see trays and trays of shondesh with different toppings displayed in Bengali sweet shops. This sweet is also eaten both as a snack and as dessert and is as common as the roshogolla. It is a simple dish to cook and describe. Freshly made chhena is mixed with sugar and lightly cooked, mildly flavoured with cardamoms, and shaped into cookie-shaped discs for serving. Most sweet shops will also add some toppings, e.g. chopped pistachios, to add colour and taste.

Kolkata is the home of the unique Indo-Chinese cuisine. In the nineteenth century, when Calcutta was the capital of the British empire in India and a major port for trade, the opium trade established close links between Calcutta and the Canton region (modern Guangdong province) in China. A small community of Chinese people have lived in Calcutta ever since. This community is credited with adapting Chinese food to Indian ingredients, mainly with greater use of vegetables and spices and the use of chicken and fish rather than pork and beef. Indian Chinese or Indo-Chinese is a cuisine by itself, popular across India and is often the first taste of 'foreign food' that most Indians get. While this is not strictly Bengali food, I've included it in this chapter as its most logical home.

Chinatown in Kolkata still has a number of Chinese restaurants. Going to eat there gives you the feeling of eating something authentic, though 'authentic' may not be the right term for the home of food which is in reality a corruption of the original.

The most famous Indo-Chinese dish is **Chicken Manchurian** or its vegetarian equivalent **Gobi (cauliflower) Manchurian**. The preparation of this dish follows the Indian convention of frying ginger and garlic pastes with red chilli powder as the starting point for a thick curry, but instead of powdered spices you add soya sauce to the paste. The main ingredient, chicken or cauliflower, is fried in this paste. The soya sauce makes the dish taste like a Chinese dish and the rest of the flavours satisfy the Indian palate. As good an example of fusion cuisine as you will ever find.

Chicken manchurian is an easy introduction to foreign food for most Indians, considering that it is actually not foreign. It has been a favourite Chinese dish in India for ages. It is also the cause of dismay when Indians go to Chinese restaurants outside India and don't find it on the menu. Sadly, as more and more Chinese restaurants serving authentic regional Chinese food have come up in the major cities in India, chicken manchurian seems to be becoming unfashionable and often not available.

My personal experience with Indo-Chinese also includes a dish which you will rarely find in restaurants. One of the most visible packaged food products in India is Maggi® noodles. Noodles are of course originally Chinese and are an integral part of Indo-Chinese food. Maggi® 2-Minute Noodles, like pot noodles all over the world, is sold as a quick to prepare light meal. You only need boiling water to cook it and the quickness is captured in its sub-branding of 2-Minutes. It has been thoroughly Indianised and its main variants are branded '**Masala Noodles**'. The flavouring is provided in powder form in a separate pack which you just add to the noodles. Variants include Special Masala, Green Chilli, Chilli Chicken, etc.

When I was in Calcutta as a student, our hostel had a night canteen run by one of the dining hall workers, Kasim. It used to run for a couple of hours from 11 pm onwards, mainly to serve tea and coffee to students needing a boost in the middle of late-night studies. For people needing a bit more sustenance, Kasim provided a plate of plain noodles or a special variant of noodles topped with **Anda (Egg) Bhujia**. Egg bhujia is a dish made of beaten eggs, fried and scrambled with chopped onions, tomatoes, green chillies and spices. In my mind, the combination is forever etched as Kasim's Maggi® noodles with anda bhujia, a very satisfying light dish to eat either as a meal or to top-up a disagreeable hostel dinner. I am sure many Indians would have experienced this dish in other student canteens and smaller eateries. I was delighted to find that the dish continues to be served in the college's night canteen when I was there a few years ago for a reunion, though Kasim sadly seemed to have moved on.

Machher Jhol with Bhaat

Kosha Mangsho

FOODSUTRA

Jhaal Murhi Vendor

Roshogolla

2
Bihar

My home food

Bihari food is rarely given a separate chapter in a book on Indian food. But I am from Bihar and a lot of the food that I ate at home is what people across the states of the Gangetic plain eat on a regular basis. So, a description of the everyday food of my home provides a good description of not only everyday Bihari food but also that of Jharkhand (which was part of Bihar when I was young), Uttar Pradesh (especially eastern UP), Chhattisgarh, Madhya Pradesh and parts of Bengal.

Breakfast, lunch and dinner were all freshly cooked meals at home. Lunch and dinner were actually quite formulaic, except on weekends and festivals. Lunch on most weekdays, even during school (I used to come home for lunch), would be bhaat (rice), daal of lentils, a couple of cooked vegetables called **Tarkari** (Torkari in Bengal, which is the same word pronounced differently), accompanied with one or more of pickles, chutney and papad. The main cereal for lunch was boiled rice or bhaat. Roti was optional and was regularly skipped. Tarkari is the collective term for vegetable dishes where a single vegetable is generally lightly fried with onions and spices and may be served dry or in a curry. The vegetables were generally seasonal then, though with better storage now there is year-round availability of most of the popular vegetables.

The common vegetables in Bihari food are, in their Hindi names: bhindi, karela, parwal, baingan, kaddu, nenua, gobhi, saag, beans, matar and aloo. The

English names given to most of these vegetables are an attempt at the impossible since the Indian English names are rarely used in India and are not known outside India.

Bhindi, generally known as okra in the west, is delightfully called lady's finger, probably a description of its shape but a name rarely used outside the Indian sub-continent. It is by far the most popular green vegetable in many parts of India and was definitely so in our home, making an appearance in meals multiple times during the week. We generally had a dry bhindi dish, called **Bhindi Bhujia**, where the bhindi is cut into small pieces and fried with spices. It is a simple dish but takes time to make as the bhindi has to soften to the right texture. I am not a great fan but if popularity is proof of taste then it must be considered a very tasty dish.

Karela is a popular vegetable in spite of its bitter taste. It takes getting used to and has always been more favoured by older people and not very popular with children. It is also considered very healthy, though in the absence of any scientific evidence, I think it is a claim made up to compensate for its bitter taste. It is probably no more or less healthy than other green vegetables. Its English name is not commonly known. Many years ago, my in-laws were visiting us in London, and we found a vegetable which looked like karela in the fresh vegetables section of the supermarket. We picked up a few but forgot to check the label card. At the check-out, when asked what the vegetable was, after a bit of head-scratching my father-in-law remembered the English name 'bitter gourd'. That name, however, was not on the check-out system. We had to go back to the vegetable section to look up the card, only to discover that it was listed, quite comfortingly, as 'karela'.

Similarly, **Parwal**, a vegetable found mostly in south Asia, is called 'pointed gourd' in English, though you would get quizzical looks if you ever asked for a vegetable by that name anywhere. A similarly named vegetable, Padwal (where the d is a hard 'r' sound), used in Maharashtra is a different vegetable called 'snake gourd' in English. Parwal is unusually also used to make a sweet. The vegetable is peeled, split, cleaned, boiled and then soaked in sugar syrup. Thus prepared, it is stuffed with sweetened khoya flavoured with almonds and cardamom for a dish which is simply called **parwal ki mithai** (sweet of parwal). Khoya or khoa, called mawa in other parts of the country, is a milk preparation widely used as a base in a variety of Indian sweets. It is what remains as white or pale yellow solids after full fat milk is simmered for a long, long time. It will come up as an ingredient in a number of dishes in this book.

Baingan, on the other hand, due to wide availability in the west, is known by not one but three English names – aubergine in Europe, eggplant in the US and brinjal in India. Like its names, it is quite a versatile vegetable and can be cooked as tarkari in fried form or added to various curries or, most commonly in Bihar, boiled and mashed up as a bharta or chokha. It is one part of the famous Litti Chokha dish from Bihar which I describe later. The other interesting bit about baingan is that the local varieties grown in India are so purple that the Hindi word for purple is 'baingani', literally the colour of baingan.

Kaddu is another vegetable quite common in Bihari food, though what is called kaddu in Bihar is called **Lauki** in the rest of north India and known as 'bottle gourd' in English. Pumpkin, or specifically red pumpkin (which is actually orange in colour), is eaten as kaddu in north India and is not that common in Bihar. If you do find it, it is likely to be called **Kohra**. Completing the list of vegetables from the gourd family is **Nenua**, called **Torai** in north India, and 'ridge gourd' in English. These gourd family vegetables are all cooked in a similar fashion. There is some upfront preparation required in skinning the vegetables and cutting to bite-sized pieces. Then the vegetables are cooked in oil with spices till they become soft.

Gobhi or phool (flower) gobhi, non-controversially known as cauliflower in English everywhere, was available only during the winters in my childhood as it does not grow well in hot, tropical summers. It was one of the vegetables that my mother would grow in our kitchen garden and, seeing the white head emerging and growing within the green leaves, is an abiding childhood memory. We also had bund gobhi (literally, 'closed' gobhi) which is the name for cabbage. Broccoli was not known to us when we were young, though it is quite widely and easily available now. Given how similar it looks to gobhi, it is sometimes not surprisingly called hari (green) gobhi in Hindi. One more comment on the name of these vegetables – I've spelt gobhi with a 'g' as it is called in most of north and east India. However, in Bihar, it is sometimes pronounced (or mispronounced) with a 'k' sound in front, as in kobhi. Just so you know.

Saag is the name of the dish made from leafy vegetables, commonly spinach. Spinach is called **Palak** in Hindi and, since saag in Bihar and most of eastern India is mostly made of palak, the two names are often used interchangeably. Palak is a widely available vegetable and is had on its own or in combination with other foods. **Palak Paneer**, spinach with cottage cheese as a curry, is common both in households and restaurants. **Saag Aloo**, spinach with potatoes also as a curry, is a must-have on the menus of Indian restaurants in the UK and also widely available as packaged food in supermarkets. I am not sure the combination of spinach and potato actually works but there are many paying diners proving me wrong every day.

Beans of different types are also used as tarkari in Bihari meals. One type is locally called barbatti and another is called France or French bean. I don't know for sure if the latter has anything to do with France, but it may be believed to have originated there. Beans are also cooked either as stand-alone tarkari or added to other dishes, especially in lentil-based vegetable stews.

There was always an aloo, i.e. potato, dish at our meals at home. This was mainly because my brother and I would refuse to eat any vegetables without the mitigating taste of aloo. Thankfully nobody worried too much about carbohydrate consumption those days. The two most common aloo dishes that we find in Bihari cuisine are the aloo bhujia and aloo curry. **Aloo bhujia**, like other bhujia dishes, has small pieces of the vegetable, sometimes as thin as crisps, spiced and fried. Aloo curry on the other hand has slightly bigger pieces, often boiled before-hand to reduce cooking time, cooked in a curry of onions and tomatoes. It is also common to have tarkari of aloo in combination with other vegetable such as gobhi and palak.

Daal, made of various types of lentils, is always served along with bhaat, otherwise the meal would be considered too dry. As a source of protein, it is an essential part of the vegetarian diets of a substantial number of Indians. The daal at my home was made by boiling a single type of lentil or a combination of different types of lentils in water with turmeric powder and seasoning. The main lentils used for making daal are arhar or toor (pigeon pea), moong (green gram when whole, and yellow gram when dehusked and split), masoor (red lentil/red split lentil), urad (black gram or lentil) and chana daal (dehusked and split brown chickpea or Bengal gram). The proportion of lentil and water and the cooking time are key to get a daal dish of the right liquid consistency. In our home, the daal was cooked till the lentil grains were completely absorbed, yielding a thick and consistent liquid dish. Having grains too visible was considered a sign of incompetent cooking. The cooked daal is normally topped with chhonk, called tarka in north India, which at its simplest is just cumin seeds, asafoetida and red chillies roasted in hot ghee.

The Hindi word for cumin is 'jeera' which sounds similar to 'keera' which means insect. A chhonk of cumin seeds in the daal leaves the black seeds floating on the surface. When I was a child, I was fooled into believing that these were insects. I'd righteously insist on these 'insects' being taken out of my daal and my poor grandmother or mother would have to indulge me by painstakingly scooping out the seeds. Thankfully I grew up.

We always had **Papad**, called **Poppadum** in other states of India, at every lunch. We used to add crushed bits of papad to each morsel of bhaat, daal and vegetables. I don't recall ever having papad as a starter at home, as is common in Indian restaurants in the west. I don't think I've ever eaten papad as a starter anywhere else in India either. I am not sure of the origins of this practice in the curry houses of the UK, but my theory is that it was adapted for western eating habits as we don't have the concept of starters in north Indian cuisine. Papad continues to be a favourite for me and on many days, a comfort lunch is nothing more than bhaat and daal with papad crushed into the mix.

An unusual accompaniment to meals is a Bihari speciality called **Tilori** or **Tilauri**. These are small, reddish brown, crunchy drops of lentil and til (sesame seeds), deep fried in oil. A smooth batter of ground urad daal mixed with sesame seeds and salt is poured as small droplets over a sheet of cloth and dried in the sun. Once dried, the raw tilori droplets can be stored for months. A cup full can be quickly deep fried before a meal. We would often have both papad and tilori as accompaniments to a lunch of bhaat, daal and vegetables, both serving the same purpose of adding crunchy texture and additional savoury taste to each morsel.

Dinner on most days was the same formula as lunch, but with bhaat replaced by roti. **Roti** or **Chapati** or **Phulka**, as it is variously known, is common all over India, except the extreme south. The Bihari roti is similar to the one found across all of north India, a flatbread made from a dough of moistened unleavened wheat flour, called atta, rolled to a circular shape about 20 cm in diameter (though the size can be variable). Roti is traditionally cooked on a cast iron griddle, called a tawa, on high heat. Each roti is cooked on both sides till the surface is lightly browned and the roti starts to puff up. In our home, each roti would then be transferred for a few seconds on to a wire mesh held over an open fire for the roti to fully puff up, to ensure that it was properly cooked inside. This last step is indulgence and can be skipped as the roti can be made to puff up on the tawa itself, with a bit of skilful pressing on the edges with a spatula.

Rolling of pieces of dough into the perfect circular shape of roti requires a lot of practice. Most Indian children, at some stage, have given rolling roti a try. It is not easy to get right and the shapes that I ended up creating were cause for much mirth in the kitchen.

Roti is best had freshly cooked and, as a result, creates complications during dinner time. While better-off families in India have cooks, it was and is still common practice in most households for the mother to make hot and fresh rotis for the rest of the family while they eat. I've always considered this an unsatisfactory arrangement, as it is not much of a family meal if one member is missing. A perfectly workable solution, increasingly practised, is to store cooked rotis in a container with a lid, with a cloth lining, to ensure that they remain soft and somewhat warm. They still need to be prepared just before dinner but at least the whole family can have the meal together. With the effort required to make rotis, it is not surprising that there are packaged options available now. They tend to be good solutions for time-pressed modern families but rarely taste as good as freshly made ones. We now have packaged roti as normal routine at our home in the UK. As a result, my children go gaga when they get freshly made rotis on our visits to India.

In my childhood, our meals were mostly vegetarian. Non-vegetarian food was expensive, took time and effort to cook and was had only two or three times during the week and on special occasions. Typically, this would mean mutton, chicken or fish curry, added to the menu at dinner time. Mutton or lamb in India is generally goat meat and just called meat, or maans in Hindi. On the days when mutton or chicken was planned for dinner, I'd accompany a parent to the butcher's shop. Buying fresh meat was an interesting experience as a child. We would select our portions from the carcasses hung in the shop and there was never any doubt that these were recently butchered animals. The butcher shops would often have the abattoir right at the back of the shop and you could hear and sometimes, if curiosity got the better of you, see the animals being slaughtered. I guess one could call it educational – we should know where our food comes from. I don't remember having any qualms about eating meat thus bought for most of my childhood. However, I did get quite disturbed by one particular episode when I was a teenager and it led to me to give up mutton for a period of time. Perhaps it was just a growing up phase.

The **Mutton Curry** made at home had a long list of ingredients and a long cooking time. A key ingredient in Bihari mutton curry is the use of mustard oil or kadua tel (bitter oil), something that Bihari and Bengali cuisines have in common. Mutton pieces on the bone are marinated and then fried with onions, ginger garlic paste and spices. The list of spices used is not long by the standards of Indian cooking: first, powdered turmeric, cumin, coriander, pepper, chilli and then, garam masala which was often prepared from its roasted ingredients – clove, cinnamon, black and green cardamoms, bay leaves, cumin and coriander seeds. Water for the curry is added last. When we were young, we would be given a taste of the meat at an intermediate stage, with a small piece which would be fully cooked, as an appetiser but also to make sure that the seasoning was right. The cooking after that can take about an hour and these days most cooks will speed the process by cooking in a pressure cooker. The aroma of the cooking curry is special as it spreads out of the kitchen and whets the appetite for the meal ahead.

There is a region in north Bihar called Champaran and the mutton curry from the region has gained fame as the **Champaran Mutton Curry**. Champaran is well known historically, as the region from where Mahatma Gandhi first launched his famous non-violent civil disobedience movement, Satyagraha, against the British Raj in 1917. In this case, it was specifically against forced indigo cultivation in the region. As far as I know, there is no association between the mutton curry and Satyagraha! The dish pre-dates the movement. The distinctive feature about this mutton curry is that it is slow cooked in a sealed earthenware pot. The ingredients are similar to the standard mutton curry described earlier, though as a richer dish, the Champaran Mutton Curry has a dose of ghee and a few extra spices. The whole mix of mutton and other ingredients is put in an earthenware pot, covered, sealed, and then cooked for a few hours over low heat. The resultant dish has very soft meat and a thick flavourful curry. I recently discovered that Moroccan tagine is also cooked in a similar way.

The standard **Chicken Curry** at home was similar to the mutton curry in both ingredients and cooking process. Chicken is a softer and blander meat, so the meat is marinated longer but needs to be cooked for less time. Like in the mutton curry, the chicken is initially fried with the rest of the ingredients till you get almost cooked chicken with a dry gravy. This intermediate step was a very important one for me personally, as I've mentioned, because at this stage we would be given a small piece as an appetiser. I'd be lurking somewhere close to the kitchen waiting for this stage to be reached so that I could get my first taste. Sometimes my greed would get the better of me and I'd go in and self-importantly ask my mother "if the food was ready for me to inspect?".

When I've researched recipes for Indian mutton and chicken curry, apart from the use of mustard oil, the Bihari curries differ from other north Indian recipes in not using lots of tomatoes in the curry. Tomatoes add a distinctive sourness and also soften the spiciness of the curry. They lead to a somewhat different tasting curry. Absence of tomatoes also means that the curry gets its colour from fried onions and can be a darker shade of brown. Typically, such a chicken curry will not have an exotic label in cookbooks. When I first looked up the recipe for a standard chicken curry in a book, by the doyen of Indian cooking in the west, Madhur Jaffrey, she called it her 'everyday' chicken curry. I somehow felt offended. My childhood memories associate this chicken curry with special and memorable meals, not a humdrum everyday happening and, trust me, while you can have this regularly, in taste it is anything but 'everyday'.

I had mentioned in the previous chapter that **Fish Curry** was a regular dish at home. The Bihari fish curry is only marginally different from the Bengali fish curry and the most popular fish are the same, rohu and katla. The similarity is that in preparing the dish, the fish pieces are first marinated using salt, turmeric and red chilli powder and then fried in mustard oil. The curry, called jhor in Bihar, is cooked independently. Yellow mustard seed, either powdered or as a paste, is a key ingredient and makes the Bihari fish curry taste somewhat different from the Bengali machher jhol.

This two-step process used to be key for a unique way of cooking this dish at home for a period of my childhood. When we moved from Haldia to Barauni, we lived in the company township which was only about twenty kilometres away from my ancestral village, where my paternal grandparents lived. The village was on the banks of a river (the intriguingly named Burhi Gandak or Old Gandak) and also had a large fishery pond. A person we knew from the village, Sohan, used to be a lunch 'dabbawala' in the company. Every day he would carry lunch boxes from the township to the office for employees who preferred hot, home-cooked food to what was available in the office canteen. What made the job arduous and remarkable was that he used to cycle every day from the village in the morning and then cycle back in the evening after doing his lunch run between the township and the office. My guess is that he was cycling about fifty kilometres every day, every week, year after year. He was well-known to my grandparents and parents. He used our house in the township as a pit stop during his long working day, first as a late morning tea break when he came in from the village and then for a rest and refuelling break before he went back to the village in the evening.

Since Sohan was cycling to and from the village every day, he was a perfect, personal courier for my family, for messages and letters sent between my grandparents and parents but also for food items prepared by my grandmother. Among other things, fairly common was fish, caught in the morning from the river or the pond, fried as in the first of the two-step cooking process and then sent in a lunch box. We could have a few pieces of the dry fried fish for lunch, but mostly my mother would prepare the curry in the evening. Those were the rare times that we had bhaat for dinner because, of course, fish curry just does not go with roti. Having grown up on a regular diet of fresh fish curry, it is no surprise that I've had great fondness for fish dishes all my life.

Apart from the vegetable dishes called tarkari, we also had a number of other vegetarian dishes such as **Matar Paneer**, peas and cottage cheese in a curry; **Malai Kofta**, creamy curry with potato balls stuffed with cottage cheese; and **Chhole**, white chickpeas in a curry. A frequent dish, **Karhi Badi**, is popular all over north India. I find the name of the dish interesting as it is one of the few dishes which has the word 'Karhi' in its name. Karhi (kari in Tamil) is a generic name for the gravy or liquid which is part of most Indian dishes and from where the English word curry is derived. But the word is not commonly attached to the name of a dish in local languages. Karhi Badi is one of the few, perhaps the only one in Hindi, with the word karhi in the name and in fact refers to a specific dish.

Also, a note on the spelling of badi. The 'd' in the word is a hard 'r' sound in Hindi and other Indian languages with no equivalent in English. It could be spelt barri or even barhi in English. I've used the common convention in this case as well as for the other similar dishes such as vada, vadi, etc. later on in this book.

Karhi Badi has two parts. The key ingredient for both is **Besan**, which is flour made from dried and lightly roasted chana daal (Bengal gram, or dehusked and split brown chickpea). It is sometimes called chickpea flour in English translations but that is not strictly correct. Chickpea or chola is different from chana. Besan is widely used in Indian cooking, especially for snacks and sweets, and most familiar as the batter in Pakora of all types. For the badi, lightly spiced besan batter is whipped and then small round dollops of the batter are deep fried. This results in spongy balls of fried, spiced besan. Karhi is made of besan flour, yoghurt and water mixed together into a gruel and cooked with ghee and spices, especially turmeric. Karhi thus has a striking yellow colour. The badi balls are then soaked in the liquid karhi for a bit till they become very soft. The dish is generally eaten with bhaat at lunch time.

It was quite common for large quantities of the spiced besan batter, used for badi, to be shaped into balls and dried in the sun. Once dried, they can be stored for long periods of time. The sight of besan balls being dried on wicker trays in the sun will be familiar to many Biharis of a slightly older vintage.

One of the better known Bihari dishes is **Litti Chokha**. **Chokha**, as we have seen earlier, is a generic name for a mashed vegetable dish, also called bharta. In litti chokha, the chokha is generally made of baingan or brinjal, though in more elaborate forms, chokha made of potato and tomato may also be served. The key difference between the Bihari chokha and the more common bharta is that, apart from the main vegetable, all other ingredients in the chokha are raw. Thus, roasted brinjal is mashed and mixed with raw chopped onions, green chillies, garlic, coriander leaves, lemon juice and a bit of mustard oil and the chokha is ready.

Litti is not as simple to prepare. A key ingredient of the stuffing is **Sattu**. Sattu is a Bihari speciality, widely available but generally considered a rustic preparation and sometimes called a 'poor man's protein'. It is a flour made from grinding fully roasted chana (brown chickpea), though it may also have some other pulses added. Because the chana is roasted properly before being ground, sattu may be considered a ready-to-eat preparation, not just an ingredient. At its simplest, sattu mixed with a bit of water and salt or sugar makes for an easy porridge. For a slightly tastier option, milk is used instead of water. I've memories of having a bowl of sattu with milk, sugar, raisins and nuts for a substantial evening snack. Dry sattu flour mixed with onions, chillies, salt and a bit of mustard oil, with pickles on the side, is widely eaten as a full meal by farmers and labourers in Bihar. In recent years, sattu has been 'discovered' as a healthy food option in Indian cities. You may find a sattu protein drink on the menu in some restaurants and bars. This is sattu with water, jazzed up with a few spices and presented colourfully with a slice of fruit or two to justify the hike in price.

For a properly made litti stuffing, sattu is mixed with an elaborate list of ingredients – seeds of fennel, cumin, nigella and carom, red chilli powder, green chillies, ginger, garlic, coriander leaves, a bit of mustard oil and a little bit of water to allow the stuffing to hold together. This stuffing is put into flat portions of wheat dough and then shaped into balls. Traditionally, these balls were baked over open fire but now are also cooked in an oven or an open grill. Once properly baked, it is customary to slightly crack each litti and pour a teaspoon or two of hot ghee on each before serving. When eating, the litti is broken into smaller pieces and had mixed with the chokha.

The funny thing for me about litti chokha is that I've no memory of eating it at home. When I was young, I knew the dish mainly as a boring, low cost meal served in roadside eateries. The few times I tried it, neither the litti nor the chokha impressed me. It has been somewhat of a surprise then that, of all the dishes that I remember from my childhood in Bihar, it is litti chokha which has become a symbol of Bihari cuisine. In my view, a variant of litti chokha, which deserves a little more publicity, is a non-vegetarian variety which can be called **Litti Keema**. **Keema** is minced mutton curry available across most parts of India. It is a really wonderful accompaniment to litti. So, if after having tried litti chokha, if you also wonder what the fuss is about, do give litti keema a try.

Keema curry was often made at my home, sometimes with peas as **Keema Matar**. Minced mutton could be bought straight from the butcher, who would mince our selection of meat pieces on request. For a good keema curry, the mince should be marinated to soften it. A particular flourish is to add raw papaya to the marinade, which is supposed to make the meat extra soft. The dish is cooked in a fairly standard sequential way with whole spices such as clove, cinnamon, peppercorn and bay leaves being roasted in mustard oil as a first step, then sliced onions, ginger and garlic are fried in the same oil. To this mix, tomatoes and the standard powdered spices of coriander, cumin, red chilli and turmeric are added. Once this curry base is fried to a mush, the mince is added to it. When the meat is browned, water, seasoning and garam masala are added. The cooking time after that can be long because the meat takes time to be cooked. At home, we now shorten the process by using a pressure cooker. Keema is a versatile dish and can be eaten with roti, paratha, bhaat, poori or indeed litti.

As an aside, Bihari keema and kabab are popular dishes in Pakistan. These dishes travelled with Bihari Muslims who migrated to Pakistan during Partition. They use a complex spice combination, called Bihari kabab masala, which has many more individual spices for taste and aroma. While these dishes have roots in Bihar, they have evolved in Pakistan and should be seen as Pakistani dishes rather than Bihari.

Breakfast at home on weekdays was not generally anything special. However, on most weekends we would have a heavy breakfast and a lighter lunch and, sometimes, combine the two into a brunch. A favourite weekend brunch was **Poori Aloo**. The **Poori** eaten in Bihar is about 10 – 15 cm in diameter and prepared by deep frying circular pieces of rolled dough made from atta. In frying, a well-made poori puffs up beautifully and generally stays puffed for a short period of time. The first thing to do when eating a freshly made poori is to poke a small hole on the top and, as the hot air hisses out, to smell it. It is a great way to get started. Poori, like roti, can be eaten with many types of dishes. At breakfast at home, it was generally always paired with aloo bhujia, which I've described earlier. It is not a particularly healthy meal and does take a bit of effort to cook, so it tended to be only a weekend or special occasion indulgence. Poori Aloo can also be had as a light meal and is very popular on railway stations as a quick meal for passengers on long-distance train journeys. When I used to travel by train from Delhi to home, during my undergraduate years, Poori Aloo served at Mughal Sarai station (Banaras) used to be a meal to look forward to during the journey.

In the 1990s, my wife and I moved to the US for a couple of years. Till then, living in India and as a working couple, we had a cook. So, while we enjoyed our cook's food (or otherwise when she had a bad day), we didn't need to worry ourselves too much about recipes etc. That changed in the US and we, like many before us, discovered recipe books and recipes dictated over the phone.

One day we decided to make poori at home. The recipe didn't seem too complicated – prepare the dough, roll small lumps into poori sized circles and then deep fry. We got stuck at the first stage. I thought that the dough is prepared by mixing wheat flour with water. But my wife insisted that poori should only be made with dough prepared with flour and milk and that is how poori dough is different from roti. The pooris made this way came out really nice. But I still had a nagging doubt. As I've said earlier, I did spend a lot of time as a child in and out of the kitchen and remember flour being mixed with water to prepare dough for both roti and poori. Sometime later, I got the chance to check with my mother-in-law. It so happens that, at my wife's home, poori prepared as 'prasad', or offerings for religious ceremonies, was made with milk but otherwise would be prepared with water. I am guessing that the festive occasions must have stuck in my wife's memory. You don't have to use milk for the dough, but the pooris taste better that way.

During winters, a popular snack in Bihar is **Gughni Chura**. **Gughni** is made mostly with matar (peas), though chana (brown chickpeas) can also be used. The process is similar to that of frying vegetables. Boiled peas are cooked with onions and spices in mustard oil. **Chura** (also written as chiwra) is flattened, lightly roasted rice. For this dish, it is roasted further before being served with the gughni, providing a nice contrast of crunchiness to the softness of the gughni. It is a snack common both with street vendors and in homes. It was routinely served with tea when we visited or were visited by family friends. Somehow, we easily managed to finish off a bowlful and still have a proper dinner a couple of hours later. I've also been served this dish many times in my days as a sales manager in Uttar Pradesh when visiting distributors in far-flung towns. It is a safe and satisfying snack option on the road in most of north India.

Daal with Bhaat

Roti or Chapati or Phulka

Litti Chokha

Poori Aloo

I was uniquely placed in one particular way as a child. Both my paternal and maternal grandparents had houses neighbouring local sweet shops, so I had literally a direct view to the preparation of some of the most popular sweets of the region. These shops are not the sanitised sweet shops that you find in cities, but kitchens doubling up as shops. Right in front of each shop there were massive cooking pans filled with bubbling oil or ghee in which the sweets would be prepared multiple times during the day. The cook is called a 'halwai' and the shop, 'halwai ki dukaan' or halwai's shop, is also often shortened to just halwai. The halwais would sit on a stool or bench in front of their assigned pan, each responsible for the preparation of something specific. As in other kitchens, there were a number of other cooks and helpers, preparing ingredients, washing up, serving customers and generally beavering about. These were busy places. There were always a few benches for customers, as it was common practice to have a plate or two of the freshly made sweets as a snack. Since the shops were next door, we knew when the sweets would be freshly made and often bought hot sweets as they came out of the cooking pans.

A favourite was **Jalebi**. This sweet dish is so well-known that it is almost a symbol of Indian sweets. It is made from maida, very finely milled wheat flour. A viscous and fermented batter of maida and water is used. Circular, spiral strings of the batter are poured directly into hot oil to be deep fried. Making the spiral shapes requires a little bit of skill and quite a lot of practice. The halwais in those sweet shops would transfer the batter into a thin cloth holder with a small hole and squeeze out the batter through the hole in a circular motion. The jalebis are fried till they are golden and crisp. In another pan, sugar syrup is prepared with a bit of saffron and cardamom for the special jalebi flavour. The jalebis are transferred directly from the frying pan to the syrup pan, held in the syrup for a few minutes and then transferred to large plates ready to be served or sold. This is a process that I've watched with fascination, mouth salivating (even writing about it makes me salivate), many times as a child when buying jalebis from the neighbouring shops. We would buy jalebis mostly to have as an evening snack but sometimes, as a special treat, jalebi would be served as the dessert after a big breakfast or brunch. I had never eaten a breakfast only of jalebis but discovered later that it is not uncommon in north India. What a delight!

Another favourite from the local halwai was a combination snack called **Sev Bundiya**. **Sev** is a savoury snack made of fried besan, shaped as thin noodles. When eaten as a stand-alone snack, it is made quite spicy but when added to chaat or other snacks, it is what one could call the plain-salted variety. **Bundiya** or **Boondi** are sweet pea-sized balls of fried besan. The batter is poured into the oil through ladles or cooking spoons with perforations, forming the droplets which fry fairly quickly in the oil. The name derives from the Hindi word 'boond' which means a droplet. In its sweet form, after frying, the droplets are dipped into a sugar syrup, similar to the one used for jalebi, to make them sweet and crunchy. Sev Bundiya is a savoury and sweet combination and is a snack rather than a dessert.

Jalebi and Sev Bundiya are widely available across India. Khaja and Lai are more regional specialities. I find the name **Khaja** especially intriguing. It translates as 'go eat'. What else would you do with it? It is a well-known sweet dish, its fame comes mainly because it is an essential part of the prasad or holy offering in the famous Jagannath temple in Puri, in the state of Odisha. The preparation of the dish requires quite a bit of work. Layers of maida dough are delicately stuck together, rolled and cut into rectangular pieces and deep fried. The flaky fried pastries are then soaked in sugar syrup and patted dry. One can get khaja of varying dryness. I've had pieces dripping with the syrup and also sweet but completely dry, and hence less messy, ones. Wet khaja can be similar in feel and appearance to Turkish baklava, though there are no nuts in khaja and they are larger in size.

Lai or **Ramdana laddu** is a Bihari speciality. Laddu is a generic name for a range of sweets, all spherical in shape and about the size of a table tennis ball. Inevitably, the word laddu is also used colloquially to mean fat. Lai is a laddu made with Ramdana or Rajgira seeds, amaranth in English. The seed is considered quite healthy and used for religious meals. Its names are indicative of its perceived value: Ramdana means Ram's seed or God's seed and Rajgira means royal seed. The seed is used in a number of dishes. But in Bihar you will find it most commonly as lai or Ramdana laddu, sold by street-side vendors and in sweet shops. It is not complicated to make. The seeds are roasted to puff them up and mixed with either cooked gur, jaggery, or khoya and sugar syrup. The mixture is then shaped by hand into individual laddus.

Continuing with Bihari specialities, there is a sweet dish called **Thekua** which is prepared during the annual Chhath festival. Chhath is celebrated only in

Bihar and neighbouring areas, where it is as big a festival as Diwali. It is celebrated a few days after Diwali when the weather is just beginning to cool. It is a very old festival with Vedic rituals involving worship of the sun over four days, one of the few Hindu festivals still practised which does not involve idols.

Thekua is a sweet dish prepared as part of the daily offerings made to the sun, eaten as a prasad first and then as a snack for many weeks after. The dough is prepared by mixing whole wheat flour with sugar syrup or cooked jaggery syrup and flavoured with ghee, cardamom and fennel seeds. In some variants, grated coconut is also added. The dough needs to be quite stiff to ensure that the thekua retains shape when being fried. Bits of the dough are rolled and shaped or cut into either round discs or a leaf-like shape and often embossed with designs. These are then deep fried. The cooked thekua is a deep, reddish brown in colour, soft when it is hot but hard when cold. It is mostly eaten cold. The outer crust can get quite tough to bite into. Thekua is practically unknown to non-Biharis. This is not surprising. While it is comfortingly tasty, it is a fairly simple preparation and lacks subtlety in flavour. One other quirky bit. We called it khorma, not thekua. There is a local dialect spoken in my village and surrounding areas, one of those which pre-dates Hindi and stubbornly refuses to die. The dialect is a mix of two other Bihari languages, Maithil and Magahi. In this dialect, thekua is called khorma. So it was in our home.

The Chhath festival food includes a sweet called **Pirakia** or **Perakia**, more commonly known as **Gujia** in north India. This is made for many festivals, including Holi and Diwali. It is a stuffed, fried pastry and has a distinctive semi-circular shape with a crinkled edge. In appearance, pirakia or gujia is very similar to the Latin American empanada but smaller. The pastry crust is made of maida or a mixture of maida and atta flour. The stuffing varies by region. In Bihar, the stuffing is made of suji or sooji (semolina), cooked in ghee with cardamom powder, sugar and dry fruits, such as cashew, coconut and raisins. Sometimes khoya is also added to the suji. In gujia made in other parts, the stuffing may be made entirely of khoya with dry fruits, etc. In all cases, the stuffing is spooned into circular pieces of the dough but only on one half, and then each piece is folded and crinkled to seal along the folded, curving edge. This gives the sweet its distinctive shape. The pieces are deep fried till the crust becomes golden and crisp.

Pirakia or gujia is one of the sweets that is now sold in packaged form in Indian sweet shops all over and available on online stores. Large quantities of thekua and pirakia would be made at my grandparents' place for Chhath. We would have jars of both at home after the festival, to be eaten with the evening tea or when feeling peckish anytime during the day. That was one way of making the festivals last longer than just a few days. When the thekua and pirakia finished, so did the festive feeling. Till the next one came along.

Jalebi

Thekua

3
Punjab and Delhi
Familiar stalwarts of North Indian food

I've grouped the foods of Punjab and Delhi together in this chapter after a bit of deliberation. Traditional Delhi food has its roots in the centuries that Delhi was the epicentre of the Mughal empire and, before that, the Delhi sultanate. However, the settlement of large numbers of Punjabis in Delhi, after the Partition of Punjab between India and Pakistan in 1947, has altered the nature of Delhi food. There are still families who have lived in Delhi for many generations and are custodians of Delhi's traditional food, but they are relatively small in number. Madhur Jaffrey belongs to one such family and the food she describes as 'home food' in her books is representative of the upper-class kitchens of Delhi before 1947. But Punjabi food is now a widespread and integral part of Delhi and it can be quite difficult to differentiate traditional Delhi food from Punjabi food. Indeed, the rest of the country knows this food as an amalgamated 'North Indian food'. At a minimum, a more nuanced approach is to separate Punjabi food from Mughlai food, and I will attempt to do so in this chapter and the next.

My first experience of North Indian food was many hundreds of miles from Punjab and Delhi, in Calcutta, in a restaurant called Anarkali in the centre of the city. The restaurant's name is misleading. Anarkali was the name of a Mughal period beauty who was supposedly an early love of Prince Salim, later Emperor Jahangir. Their tragic love story was popularised through a Bollywood super hit in the 1950s called *Mughal-e-Azam*. One would expect a restaurant with such a name to specialise in Mughlai food. But the food served in the restaurant was mainly Punjabi. It was a typical no-frills, low-cost restaurant, similar to many dotted around the cities of India in the 1960s and 70s. Many of them had menus based on what one would find in a 'dhaba', a roadside eatery, serving mainly Punjabi food. It is generally believed that these dhabas had sprung up to cater to the needs of truck drivers, providing a place for food and rest. Since the earliest truck drivers were Punjabis, the food served was Punjabi. These dhabas introduced Punjabi food across large parts of India, especially on the main transport routes in the north, west and east. Restaurants like Anarkali were an offshoot of this phenomenon, a more middle-class version of the dhaba, catering to the local population rather than the itinerant truck drivers. The restaurant still exists in Kolkata, an upgraded version of what it was in the 1970s.

We used to pass through Calcutta every time we went on a holiday away from Haldia. We would arrive in the morning, spend the day in the city sightseeing and shopping, and then catch a train from Howrah station in the evening. Lunch at Anarkali, once we discovered it, was a key part of these special days. This was my first introduction to the Punjabi food staples: Tandoori Roti, Tandoori Murgh (tandoori chicken), Murgh Makhani (butter chicken), with sides of Daal Makhani (creamy daal) and Raita (spiced yoghurt with vegetables). Anarkali was a popular restaurant then, very often with queues of waiting diners. The fast turnover ensured the food was freshly made and mostly hygienic. The kitchen, at that time, was just at the back of the restaurant and we could see, and smell, the food being cooked.

Tandoori dishes get their names from being cooked in a tandoor, which is a traditional clay oven with a live fire of charcoal inside it. But it was rare to find a tandoor in a domestic setting even in Punjab. Communities there would have a shared tandoor, but these were not common outside the region. For people like us, living far away from Punjab, tandoori food was only available in dhabas and restaurants.

Tandoori Roti is cooked by sticking flattened pieces of wheat flour dough to the inside of the tandoor. The tandoori roti is often shaped by the cook just with his hands and is thicker than the chapati or roti cooked on a tawa. The shape of the tandoori roti can be circular or oval, though I've known cooks to experiment with the shapes, especially when you ask them to show them how these are made. The intense heat of the tandoor makes the surface of the tandoori roti crisp and charred in places, so it feels quite different from chapati. Hot ghee can be smeared on to tandoori roti for a bit of added indulgence.

Tandoori Murgh, or **Tandoori Chicken**, was a revelation the first time I had it. As I've described in the previous chapter, chicken at home was normally made with curry. Even the dry chicken that I was given as an appetiser would still have a thick gravy of cooked onions and spices. In Anarkali I tasted a completely dry chicken dish for the first time. Tandoori chicken is a dish prepared by marinating whole or pieces of chicken in a blend of yoghurt and spices. A key element is Kashmiri red chilli powder which has a strong red colour. The marinated chicken is put on skewers and cooked in the tandoor over high heat. The cooked meat tends to be reddish in colour due to the red chilli. This has led to the unfortunate practice in modern restaurants of adding red food colour to the marinade to ensure that the dish comes out looking fiery and unnaturally red. It is quite unnecessary.

Tandoori chicken is normally served either whole or in big, chunky pieces. As a main dish, it needs daal or raita as a side dish, otherwise just the tandoori chicken and roti can be dry. It is common practice to serve raw, sliced onions with a bit of mint chutney as an accompaniment to the tandoori chicken. A strong mouth wash after the meal is a good idea!

As an aside, if the chicken pieces are cut into small, bite sized pieces before marinating and cooking, the dish is called **Tandoori Chicken Tikka** or just **Chicken Tikka**; the word tikka simply means a small piece. Chicken tikka is a dish which can be served as both a main dish and, in a smaller quantity, as an appetiser. It is also a very popular cocktail and party snack in India, served on trays carried around by waiters, with toothpicks to pick them up. It is best had with a mint chutney, which always poses a behavioural conundrum for me. Is it polite to dip your chicken tikka in the chutney bowl on the tray carried by the waiter? If not, then do you hold up the waiter while you delicately spoon out a bit of the chutney onto a single piece of the tikka?

Tandoori chicken is probably the best known of Punjabi dishes. As teenagers we used to joke that if Punjab were a country, tandoori chicken would be its national bird! The dish also has historical provenance. The Indus Valley civilisation sites, found all over north west India and Pakistan and dating about 3000 BCE to 1500 BCE, have remnants of clay ovens similar to the tandoor. There is also evidence that chicken or fowl was part of the diet at that time. Something similar to the tandoori chicken would, not too improbably, have been a part of their food, as has been claimed by some historians. The key difference would be the absence of red chillies, since these came to India from the Americas only in the sixteenth century CE.

The other iconic Punjabi chicken dish is **Murgh Makhani** or **Butter Chicken**. This dish was actually created by a restaurant in Delhi, Moti Mahal of Daryaganj (one more reason for combining Punjabi and Delhi food). The restaurant was set up by Punjabi refugees from Peshawar, now in Pakistan, after Partition. They may have created the dish in their restaurant in Peshawar, but it was first introduced as a menu item by the Delhi restaurant in the 1950s. The story is that they wanted to find a way to prevent leftover chicken tikka from drying out, and found that it could be kept well enough to be served again in a thick tomato based gravy with butter and cream. The family of one of the original restaurateurs still runs the Moti Mahal Deluxe restaurants in Delhi, though the Moti Mahal in Daryaganj is now owned by another restaurateur. Both are good places to try the original murgh makhani.

The curry for butter chicken is made with onions, tomatoes and spices, with large dollops of butter and cream. The curry is made really smooth and thick, by either using puréed ingredients or by blending the curry at an intermediate stage of the preparation. The chicken in the dish should normally be tandoori chicken in medium sized pieces. However, when the dish is prepared at home, the chicken maybe pan-fried or grilled.

Butter chicken is best eaten with tandoori roti, with roti pieces used to scoop up the gravy. Inevitably you will find yourself licking the gravy off your fingers, during and at the end of the meal. It is a very rich dish and generally does not require a supporting cast of side dishes.

Butter chicken is a close cousin of **Chicken Tikka Masala**, arguably the most popular Indian dish in the UK. There are many claimants for its invention. One popular story says that it was created in a Glasgow curry house when a customer asked for curry with his chicken tikka. The cook added some tomato soup to a pre-prepared curry, and the resultant dish seems to have delighted that customer and many to follow. Another version has a cook in Birmingham trying to make the surplus chicken tikka keep better and discovering, like the inventors of butter chicken, that chicken tikka keeps well in a tomato and cream-based curry. Chicken tikka masala recipes have many variations, though most will have small pieces of boneless chicken and a mild curry with tomato and cream.

Going back to Anarkali, **Daal Makhani** was another popular dish. Punjabi daal makhani is made with urad daal (black lentils). Sometimes a little bit of rajma (red kidney beans) is also added. The daal is initially prepared in the standard way by boiling with the right proportion of water for the right amount of time, preferably after soaking the lentils overnight. Separately, the chhonk, called tarka in north India, is prepared with a small quantity of onions, tomatoes and a number of spices, fried in generous quantities of ghee or butter. In some of the restaurant varieties of daal makhani, a really long list of spices is used for the tarka. I've seen recipes which include ginger, garlic, green chillies, cumin seeds, cloves, green and black cardamoms, bay leaves, cinnamon, red chilli powder, onions and tomatoes. The tarka is added to the daal which is then further cooked over low heat with lots of cream added at the last stage. Daal makhani, like the curry in butter chicken, is smooth and creamy. It is a fantastic side dish in most Punjabi restaurant meals and goes well with both roti and rice. And personally, I love the fact that there are no visible jeera (cumin) seeds floating on the surface to put me off.

As I've described in the previous chapter, daal is generally always made with chhonk or tarka in north India, otherwise it would be too bland. So, when I first came across the dish called **Tarka Daal** in a Delhi restaurant, I found it intriguing. I half expected to find a plain daal dish on the menu but didn't. Since it is rare to have daal made without a basic chhonk or tarka, I am still not sure if the additional qualification is necessary. In my opinion, the tarka adjective really stands for an elaborate tarka of onions and tomatoes fried with ginger, garlic, chilli, and lots of whole and ground spices. And I suppose that on a restaurant menu 'tarka daal' sounds better than just plain 'daal'.

Raita is also a regular side dish in Punjabi meals, and in most north Indian households. At its simplest, it is yoghurt mixed with salt and a couple of spices, such as jeera powder and red chilli powder. At home, my wife rustles up a pretty-looking raita dish in a few minutes by sprinkling these spice powders in straight diametric lines over a bowl of yoghurt, for us to mix and spoon out when eating.

A more common variety is the cucumber raita with grated cucumber mixed into the yoghurt. The restaurant varieties tend to be a little bit more complex. The vegetable raita has chopped onions, tomatoes, cucumber and green chillies along with spices. Another variety is the boondi raita, where boondi drops, described earlier in Sev Bundiya as small drops of fried besan (Bengal gram flour), are added to the yoghurt.

Raita can be had as a side dish in most north Indian meals. It is generally eaten to cool and refresh your palate in between the morsels of the main dishes. A mild raita is especially useful if you have a particularly fiery curry as your main dish. A raita will always be a part of a meal with multiple dishes, but it is rare to eat it as a main dish. However, I've sometimes eaten rice, daal and a vegetable raita as a full meal, mixing all three dishes together into a gooey mess. It can be a surprisingly tasty lunch, and easily put together if you have rice and daal left over from a previous meal. Apart from north Indian food, I've found yoghurt-based dishes being so extensively used only in food from Greece, Turkey and the Levant. Greek Tzatziki is in fact very similar to cucumber raita.

After we moved from Haldia to Barauni, my chance of eating Punjabi food was reduced. We'd go to Punjabi restaurants during holidays, but these were infrequent. I had a couple of friends from Punjab in school but most of us went home for lunch, so there was no sharing of lunch box food. Meals in friends' places were mostly pan-Indian snacks. Of the few meals that I can remember at my Punjabi friends' houses, we didn't have food like I'd eaten in Anarkali. As I've said earlier, most households don't have a tandoor, so this was not surprising. The two dishes that I most remember from those meals are both vegetarian – rajma (red kidney beans) curry and matar paneer (peas and cottage cheese) curry.

Rajma Curry is made in many northern states, so in classifying it as a Punjabi dish, I am talking specifically of a thick, spicy curry dish called rajma masala or simply rajma. The dish is prepared in a fairly standard way with onions and tomatoes fried with ginger and garlic paste and a range of spices for the masala. This masala is then cooked with the beans and a proportionate amount of water to make the dish. Rajma curry, as a dish, is somewhere between a daal and a vegetable dish. Its most common combination is in rajma chawal, a simple meal of boiled rice and rajma curry, comfort food for most Punjabis.

Matar Paneer, peas and cottage cheese, is also a very well-known vegetarian curry dish, often made at home and widely available in north Indian restaurants. Paneer is a dairy product, hence vegetarian but not vegan, and very popular in Punjab. It is a whitish, unsalted, spongy cheese. Once made, it keeps quite well and doesn't melt when cooked. It can be prepared at home with a bit of effort but is more easily bought in packaged form or freshly made from dairy shops. Paneer and chhena (used to make Rasgulla among other things) are similarly made. Chhena is softer and crumbly whereas paneer is made as a solid slab and can be cut into small cubes for dishes like the matar paneer. Matar paneer has a base curry similar to other curries, onions, tomatoes and spices, with cream sometimes added for greater smoothness. The paneer may be separately lightly fried before being added to the curry or added to the curry at the last stage for a few minutes. The dish can be served with roti or rice. I've eaten matar paneer at home, at other people's homes and in many different types of restaurants. It tends to taste similar everywhere, consistent but hardly ever exceptional. That may in fact be the reason for its popularity.

I discovered north Indian **Paratha** (also spelt parantha or parontha) when I moved to Delhi during my undergraduate years. I had eaten both plain paratha and aloo paratha (paratha stuffed with potatoes) at home. Paratha is a type of flat bread and, at home, we had it as a breakfast dish, either with a vegetable dish or with yoghurt. But the parathas at home were the size of rotis and, in the case of aloo paratha, only lightly stuffed with mildly spiced potatoes. In Delhi, stuffed paratha is a much more substantial dish, regularly had for breakfast, weekend brunches or even for meals.

Plain Paratha can be made in two ways. The simpler way is to roll wheat flour dough somewhat thicker than a roti, lightly brush with ghee or oil on both sides and then cook on a tawa. A stricter method requires the paratha to be layered. At home, the plain paratha would be made first by rolling out the dough into a circular shape larger than for a roti, then applying ghee and folding it twice into a triangular shape; then rolling it out while maintaining the shape and finally frying on a tawa. Plain paratha at home was always triangular and hence visibly different from roti. Punjabi plain parathas are always layered, though not necessarily triangular, with most cooks using various techniques in the intermediate step of folding the dough to create parathas of varying flakiness.

The best known north Indian stuffed paratha is the **Aloo Paratha**. The filling of mashed boiled potatoes with spices is separately prepared. This is stuffed into ball-sized pieces of wheat flour dough, then the dough is rolled out and cooked with coatings of ghee or oil as in the plain paratha above. Like rotis, aloo parathas are circular and can be of varying sizes, between 20 – 30 cm in diameter. A single large aloo paratha had with yoghurt and pickles makes for a very full breakfast. A large aloo paratha is also somewhat more difficult to cook as flipping the paratha weighed down with potatoes on the tawa can be difficult. Most cooks will hence settle for sizes between 20 – 25 cm. The stuffing can be prepared with many variations. Most commonly, the stuffing will also have some chopped onions, green chillies, coriander leaves and spices mixed in with the boiled potatoes. Cooks have their own preferences in the specific mixture of spices used, but generally the stuffing is only moderately spiced.

One of my close friends from college, Vivek, is a Delhi Punjabi. He was my guide to aloo parathas in Delhi. The college rules required all students to lodge in college hostels. The curriculum was quite rigorous and studying till late at night was very much the norm. To provide for peckish young people, there was a canteen in the campus which stayed open till midnight. But we often found ourselves awake after midnight and hungry. Vivek, as a local, knew many roadside eateries which would be open late at night. These were small eateries, sometimes nothing more than a tent with a charcoal-fired stove and a few benches for customers to sit on. They catered mainly to truck, taxi and auto rickshaw drivers on night shifts and also students from nearby colleges. I don't call them dhabas, as they served a very limited fare and operated out of almost temporary premises.

The two best known aloo paratha eateries close to the college campus in south Delhi were on the road crossings at Dhaula Kuan and Moolchand. Dhaula Kuan at that time was a simple road crossing, with none of the current loops and spirals of flyovers. On the southern side of the Ring Road were a few of these eateries, serving plain parathas, aloo parathas, boiled eggs and omelettes round the clock. Similarly, there were a couple of such eateries below the Moolchand flyover, also on the Ring Road. (Permanent eateries in the shopping arcades at the Metro stations have replaced those roadside shacks now). Later on, we found a paratha vendor even closer on Aurobindo Marg. This guy would set up shop every night at about 10 pm and pack up at about 3 – 4 am in the morning. Catering mainly to auto rickshaw drivers, he used to set up shop next to a bus stand with a portable stove and a bag of his cooking necessities and ingredients. The paratha was served on paper and we ate standing. The aloo parathas in these places were made to be filling, large in size and with a good quantity of stuffing, though it helped to remind the cook to be generous with the stuffing when making your aloo paratha.

Vivek's parents lived not far from the college campus and he would usually go home for the weekend. He was very fond of aloo parathas then (and still is, though a bit more calorie conscious now) and claimed that his mother made the best. It took some persuasion, but I did manage to get him to invite me home for Sunday brunches a few times. The aloo parathas that I had at Vivek's place, fresh off the tawa and served with butter, are probably the best that I've ever had. As far as I know, there was no secret ingredient, just a what a perfect aloo paratha served with butter is: a harmonious medley of carbs, fat and spices on your palate!

There are many other varieties of stuffed paratha. In the roadside eateries, I discovered the **Anda (egg) Paratha**. This is trickier to make than the name suggests. The paratha dough is prepared as for a plain paratha and, separately, the egg is whisked and mixed with some chopped onions, green chilli and spices in a bowl. The dough is then cooked on the tawa as a plain paratha. While it is cooking, when it is crisp enough but not fully cooked, a small slit is made on one side and half of the egg mixture poured in. Once this side is cooked, the process is repeated for the other side. This step, which requires slitting the paratha and pouring the egg in, is the tricky part, something I've rarely managed to pull off when trying to make egg paratha at home. One can take the easier route of pouring the egg mixture on the sides, rather than inside, and make what is the paratha equivalent of French toast or eggy bread, but it is not the same.

After aloo paratha, the second best known stuffed paratha is **Mooli Paratha**. Mooli is a long, white radish-like root vegetable, widely available in Asia. It can be cooked as a vegetable, but is mostly eaten raw, with seasoning, on its own or mixed with onions and cucumbers as a salad side dish. The stuffing for the mooli paratha is made of grated mooli with green chillies and spices. It is lighter than the aloo paratha. It is often preferred over aloo paratha for being 'healthier'. That is a relative term – a healthy stuffed paratha is otherwise an oxymoron. Similar to the mooli paratha is the gobhi paratha, paratha stuffed with cauliflower. The cauliflower needs to be finely grated before being mixed with green chillies and spices. The raw cauliflower gets mildly cooked inside the paratha. This is not to everyone's taste and an alternative way of cooking requires the cauliflower to be separately fried with the other ingredients and mashed before being stuffed into the paratha dough.

As is evident from the preparation of mooli and gobhi paratha, the stuffing for paratha can be made from many different things. There is a small street in Old Delhi, just off Chandni Chowk, called Paranthewali Gali, literally 'the street of parathas'. While aloo paratha is considered a classical Punjabi dish, stuffed paratha itself is much more a part of traditional Delhi cuisine. The oldest paratha restaurant in Paranthewali Gali is from the 1870s. There are still a number of small restaurants in this crowded and narrow street, a few running continuously from the nineteenth century. These places serve a long list of parathas. Apart from the standard, aloo, mooli and gobhi, the stuffing can also be of mint, just green chillies (!), carrots, tomatoes, peas, lemon, paneer, besan, even karela. Most of the parathas in these shops are deep fried, rather than pan-fried like those I've described so far. The first time I had a paratha here, I was quite surprised as I didn't expect the crispiness that you get from deep frying. But this is how parathas have been made in Delhi for a long time. These deep-fried parathas are thinner than pan-fried parathas and crispier.

You also get sweet parathas in the Paranthewali Gali restaurants. These are parathas stuffed with sweetened dairy preparations such as khoya. These sweet parathas bring back memories of mitha (sweet) paratha I ate as a child. Instead of filling the dough with a savoury stuffing, you just add a small amount of fine sugar. Then roll the dough and cook as you would any other paratha. The heat of the cooking melts some of the sugar, so the paratha has a nice sweet consistency. Like sweet crepes, this one is mainly meant for kids. I haven't had one since I was a child and I think may find the taste a bit dodgy now.

For a relatively uncomplicated dish, aloo paratha can command very fierce loyalties. I've known people outside India who have driven hundreds of miles for aloo parathas made at a friend's house by a visiting parent. I personally need a regular dose of aloo paratha. Since we rarely attempt to cook it at home, I've had to make innovative arrangements. In one instance, I convinced my local chippy (fish and chip shop) in London to try their hand at making aloo parathas, a reasonably successful attempt before they went out of business (for unrelated reasons I must clarify!). In a more recent attempt, I convinced a nearby south Indian restaurant to add aloo paratha to the menu. That proved to be a longer lasting arrangement.

Such behaviour is not just restricted to Indians outside India. An episode from my days in Delhi will help illustrate. I was working as a sales manager for a large consumer goods company, based in their Delhi branch and responsible for sales in a part of Uttar Pradesh including Agra. Agra has a number of fine paratha shops and one in particular was a favourite of the national sales manager of the company. He was based in Mumbai (then Bombay), and only got a chance to go to Agra once in a while.

He was attending a sales meeting in Delhi. Late in the evening, after a few drinks, he was waxing eloquent to another senior executive, also from Mumbai, about this paratha shop in Agra. Either due to the lure of the parathas or the effect of drinks or both, they decided that they had to have parathas at that shop next morning. I was immediately summoned to organise the visit. Arranging a car to take them to Agra in the morning for a paratha brunch was not a problem, but the ethics of doing this on a company expense account definitely was. The senior executives 'solved' the problem by deciding that it would be a 'market visit' and hence company business. That meant I had to go along with them. We set off early next morning and duly managed to have a delicious brunch of deep-fried stuffed parathas. Such can be the attraction of a well-made paratha.

Just to complete the story, since it was a 'market visit', we also stopped by at a few shops to check the displays of the company's products. This included a paan shop near the paratha shop. **Paan** is a preparation of betel nut leaves and had as a post-meal mouth freshener and stimulant. The leaf is cleaned and stuffed with chopped areca nuts, a spicy paste of rose preserve called **Gulkand**, chutney and other stimulants, before being rolled into a conical shape. You are supposed to chew and then spit out the resultant red liquid. This leads to the disgusting paan spits, red coloured splotches, seen on many paths and walls in India. Thankfully the practice of eating paan seems to be on the decline at least in the cities. A paan shop is a small kiosk selling paan, of course, but also cigarettes and a few other small items. They would not normally sell any of this company's products. As one purpose of a 'market visit' was to provide guidance to the young sales manager (me), I remember getting some sage advice from the recently well-fed senior executives, keen to keep up the façade of a market visit, on how to get paan shops to stock and sell the company's grocery products.

One summer in college, I enrolled for a National Social Service (NSS) project. As part of the college curriculum, we were required to do 100 hours of either NSS or National Cadet Corps (NCC) activities. NCC was run on campus but required waking up very early on Saturday mornings continuously for a couple of years. NSS had greater flexibility. You could collect hours doing a number of different types of social service projects, including participation in adult education, rural development, health awareness and blood donation programs. The program I chose was a rural development one, requiring a couple of weeks' stay in a village for a road building project, with the benefit of completing the 100 hours curriculum requirement in one go. The village was in Haryana, north of Delhi. Haryana used to be part of the larger Punjab state, before the state was divided into smaller states in the 1960s. The village was close to Punjab and the food there was mostly Punjabi.

It is customary to mention **Makki di Roti** (roti made of maize or corn flour) and **Sarson da Saag** (cooked mustard leaves) when talking about Punjabi food. I've never had them in my years in Delhi or in visits to cities in Punjab. These dishes are associated with rural Punjab and eaten in the winter months when both corn and mustard are available fresh. We were at the village during the summer and these dishes would not normally be cooked at that time. But as part of the project's aim of introducing us to local food, the cook used packaged ingredients bought from a nearby town to give us authentic (!) makki di roti and sarson da saag meals.

Makki di roti is roti made of corn flour, prepared the standard way over a tawa. The saag dish is made of mustard leaves. As I've mentioned earlier, saag is more commonly a dish made with palak (spinach), so the Punjabi sarson da saag is definitely different. Spinach is sometimes added to dish to reduce the bitterness of the mustard leaves. The Punjabi saag is very different from the tarkari that is had in the eastern states. The leaves are cut into small pieces, boiled in water and cooked till they get of puréed consistency, unlike palak saag which remains leafy. This calls for cooking for a long period of time, and modern cooks will shorten the time by using pressure cookers and blenders. In the traditional way of cooking, a tarka of ghee and garlic is also added at the end.

Most of the meals during our stay in the village were otherwise standard fare of roti, daal and vegetables. One new dish that I first tasted during this stay was **Mushroom Masala**. This is a recent addition to Punjabi food, fuelled by the uptake of mushroom farming in India's northern states in the 1960s and 70s. Mushrooms were grown mainly for the cities and export markets then and were still considered an uncommon ingredient. The dish itself was a typical vegetable curry, button mushrooms cooked in a gravy of onions, tomatoes and spices.

The reason we got to try the dish in the village was that the village headman, influenced by his entrepreneurial son, had switched some of his land to mushroom farming. I remember having an enlightening conversation with him about mushroom farming. He and his family were doing were very well from the switch to mushrooms and he was deservedly proud of his son, who handled commercial aspects from Delhi. When talking about his son, he let it drop that his son had recently bought a Japanese car. The Maruti Suzuki had only recently been launched in India, an Indian-made car produced in collaboration with Suzuki of Japan. Owning a car was at that time quite a prestigious thing, even in cities, so I was suitably impressed. Since he couldn't remember the name, I helpfully (and with a bit of urban condescension) prompted, "You mean the Maruti?". His response was a put-down to last a lifetime. "No, no. Maruti is an Indian car. I mean a Japanese one, something which is called Tyotta (Toyota) or something".

Tandoori Chicken

Murgh Makhani or Butter Chicken

Matar Paneer

Aloo Paratha

Punjabi and Delhi food have a number of dishes which fall under the street food category. These include Gol Gappa, described earlier, Chhole Bhature, Samosa, Pakora, Aloo Tikki, Kachori, Dahi Bhalla, etc. Most are now widely available across India in restaurants and shops. It is rare to find these dishes, with a few exceptions, being cooked at home and most people experience these as outside food, sold by vendors on streets, roadside tea shops, sweet and snack shops and smaller restaurants.

One of the best-known is **Chhole Bhature**. This is a dish of two parts: **Chhole** is a spicy curry of chickpeas and **Bhatura** (plural **Bhature**) is a deep-fried, puffed up bread made of maida and yoghurt. The bhatura can be round or oval shaped. When round it looks like a poori, but it tastes different and has a different texture because it is made of maida and has baking powder or yeast mixed in the dough for greater lightness. Depending on the quantity of chhole and the number of bhature served, this dish can be eaten as a snack, for breakfast or even as a full meal.

The chhole served in most Delhi restaurants can be very hot. When I was an undergraduate student in Delhi, I was a member of global student organisation called AIESEC. One of the main activities of this organisation then was to arrange internships for students from other countries on an exchange basis. This meant that, as local members, we played host to many students from other countries, especially from Europe, on internships to Delhi. A number of the foreign students would be keen to try Delhi street food. I am not sure what advice they were getting from their travel guidebooks since the best way to try Delhi street food then was not from street vendors, where the hygiene standards are not great, but at selected restaurants. Our first task with the AIESEC trainees used to be to explain that street food does not have to be literally street food.

During these meals, I've watched many different reactions to chhole bhature: from sheer delight to absolute distress, sometimes one after the other. One thing to remember – there is a reason why the dish has two parts. You have to have the chhole scooped in pieces of the bhature which helps to soften the overall spiciness and heat of the dish. If you attempt to have them separately, the chhole will be too spicy and sharp and the bhatura too bland.

Samosa is one of the most widely available north Indian street foods. It may be originally a Persian or Middle Eastern dish, though it is mentioned in Indian medieval texts as something eaten by both kings and the general population. It used to be made with a filling of minced meat with dried fruits. Such a dish can still be found in Middle Eastern food. Similar preparations using minced meat or vegetable fillings in fried pastry can be found in many countries in Asia and Africa. I remember eating something similar called zamoosa in Kenya.

It is the Indian samosa though which is best known. In its most common form, it is a triangular deep-fried pastry filled with a stuffing of spiced potatoes. The stuffing can be varied, so you can also get a stuffing of potatoes and peas, only peas, or cooked lentils, etc. It is rarer but not impossible to find samosas with stuffing of meat in India. There is a samosa-like dish called **Lukhmi** found in Hyderabad which has minced meat as the stuffing. The outer layer in all types of samosa is made of wheat flour, made crisp by deep frying. A modern, healthier practice is to bake the samosa rather than deep fry. Samosa is eaten with a chutney of mint, tamarind or tomato, or even with tomato ketchup. Like other street food, the magic of samosa is in the multiple tastes and textures that it combines in each bite: crispiness of the crust, softness of the boiled potatoes, flavours of the spices, sharpness of the chillies, and the balancing sweet and tangy taste of the chutney.

Samosas are mostly sold by sweet and snack shops, but also roadside tea vendors. They are rarely made at home, may be only during festivals and special occasions, as they can be easily bought locally in most neighbourhood markets. The best time to buy and eat samosas is early evening when a fresh batch is usually prepared at the shops. The preparation is timed with the popularity of samosa as an accompaniment to evening tea. When I was working in Delhi, it was quite common for us in the office to ask for samosas with our evening tea service. It sounds quaint but we used to have fixed tea times during office hours. Tea would be prepared in the office kitchen and tea bearers would go around serving it to everyone in the office. It was customary to serve biscuits or snacks along with the tea. In the evening round, we would once in a while ask for samosas and pakoras instead of biscuits. This must have been happening in other offices also, as the roadside tea shops outside the offices seemed to have good custom for their evening output of samosa and pakora.

Pakora or **Pakoda** is also very widely available in north and east India. A similar dish called bhajiya is eaten in western India (the names can be confusing – the similar sounding bhujia, described in earlier chapters, is a fried vegetable dish quite different from pakora). Pakora is a dish in which pieces of vegetable, most commonly potato or onion, are coated with a savoury and spicy batter of besan and then deep fried. The core of a pakora can also be spinach, cauliflower, brinjal, peppers and paneer. While it is not very common to use meat as the core for pakoras, one can find chicken pakora and prawn pakora in many places. Unlike samosa, which can be considered a north Indian dish, I am not sure any particular region in India can claim to be the home of pakora.

Pakora is routinely made both at homes and in restaurants. Most households have a favoured, traditional mix of spices which are added to the besan batter, passed on from one generation to the next. This breeds strong loyalties to pakora 'as cooked at my home'. For some reason, pakoras have always been considered great snacks to have during the monsoon season, on days when it is pelting outside and children are stuck indoors. It must be due to convenience. The ingredients are staples of Indian kitchens and, if the rain prevents one from going out to the shops for samosas and the like, churning out platefuls of potato or onion pakora at home is not difficult.

Vatsala, a friend from college, writes newspaper columns and blogs about food and this is what she has to say about pakoras on rainy days:

'Every family has a particular style of bhajia or pakoras they prefer. But, in all humility, I will offer that the best pakoras of all time, with absolutely no debate, were the ones my grandmum made on rainy days. Potatoes and onions were diced along with tiny slivers of green chillies. These weren't dipped into batter and fried like regular pakoras. Instead, a small amount of dry besan would be added to the diced vegetables, and then barely moistened with just a little water so that the besan paste acted as an adhesive, not as a coating. Hand smoothened clumps of this would then be fried to a wicked crisp and served hot to the panting, drooling family. Crispy bits of the outside with little crunchy besan blobs would intersperse with soft bits of potato and onion, and the slivers of green chillies in the mix would have our ears burning and our eyes streaming while we demolished mound after steaming mound.' (Indian Express, July 29, 2018)

There are many sweet dishes popular in north Indian food. It is difficult to associate most with any specific state or region. In this chapter, I've selected a few which are common in Punjabi food, if not necessarily specific to the state. Post-independence, Punjab has been a major producer of milk and dairy products and has the highest per capita consumption of dairy products among Indian states. Sweets made from milk are, hence, an integral part of Punjabi food.

Kheer is a sweet dish prepared by boiling rice, milk and sugar together, flavoured with cardamom or saffron and topped with chopped nuts and raisins. Rice pudding of various kinds, found in Middle Eastern and European cuisine, are believed to be derived from kheer. The name itself is derived from the Sanskrit words for milk and milk products. Like other north Indian sweet dishes, kheer can be had as a snack or a dessert, though it is one of the few generally had as a dessert. Most Indian restaurants will carry some version of the kheer as a dessert item on the menu. As a popular festival food, it is also often also served as 'prasad', a religious food offering. Kheer can be both white and brown in colour, the latter when jaggery is used instead of sugar. It can be had warm, at room temperature or chilled, depending on personal preferences.

I discovered **Rabri** surprisingly late in life, when I was working in Delhi. It is not something that was made at my home and the name somehow was never enticing enough on restaurant menus. It is made by boiling full fat milk till the milk becomes viscous, with all the cooked bits added back. It is flavoured with cardamom powder and/or saffron. Like kheer, it is served with a garnishing of chopped nuts, any combination of cashew, pistachio and almond. Rabri can be eaten on its own but also is a great balancing accompaniment to other sweet dishes which is how I had my first few experiences of it.

Halwa or **Halva** is a dish found in many countries, though the name can refer to different types of dishes in various countries. In Hindi, the word halwa, taking a cue from the physical appearance of the dish, has also generically come to mean making a mash of things, in a slightly negative way. In north India, the main type of halwa is made with a base of wheat flour or suji (semolina). The flour is cooked in ghee, with some cardamom powder, till it is nicely browned and then sugar syrup is slowly mixed in, ensuring that the cooked flour swells up but remains grainy. The dish is garnished with chopped nuts and raisins. In some recipes, the chopped nuts are added while the halwa is being cooked, so the nuts come out nicely roasted. Halwa is also a popular festival food and also used as prasad. While it is mostly eaten as a dessert, it is makes for a surprisingly good snack with pooris.

A variant of the halwa is the gajar (carrot) halwa, a dish supposed to be Punjabi in origin. It is called **Gajrela** in Punjab. Grated carrots are boiled in milk till the mixture reduces to a thick consistency and the carrots soften. Then the mixture is cooked, as in the other varieties of halwa, in ghee with cardamom powder for flavouring. Khoya may be added to the mixture at an intermediate stage for a bit more body to the dish. The dish is normally served as a dessert. But in some cases, a drier variety is shaped into small rectangular pieces and served as a stand-alone sweet.

As mentioned earlier, **Laddu** is a generic name for a range of sweets, all spherical in shape and about the size of a table tennis ball. This is a very ancient Indian sweet dish; its Sanskrit name, ladduka, is mentioned in the *Mahabharat* and *Sushrutha Samhita*. The latter was a medical treatise, dealing mostly with surgery and along with *Charaka Samhita* is considered the foundation of Ayurveda, the ancient Indian medicine system. The *Sushrutha Samhita* recommends medicines to be added to laddus made of sesame seeds and jaggery, called **Til ka Laddu**. This is similar to medicines added to sugared pills in Homeopathy, probably with the same purpose of camouflaging the taste of the sometimes bitter medicine and also helping with the absorption.

The most popular laddu in Punjab and Delhi is the **Motichoor Laddu**. This is a laddu shaped from bundiya, described a couple of times earlier as fried besan droplets. Sweet bundiya is fried besan droplets soaked in saffron flavoured sugar syrup. In making bundiya for motichoor laddu, the bundiya is not fried to crispiness as it is for sev bundiya but taken out while still soft. The soft and sweet bundiya spheres are gently broken into even smaller balls. Then they are shaped into laddu spheres, perhaps with additional flavouring in the form cardamom seeds or chopped nuts. The dish is golden in colour and sparkles when freshly made. The name motichoor essentially means 'crushed pearl', an apt description of the physical appearance of the bundiya used in this laddu.

Motichoor laddu is a festival food, especially popular during Diwali. But it is available in sweet shops all year. The laddu balls are easily packed into cardboard boxes and are often used as gifts and for celebrations. A laddu box or two brought by a colleague to office often meant some personal happy event, ranging from birth of a child to purchase of a white good or a promotion, etc. It is one of my favourite sweets. My daughter also loves it and, when we buy motichoor laddu for Diwali and other festivals, we have to agree on a fair split. She is disciplined about her eating, I am not and she has learnt with experience that agreeing a split up-front is the best way to ensure her fair share.

Barfi is a sweet similar in usage to laddu. It is as popular as a gift during Diwali and festivals and also for celebratory occasions. Different types of barfi are easily available in sweet shops all year. The name is derived from the word 'barf' which means 'ice' in many north Indian languages. It might be an allusion to the common milk barfi which is somewhat like an ice cube in appearance, if you are willing to stretch your imagination.

The milk barfi is made by cooking chhena (crumbly cottage cheese) in lots of ghee with sugar. The tricky bit is to get this mixture to a consistency that will set into a medium soft, not hard, dough that can be cut when fully cooled. It is practically always flavoured with cardamom. When fully set, the barfi is cut into small rectangular or diamond shaped pieces. An equally popular variant is the kaju (cashew) barfi which uses powdered cashew as its main ingredient. Barfi is easily packed into cardboard boxes and keeps well. Half a dozen or a dozen barfi pieces, packed in colourful packaging, are a very common way of gifting sweets in north India. It is so common that during Diwali, people often receive barfis in a box from guests and will in turn serve the guests barfi, sometimes bought from the same local sweet shop.

Barfi was, in the past, covered with a very thin layer of silver foil on the top surface. This silver foil is called vark or varq. The practice is a hangover from a medieval belief in medicinal properties of silver and desire to show off wealth. There is pretty good evidence that the foil has no practical use and may even be harmful. The making of the foil used to be a time consuming and skilled manual process. I was once taken to a vark workshop in Lucknow. The process requires very gentle hammering of sliver powder placed between thin parchments. It takes a good few hours for a small sheet of the vark to be ready. The workers in the workshop were clearly skilled but bent over and in bad health. I am not convinced that this is a skill that necessarily needs to be preserved.

No description of Punjabi food would be complete without a mention of **Lassi**. The drink in its basic form is made by mixing yoghurt with water and sugar or salt and churned with a hand blender. The blending is the key step in making good lassi and involves quite a bit of effort if done manually. Everyone now uses powered blenders. It is important to churn till the drink is of a good consistency and there is some froth on the top. The thickness of the drink is dependent on the amount of water added and it is considered bad form to make the lassi too thin, "trying to economise on the yoghurt, are you?". The sweet lassi may be additionally flavoured with cardamom powder or rose water, the salted one with some ground spices. If you add the pulp of a fruit to the mixture, you get a corresponding fruit lassi. Mango lassi is a very popular variant. The plain, lightly sweetened or salted variety is a breakfast drink and a regular accompaniment to aloo paratha.

Describing the preparation of lassi reminds me of a TV ad I saw some time back. An owner of a company making washing machines in Europe was intrigued by the soaring sales of its machines in Punjab. A young executive was sent to investigate (another market visit). The ad ends with the executive discovering that the washing machines were being used by Punjabi dhabas and eateries to make lassi. The rotating cylinder does the churning job exceptionally well, it seems. The ad seems to be based on observed practice, though I am not sure if the use of washing machines to make lassi is particularly widespread.

Chhole Bhature

Samosa

Pakora

Motichoor Laddu

4
Mughlai

From the kitchens of Emperors and Nawabs

Continuing with foods associated with Delhi, in this chapter we look at Mughlai food. The name is derived from the Mughal empire and is used as a catch-all label for all Indian food believed to have originated in the royal kitchens of the various Muslim rulers of medieval India, inspired by dishes from Central Asia and the Middle East. The foods have all been adapted to Indian tastes and use Indian ingredients. In some cases, origins are disputed, as is to be expected in most products of cultural intermingling. I will try and steer clear of controversy as far as origins are concerned. Suffice to say that the dishes that I describe in this chapter are generally accepted as Mughlai whatever their origins.

Not all of Mughlai food in India is native to the Mughal capitals of Delhi and Agra. First, there were many large and small Muslim-ruled kingdoms in other parts of India before and during the Mughal empire, which also had cultural exchanges with the Middle East. Second, when the Mughal empire was in decline in the eighteenth century, there were a number of kingdoms loosely affiliated with the empire but otherwise independent. The food of the empire continued to evolve in these kingdoms, notably in Hyderabad and Awadh (the region in and around modern Lucknow). This has resulted in either specific dishes or variants associated with these cities. Both Awadhi and Hyderabadi cuisines could cover entire chapters. To avoid repetition, I've included a few special dishes from both cities in this chapter.

The first Mughlai dish that I experienced was **Mutton Biryani**. This was again in restaurants in Calcutta. We used to have Mutton Pulao quite often at home and initially biryani looked very much like pulao to me. Biryani and pulao are different in taste and flavour but of similar construction – rice and meat cooked together and served as a single dish. I used to call biryani 'restaurant ka pulao' (pulao from restaurants) in those days. A few years later, I started having biryani during Id and other Muslim festivals, at the homes of friends, and learnt more about the dish and the effort and detail involved in its making.

The Mughlai biryani is cooked in four steps. First, mutton pieces are marinated for a few hours and, separately, rice is soaked in water. Biryani requires long-grained rice to ensure the grains don't stick in clumps but separate out nicely when cooked. That means using expensive rice, typically the best quality basmati. In the second step, the marinated mutton is cooked in ghee with onions, chillies, ginger garlic paste, tomato and a variety of spices. In the third step, the rice is cooked, almost but not fully, by boiling with water and also gently spiced with whole spices such as cardamom, cloves, cinnamon, pepper etc. The almost cooked rice is drained of all water for the final step.

In the final step, a deep heavy bottomed pan is coated with ghee and then the rice and mutton are put in in layers. At a minimum, there should be three layers, but five alternating layers are preferred. Raisins and nuts may be added in between the layers. A little bit of milk, with saffron and rose or similar fragrance, is poured on top of these layers for the distinctive biryani aroma. The pot is then sealed, typically using flour dough as the sealing agent. The mix is then further cooked, the duration of cooking often a matter of personal belief. Since both the mutton and the rice are already cooked, the final step is to further cook the meat to melting softness and ensure that the dish is consistently flavoured and aromatic. Whether this needs 15 minutes, 30 or more is often down to the cook's personal preference. The rice and mutton are mixed together only at the point of serving.

The method described above uses mutton, but chicken is as commonly used for biryani. The cooking time for chicken is a little less and the spices used may be also a little different. When making chicken biryani, you will also find recipes that skip the step of marinating the chicken and instead recommend adding yoghurt when cooking the chicken in the second step. It is a workable short-cut for home cooking.

The method of cooking in a sealed pot described above is called 'dum'. If the cooking is done over very low heat in a sealed clay pot, then it is called '**dum pukht**'. There is a famous high-end restaurant by that name, with many branches including the original in Delhi. It is the restaurant where I first experienced dum pukht food three decades ago. Dum pukht cooking is believed to have originated in Awadh in the eighteenth century. The story is that a Nawab of Awadh had set up an employment program for poor citizens during a famine (as per another version, the workers were employed in construction of the Bara Imambara, a famous monument in Lucknow). The workers made big clay pots from the soil dug up and let their food cook in these sealed pots over a slow fire throughout the day while they worked. On an inspection visit, the nawab smelt the aroma of the slow cooked food and instructed his cooks to copy the process for their dishes. This may be myth-making, but the same story is told by many sources. It may be true.

With the amount of preparation required and the long cooking time, it is not surprising that biryani is not a common household dish. I only had it at my friends' homes during major festivals; otherwise it is a restaurant dish and my original moniker of 'restaurant ka pulao' was not unjustified. In Delhi, there are a number of traditional biryani shops, especially near Jama Masjid in Old Delhi and near the shrine in Nizamuddin, which make biryani in large quantities for takeaway meals. These are not restaurants in the conventional sense of the word; there are no tables and waiters. They are like takeaway shops, except they specialise in biryani. Some even sell biryani only by weight. 'Biryani by Kilo' is in fact the name of a newer takeaway chain modelled on these biryani shops. The quality of biryani served can be variable, but there are a few which have built reputations over the years for great tasting biryani. You need local knowledge or help to get to the right shops. These shops can be an absolute blessing when you need to put a meal together for a large group at short notice. You don't need to pre-order and you are almost always guaranteed to get decent quantities to feed an impromptu gathering. A few modern ventures have added home delivery to this concept, so you can now order kilos of biryani by phone or even by app.

There are a number of regional or city-specific varieties of biryani. Apart from the Mughlai biryani described above, Delhi has another variety called Degi biryani. The other variants of Mughlai biryani which are most famous are Hyderabadi, Awadhi and Kolkata. These are not the only types of biryanis though. Many other states and cities, often where there were Muslim rulers in the eighteenth and nineteenth centuries, have created biryani variants based on local tastes and ingredients. A few notable ones are Malabar from Kerala, Ambur and Chettinad from Tamil Nadu, Sindhi from Sind (in Pakistan), Irani biryani found in Mumbai, and Moradabadi from Uttar Pradesh.

Delhi's **Degi biryani** gets its name from the vessel that it is cooked in, 'deg' being the name for a large, deep and heavy bottomed cooking pot. The dish tends to have more chilli than the normal Mughlai biryani and also has chilli pickle added as a special ingredient.

Hyderabadi biryani is believed to have been created in the kitchens of the Nizam of Hyderabad, the ruler of the kingdom of that name, which covered the modern state of Telangana. The basic difference is not in ingredients but in the method of cooking, though the Hyderabadi biryani comes out richer and more aromatic than Delhi's Mughlai biryani. Biryani made with nearly or completely cooked mutton before the last step of dum or sealed cooking is called 'pakki' (cooked) biryani. The traditional Hyderabadi biryani uses raw, marinated meat, so skipping the second step in the method described earlier. Because of this, it's also known as 'kachchi' (raw) biryani. The marinade uses all the ingredients required for the meat in one go. The meat is marinated for many hours to infuse it with the flavours of all the ingredients. The rice is only about a third cooked before being cooked with the meat in a sealed pot. The dum cooking for kachchi biryani can take a couple of hours or more. Getting the cooking time right requires experience, as there is no way to check the dish once the pot is sealed. It is a complex and difficult dish. Unless you specifically search for a kachchi biryani recipe, most recipes will recommend the Mughlai method of cooking.

Awadhi or **Lakhnavi biryani** is a slightly milder variant of the Mughlai biryani. This is achieved by marinating and cooking the mutton or chicken using fewer spices. In some recipes, green chillies are not used at all, the dish relies for heat only from a mild yellow chilli powder. The taste can also be softened by using cashew nut paste during the cooking of the meat, though this is not necessary. Finally, a small amount of cream may be added along with saffron and fragrances before the rice and meat layers are cooked in a sealed pot. The final dish is as aromatic as the other biryanis but milder and creamier. Also, the Awadhi biryani if cooked the dum pukht way, i.e. in a sealed pot over very low heat, is called ....

Dum Pukht biryani (no surprises there). This is a beautifully fragrant biryani with really soft and succulent meat, as you would expect from the dum pukht way of cooking.

The last Nawab of Awadh was deposed by the British in 1856 and ended up settling in Calcutta, then the capital of British India. A noted gourmand, he recreated his elaborate kitchens there. The Awadhi biryani was thus introduced to local chefs. Potatoes had by then been introduced in India and some intrepid chef figured that the Awadhi biryani would be improved by adding potatoes to the meat and rice. Another version of the story claims that the potatoes were added to reduce the quantity of meat, and hence the cost of the dish. Both stories may have elements of truth. And so, we have the **Kolkata biryani** (formerly the Calcutta biryani – should the name of a dish change when the city of its origin changes name?) which is mild like the Awadhi biryani and distinguished by the presence of golden potatoes. When you buy pre-prepared biryani or packaged biryani from supermarkets, you may find potatoes in them. I am quite sure these are added only to reduce cost, not because they are trying to recreate the Kolkata biryani.

Biryani is a favoured dish for wedding feasts in India. The reasons are not difficult to see. It can be made in large quantities, is considered sufficiently special and luxurious and is popular across pretty much the whole country. For many wedding feasts, especially in smaller towns and villages, a special tented kitchen is set up for the duration of the wedding festivities. Watching and smelling biryani being cooked for the main wedding reception can be a fascinating experience if you find such things interesting. For some reason, the cooks on such occasions are generally bad-tempered and don't like onlookers wandering around their domain. Unless you are a celebrity chef yourself.

I came across a YouTube video by the famous chef Gordon Ramsay where he participates in cooking a biryani for a large wedding dinner somewhere in India, supervised by an old chef of a formidable countenance. The setting is nothing unusual, though Mr. Ramsay repeatedly seems surprised that the cooking method is very different from what he has experienced in UK restaurants. What stuck in my mind was the meat preparation: boiled eggs are stuffed into cooked quails; the quails are in turn stuffed into cooked chickens and the chickens are then stuffed into two whole goats. The goats are then stitched up and cooked in the 'masallam' way (described later) for biryani. Now I've had egg and meat together many times in a biryani, but egg, quail, chicken and mutton in the same biryani? I'll need to eat this before I pass judgement.

Pulao (also written as pulav, pilao or pilaf) is believed to have originated in the Middle East. Biryani in India and Paella in Spain are both considered derivative dishes of pulao. In India, we continue to eat pulao as a dish distinct from biryani. It is also much more common than biryani for eating at home. So, what is the difference between biryani and pulao? In my opinion, the difference is mainly in the process of cooking and the range of spices used. Pulao is a simpler dish. For mutton pulao, first the mutton is separately boiled in whole spices. Then the entire dish is prepared as a one pot dish. In a deep bottomed pot, whole spices and onion are fried in ghee, the boiled mutton is added, fried a bit, and then rice is added. After a few minutes of sautéing the mixture, the right proportion of water is added. The whole mix is boiled till the rice is cooked and the water absorbed. During the cooking, the pot is covered but not sealed. Modern cooks may sometimes use a pressure cooker to reduce cooking time. Pulao is thus simpler and faster to cook than biryani. If one adds saffron and other fragrances at the end, pulao can also be very aromatic. But it is considerably milder in taste than biryani.

A common household variant is the **Vegetable**, or **Veg, pulao**. This is even simpler than the mutton pulao because the vegetables don't need to be cooked separately. After the whole spices are fried in ghee, a medley of chopped vegetables – from cauliflower, peas, carrots, beans, broccoli, potatoes – are cooked and then rice is added to the mix.

One can see why pulao evolved into biryani in the royal kitchens of the Delhi emperors. Its simplicity itself must have been a problem. Royal dishes needed to be complicated, both in ingredients and preparation, and not easily replicable in the common household. Biryani fits the bill, a simple pulao doesn't.

Funnily enough one of the more popular rice dishes in the royal Mughal kitchens was a very humble preparation called **Khichri** or **Khichdi**. This is not a Mughlai dish in any sense. It has been popular in the Indian sub-continent since ancient times and practically every state in India has some variant of this dish. It is simply rice and lentils cooked together. The basic recipe is to boil rice and moong daal in equal quantity with a little bit of turmeric powder, asafoetida and seasoning. The quantity of water used depends on the preferred consistency. The cooked dish is topped with a basic chhonk of ghee and cumin seeds.

Most Indians know khichri as food given when you are unwell or have an upset stomach. It is unlikely to figure in anyone's top ten list of favourite dishes. Yet, it is one of the dishes routinely mentioned in historic sources as a staple food of the general population. Khichri made of rice and moong daal was a fairly common Saturday lunch for me when I was young. I quite enjoyed a meal of khichri with papad and my mother must have found it an easy demand to satisfy. In my liking of khichri, I am in exalted company. It was a preferred dish of the Mughal emperors Akbar and Jahangir on days when they ate only vegetarian food. A number of varieties of the dish are mentioned in the official biographies of their reigns.

A story about Akbar and his courtier Birbal has khichri in a starring role. Birbal was one of Akbar's ministers, a famous wit and raconteur. There is an entire body of Birbal stories in Hindi and Urdu literature, mainly tales of Birbal's cunning and wit in Akbar's court.

This particular story starts on a cold winter day. While walking by the river, not seeing the usual throng of bathers, Akbar observed to Birbal that no man would be foolish enough to bathe in the cold water at this time. Birbal countered that for sufficient money, he could get a man who would not only bathe in the water but even stand in it for a whole night. Akbar took up the challenge and agreed to pay a sizeable amount of money, if Birbal could find someone to do that. Sure enough, Birbal found a poor man who was willing to risk death by hypothermia for the lure of money. (The moral dimension of Birbal's act, of asking a poor man to undertake something like this to prove a point to the Emperor, is not normally explored in the tale). The man somehow spent the whole night standing in the river watched over by a guard. Next morning he presented himself to Akbar's court to claim his reward. Akbar, though normally a generous man, for some reason balked; perhaps it was peeve from having lost an argument. He asked the man what he did the whole night while standing in the water. The man replied that, to keep himself distracted from the cold, he chanted hymns while looking continuously at a lamp burning in a cottage on the far bank of the river. Akbar seized upon the latter point, saying that the lamp must have provided warmth to the man and he had thus not adhered to the conditions of the task. No reward was given. Birbal could only watch in silence.

A few days later, Birbal invited Akbar for dinner at his home, promising him his favourite khichri. After a couple of hours of being entertained, Akbar enquired about dinner. Birbal went into the kitchen to check and came back and said that the khichri was being cooked and would be ready shortly. So passed another hour or so. Akbar was by now getting irritated, presumably with hunger, and asked Birbal to check again. Birbal went in and came back with the same explanation. Finally Akbar could take it no more and went to the kitchen to check himself. There he found a bowl of uncooked khichri hung about a metre over a lamp. What kind of a joke is this, asked Akbar? Birbal then made his clinching argument, if a lamp can provide warmth to a man from so far, surely it can cook khichri when just a metre away. Akbar, used to Birbal's ways, realised what this was all about and immediately agreed that he was wrong to deny the poor man his reward. I am sure Birbal must have then fed the Emperor with khichri, prepared and ready elsewhere. It wouldn't have been prudent to send an emperor back hungry!

The emperors and nawabs are, of course, better known for the rich and luxurious dishes that came out of their kitchens. **Kababs** (singular kabab, also spelt kebab) created in the royal kitchens are justly famous; the association aptly captured in the expression, 'kababs are for nawabs' or, as in the British Raj version, 'kabobs are for nabobs'.

Kababs are mostly eaten as starters in a big meal. In modern times, they are also very useful party snacks. A rough definition for kabab is an appetiser or snack made of small pieces of meat, first prepared with a variety of spices and then roasted, grilled or fried. A comprehensive but quite wide definition. Like other Mughlai food, kababs are mostly bought from specialist kabab shops or eaten in restaurants or cooked by professional chefs.

There are many different kababs in Mughlai food. The **Shami kabab** is most commonly made at home. In my childhood, I ate home-made shami kababs during Muslim festivals. My mother-in-law is one of the people who makes shami kebabs regularly at home, much to my family's delight.

The word 'shami' could mean 'of the evening' from the Hindi / Urdu word 'sham'. The name could also be a tip to the origins of the original chefs, from the region of Bilad al-Sham (modern Syria). The dish itself is deserving of royalty in ingredients and complexity. It is made of minced mutton (or beef outside India) which is first cooked with chana daal (Bengal gram) and a variety of spices. This takes time as both the meat and the chana daal need to be fully cooked and soft. The cooked meat and daal mince is then further mixed with onions, green chillies, chopped coriander, mint, spices, etc., and ground to a smooth consistency. A little bit of flour is sometimes added to the mix to make it keep shape while cooking. This mix is shaped by hand into small thick patties or discs, about 6 – 8 cm in diameter, and fried till the surface is somewhat crisp. In eating, the kabab is very soft to bite into and can be eaten with chutney or with Mughlai breads.

Seekh kabab is the other widely available Mughlai kabab. The word 'seekh' means a skewer; the name simply means kabab on a skewer. As befitting a royal dish, seekh kabab needs lots of preparation time. Minced mutton or lamb meat is mixed with ginger and garlic paste, onions, coriander, mint, chillies and spices. The mix is left to marinate for a long time. This softens the raw meat. The mix is then shaped into hollow cylinders, about 12 – 15 cm in length, on skewers and lightly brushed with ghee or oil. Seekh kababs were traditionally cooked over braziers but these days can be barbequed or grilled.

In the kitchens of the nawabs of Awadh, both shami kabab and seekh kabab went through a further level of refinement. A melt-in-the-mouth version of the shami kabab called **Galauti** or **Gilawat kabab** is one such dish. The story is that as a nawab of Awadh aged, he lost his teeth and demanded that his chefs make his kabab even softer. The word galauti is a straight derivation from the Hindi word for melting. The best cut of meat is generally taken for mincing and minced multiple times – some recipes claim that the meat needs to be minced up to ten times to get the right consistency. Into the meat goes masala powder of a long list of lightly roasted spices such as fennel seeds, cloves, peppercorn, cardamoms, coriander seeds, cumin seeds, mace, star anise, bay leaves, etc.; this masala is supposed to have 32 ingredients, but most recipes manage with only (!) 15 or so. Raw papaya, or papaya skins, onions and green chillies are also added. Papaya softens the meat. A large quantity of ghee is added to the mix to further soften the meat (remember this was to meet the demands of a toothless nawab). Fragrances may also be added. Before the individual kabab patties are cooked, the meat mix is gently smoked. The kababs are then shaped into discs and cooked on a special pan. The resultant dish is similar in appearance to shami kabab but much softer, so soft that it can be difficult to pick up by hand to eat and may need to be spooned.

A similar refinement was made to seekh kabab and the resultant dish is called **Kakori kabab**, named after a small town near Lucknow. The town has a small role in Indian history. A train robbery of British Raj cash was carried out there by Indian freedom fighters in 1925, with a number of well-known freedom fighters involved. If you have seen the early 2000s film *Rang De Basanti*, you may recall actor Amir Khan practicing lines, with the name of the town mentioned. Kakori kabab, like galauti kabab, is essentially a very soft version of the original Mughlai seekh kabab.

I've had the rare pleasure of eating food almost straight from the royal kitchens of Awadh. 'Almost', because the royal kitchens folded more than 100 years before I was born. But there used to be an infrequent reunion of the descendants of the courtiers of the Awadh royal court in Lucknow in the 1990s, in an invitation only event. Descendants of the royal chefs (or claimants, I am not sure there was any way of actually verifying the lineage) would cook for the occasion. As I've mentioned earlier, I used to travel in Uttar Pradesh extensively for work. I was invited to the event, as the guest of one of the very large number of people in Lucknow claiming connection with the royal court. I was invited because I had engaged the said gentleman a few times in culinary discussions, including voicing the heretic view that galauti kabab is just a variant of shami kabab. The invitation was probably to prove me wrong.

The meal on offer that evening was fit for royalty and remains, after all these years, one of the best meals that I've ever eaten. There were about five or six different types of kababs, a gosht (mutton) curry, murgh (chicken) korma, Awadhi biryani, a couple of vegetable dishes, and a variety of breads. I remember making a meal of mostly kababs with a little bit of biryani to round up the evening. The galauti kabab, as you would expect in Lucknow, was the star of the kababs. The interesting thing was that it was served straight from the cooking pan and was not shaped into patties or discs before being cooked or served. So the pan had a thin layer of cooked minced meat of paté like consistency, kept warm over very low heat. There were also similarly well-made kakori kabab, murgh malai tikka and murgh reshmi kabab. I think I did try some of the biryani, but it is the kababs that have stuck in my memory.

(I must also confess that as the years go by, in every retelling of this meal, the galauti kababs get softer, the kakori kababs more succulent and the whole spread more and more lavish!)

A more complex version of shami kabab has also come about in Hyderabad, called **Shikampuri kabab**. The obvious meaning of the name would be the kabab from some town called Shikmapur. But in this case, the word is a compound of 'shikam' meaning belly and 'pur' meaning full. The name is a literal description of the kabab: it has its belly full. This is shami kabab with a stuffing of spiced, thick yoghurt. The shami kabab patties are prepared as they would be in the Mughlai way. The stuffing is separately prepared, with care taken to make sure that the yoghurt is very thick so it does not get absorbed by the meat. Each kabab is filled with a dollop of this spiced yoghurt, shaped by hand and shallow-fried in ghee. The resultant kabab is another delight in the Mughlai kabab pantheon. The smooth taste of yoghurt and the taste of the minced meat make for a wonderful combination.

The kababs that I've described so far are all made of mutton. There are a number of chicken kababs as well. Chicken tikka, described earlier, is the most popular chicken kabab. The dish is prepared by marinating small pieces of boneless chicken for a few hours in yoghurt and spices, including red chilli powder. The chicken pieces are then threaded onto skewers, mostly with onions and peppers. The tikkas can be cooked in a tandoor, roasted over a brazier or grilled in an oven.

A delicious variant of the standard chicken tikka is the **Murgh Malai tikka**. The name is a giveaway, there is malai or cream in the marinade for a softer and milder chicken tikka. For the same reason, instead of using red chilli powder, this kabab has a smaller amount of green chilli, if at all. The preparation and cooking process is similar to the standard chicken tikka. The resultant dish looks quite different though, with a creamy appearance. The murgh malai tikka is a close rival to the shami kabab in reputation for sophistication. When well made it tends to be soft and aromatic and looks a dish which royals would have enjoyed in the years gone by.

Changing a few ingredients to the chicken tikka marinade is, in fact, the way a couple of other types of chicken kababs are made. One is **Achari Chicken tikka**. Achar is the Hindi word for pickle, so one would be tempted to think that there is some pickle somewhere in the dish. Not really. The name comes from the masala used which is the same used to make pickles. It is a combination of roasted and powdered mix of mustard, fennel, fenugreek, and nigella seeds. Add a bit of this powder to the marinade, with a few tweaks to the other ingredients and you get achari chicken tikka, a slightly tangy tasting kabab. A couple of other variants include Murgh Zafrani tikka (zafran is saffron) and Murgh Lahsooni kabab (lahsoon is garlic).

The chicken kababs we have seen so far use pieces of meat, unlike the mutton kababs which use minced meat. One example of a chicken kabab made from minced chicken is the chicken seekh kabab. The initial preparation is similar to the mutton seekh kabab. Minced chicken is mixed with ginger and garlic paste, onions, coriander, mint, chillies and spices. The mince is then shaped into cylinders and threaded onto skewers for cooking. In some places, chicken seekh kabab is also called **Reshmi kabab** or 'silky' kabab. Confusingly, murgh malai kabab may also be called reshmi kabab. I am not sure there is any easily explained reason behind this, so if you do come across the name reshmi kabab, it is best to check the details.

A chicken shami kabab may also be made by replacing minced mutton with chicken. The only difference is that you start with chicken pieces, rather than minced chicken, and then after the chicken, chana daal and spices have been cooked, the whole mix is minced to be shaped into kabab patties for frying. The chicken shami kabab is a modern adaptation, taking advantage of the popularity and lower cost of chicken in modern India. While it tastes fine, I've never eaten a chicken shami kabab as soft, aromatic and rich in taste as the best mutton shami kabab in Delhi or galauti kabab in Lucknow.

A speciality kabab is **Barrah kabab**, sometimes called just Barrah. For a change, it does not use minced mutton but chunky mutton pieces on the bone, either from the legs or ribs. These pieces are marinated in a yoghurt mixed with an array of ingredients, as we have seen in other kababs. The marinated meat is then best roasted over a brazier but can also be barbequed, grilled or even pan-fried.

Kababs were originally made only from meat. With India's large vegetarian population, it was inevitable that vegetarian kababs would be created and become popular. I will describe a couple, as they are often quite complementary to the meat kababs in an assortment of starters. The simplest is **Paneer tikka**. Paneer (cottage cheese) cubes are marinated in yoghurt mixed with ginger garlic paste, chillies and spices. After marinating for a while, the paneer cubes are threaded on to skewers with onions and peppers and roasted or grilled. They can also be gently fried in a pan. A vegetarian version of the shami kabab is called the **Hariyali kabab** (green kabab). This is made by blending spinach leaves with cooked chana daal and spices.

Kebabs are considered appetisers and snacks. So, in a restaurant, you would be expected to order some main courses after eating kababs. I find this quite restricting. A good Mughlai restaurant has at least half a dozen different types of kababs on the menu. When the mood strikes you, you should be able to make a full meal of only kababs, perhaps with a couple of Mughlai breads for balance. This is a concept which has caught on in many restaurants. One, called The Great Kabab Factory, now a chain, took this concept to its logical end. The menu is essentially a long list of kababs, where you can pick and choose which ever ones you fancy and order repeats if you so desire, all for a fixed price. If after all that, you still have capacity, the restaurant generously offers a biryani dish to round up the meal.

Biryani

Shami Kabab

Seekh Kabab

Nihari

In my description so far, I may have given the impression that Mughlai food is only about biryani and kababs. That would be a very incomplete picture and untrue given its royal antecedents. I will now describe a few main dishes. I've only ever tried these dishes in restaurants. I know of many people who cook these dishes at home once in a while, with help from recipes on the internet but haven't come across anyone who makes them at home routinely. These are dishes meant to be cooked by specialists and best enjoyed at restaurants.

Let us start with an unusual dish called **Nihari**, originally made with beef. When made with mutton, as is more common in India, it is called **Gosht Nihari**. The unusual thing about nihari is that it is eaten for breakfast. It is a spicy, rich and smooth stew, made by cooking meat over low heat for six to eight hours. The tradition is to cook it overnight and serve it as a breakfast dish. There are still shops in Delhi where you can find nihari being served only in the morning. I am not sure how such a heavy dish can be had for breakfast, but it could be useful if your next meal was going to be in the evening.

There is a story associated with nihari, which is closely linked with the evolution of Mughlai cuisine. When Emperor Shah Jahan moved his capital from Agra to Delhi, his courtiers suffered repeated bouts of illness, probably due to poor water quality in Delhi. 'Delhi belly' has old roots! The royal chef and the royal physician worked together to create many dishes with local spices especially turmeric, cumin, coriander and red chilli, all believed to have medicinal properties. Nihari was one such dish, created specifically to counter flu.

THE exact recipe for the dish is not easy to pin down, as most restaurants claim to have their own secret recipe. There are a few things that give the nihari its distinctive taste. First, the mutton pieces, preferably shanks, are fried in ghee with the usual ingredients – onions, ginger garlic paste, turmeric, coriander powder and red chilli powders. Then a special combination of masala powders, made by roasting and grinding a number of whole spices in very precise proportions – cumin seeds, fennel seeds, black and green cardamoms, cloves, bay leaves, cinnamon, peppercorn and nutmeg – is added. If there is a secret to nihari, it is in this mix of spice powders. Sufficient quantity of stock is then added to this meat mix, which is then cooked on very low heat for a number of hours. At the last stage, a solution of flour in water is added to make the stew smoother.

If you do have nihari for a main meal, the best way to enjoy and appreciate it is to have it with naan or khameeri roti and nothing else – no appetisers and no side dishes. A small dessert should be ok afterwards if you feel up to it. It will not feel like a feast but will be very satisfying, nonetheless. And you will be surprised by how full it makes you feel.

Haleem, another Mughlai main dish, is clearly an import from the Middle East and found in many places in India. However, the dish has been adapted and the Hyderabadi Haleem is well-established as a local speciality. It even has an official Geographical Indication. It is especially popular during Ramadan in Hyderabad as the dish eaten to break the fast in the evening. Otherwise, it is eaten as a starter during special occasions and elaborate meals. The dish is a stew of mutton, lentils and broken wheat. The uniqueness of the Hyderabadi haleem is in the use of lots of ghee and generous spicing. Ingredients include ginger, garlic, turmeric, red chilli, cumin, caraway, cinnamon, cardamom, cloves, black pepper, mace, saffron, jaggery, etc. It is typically cooked over low heat for a long time, sometimes up to twelve hours, with constant stirring till it has a smooth, paste like consistency. Lots of dry fruits such as cashew, pistachio, fig and almond are also added. It is served with a further garnish of sliced boiled eggs, fried onions, coriander, green chillies etc. It is a lavish dish and high in calories, the latter the reason why it is considered good for breaking the Ramadan fast. While a great tasting dish, a small serving is usually the best way to eat haleem; larger servings can be quite heavy and even uncomfortable.

Korma (also spelt Qorma), made of either chicken or mutton, is a classic Mughlai dish. This dish is mentioned in many Mughal historical sources, so the dish that we eat now definitely originated in the kitchens of the emperors. If you find it listed on a restaurant menu as Shahi (or royal) Chicken Korma, that is not just restaurant hyperbole, but an adjective often used for this dish. The word korma actually means a way of cooking, braising in this case, but it is now used specifically for this type of Mughlai dish. It has a creamy gravy and, in line with its appearance, is moderate to mild in spiciness. The creamy appearance is due to the use of generous quantities of yoghurt and/or cream in cooking the meat. The shahi version of the dish will also have cashew nuts, almonds and raisins added to the gravy.

A vegetarian version of korma, called the **Navratan (nine gems) korma**, is generally found in Mughlai menus. The name is a dual play on the word navratan.

Emperor Akbar's court was renowned for nine wise and competent ministers, collectively known as the 'Navratan' and the name of the dish thus denotes Mughlai heritage. In addition, it is made with nine different vegetarian ingredients. Paneer, potatoes, cauliflower, beans, carrots, peas, peppers, pineapple and cashew nuts are used in a typical navratan korma.

Another mainstay of Mughlai menus is **Do Pyaza**, also either of chicken or mutton. The name translates to 'two onions' or could also mean 'of onions'. As the name implies, this dish has onion taking centre stage. While many Mughlai (and indeed north Indian) dishes use onions as an ingredient, these are added early and cooked till they disappear in the curry or gravy. In this dish, apart from the finely chopped onions added in the beginning, chunkier bits of onions are added towards the end of the cooking. So, the dish has visible pieces of onions as its distinguishing element. The onions help balance some of the extra heat from the chillies in the curry. This is a dish which is altogether spicier than the korma and illustrates the point that the Mughlai chefs attempted to cater to the entire spectrum of heat in every feast.

Do pyaza is described in Ain-i-Akbari, the official records of Akbar's reign written by his court historian Abu'l Fazal. There is a fairly detailed recipe for the dish specifying that, in modern weights, you need two kilos of onions for ten kilos of meat. The interesting bit is not the recipe itself, which is in line with what you expect for a do pyaza, but the quantities mentioned. It is reasonable to assume that the recommended quantities of the recipe are an indicator of how many people a single preparation would serve, just as many modern recipes are for four servings. Ten kilos of meat in a single preparation would probably serve about 50 people, more if you had a couple of more dishes. That is actually not a very large number for a royal meal if you include all members of the extended royal family; the quantities in the recipe must have been for an everyday meal rather than a banquet.

A royal dish, deserving of the shahi title, is **Murgh Masallam**, sadly slowly disappearing from restaurant menus. Masallam refers to a whole chicken or lamb, cooked with a stuffing of minced meat and eggs or just eggs. The Gordan Ramsay video I described earlier showed the use of the masallam method for cooking meat for a biryani, though it is extremely rare to use three different types of stuffing. The typical process requires a whole chicken to be cleaned and marinated. Minced meat and eggs are cooked separately. Then they are stuffed into the chicken which is stitched up and cooked over low heat. The whole chicken is served on a large tray with its gravy, garnished with dried fruits and other embellishments. The preparation time is long and given that it is a dish that needs to be shared by the table, restaurants which serve it these days, ask for prior notice. I am afraid it is a dish which may not survive the financial constraints of a modern restaurant business.

There is no such problems with the availability of **Rogan Josh**, a dish which is Kashmiri in origin but a standard part of Mughlai menus in Indian restaurants across the world. It is one of the dishes of the Kashmiri Wazwan, a multi-course celebratory meal consisting of as many as 36 dishes. The name of the dish is interpreted in a couple of different ways. With a Persian origin in mind, the words are taken to mean 'stewed in butter'. With an Urdu interpretation it means 'red with heat'. The red colour is, in fact, a distinguishing element of the dish. In the traditional Kashmiri way of cooking, the dish gets its red colour from Kashmiri red chillies and local herbs. Kashmiri red chilli is not as hot as regular red chilli, so the dish appears fierier than it is.

There are three different types of rogan josh. All use Kashmiri red chillies for colour and ground fennel seeds for a distinctive rogan josh aroma. The first type is the traditional Kashmiri Muslim variety which uses onions and garlic to fry the meat in and give body to the curry. The Kashmiri Pandit variety caters to the somewhat idiosyncratic eating rules of the Pandits – they eat meat but no onions and garlic. Asafoetida is used as a substitute for garlic and yoghurt is used to provide a base for the curry. The Mughlai variety combines the two Kashmiri varieties using both onions and yoghurt. Trying to pin down a standard recipe for rogan josh is, hence, very difficult. Unfortunately, the rogan josh which is found in most restaurants is a bit of a mongrel; more often than not, a mutton curry with extra red food colour passed off as rogan josh.

Most of the main dishes in Mughlai food have gravy or curry; unlike western main courses, they are rarely eaten on their own. They are eaten either with a rice dish or with one of the many different types of breads that feature in Mughlai food. Plain chapati, tandoori roti and paratha can also be had with these dishes, but it is customary to pair the dishes with a Mughlai bread. I will describe a few here.

The most common Mughlai bread is **Naan**. Naan is a flatbread made of leavened dough of whole wheat flour, atta, or fine wheat flour, maida, or a mix, cooked in a tandoor. It is generally oval or teardrop shaped. The leavening of the dough with yeast gives it a softer feel than tandoori roti. To further soften the feel of the naan when cooked, cooks will sometimes add butter, milk, yoghurt or egg to the dough. Cooking in the tandoor results in charred bits on the surface, just like the tandoori roti. Naan can also be brushed with butter or ghee when eating, though it is quite soft as it is. It is also quite common to add an additional ingredient or two to flavour the naan. For example, crushed garlic in the dough creates garlic naan. Similarly, it could be flavoured with coriander or mint leaves. A slightly sweet tasting naan can be made with dried nuts and raisins.

Kulcha is a close relative of naan, so close that sometimes it is difficult to tell the difference, apart from the shape. Kulcha is mostly circular. The dough for Kulcha is made with maida and yeast with milk or yoghurt added to the dough. When cooked in a tandoor, the kulcha comes out looking and tasting very much like naan. However, it can also be lightly brushed with ghee or oil and cooked on a pan or griddle. Kulcha can also be stuffed with all kinds of things, including minced meat, potatoes, paneer, onions and vegetables. In many restaurants, kulcha is only offered stuffed, perhaps to help differentiate it from naan.

Another close relative of naan is **Khameeri roti**. This is also a leavened bread, made of atta with yeast and milk. The dough is usually flattened by hand into a circular shape and cooked in a tandoor or oven. It is generally served with a ghee smeared on both sides. It is a simpler flatbread than naan and considered a suitable accompaniment to the meat curries of Mughlai cuisine, especially nihari.

A very different looking bread is **Roomali roti**, that is 'handkerchief' roti. This is a very thin and very large flatbread, between 40 – 50 cm in diameter. Due to its size, it is served folded up like a handkerchief, hence the name. The dough is made from a mixture of atta and maida. The dough is rolled and then made thinner by repeated rotations and flipping in the air. Watching the roomali roti being flipped in the air is quite a spectacle; making it requires no small amount of practice and skill. The roti is cooked over a convex shaped griddle, called the 'oolta' (upside down) tawa. The name comes from the days when a concave shaped karahi would be turned upside down over the fire to be used as a tawa. The roti itself is very thin and bland, so as to not detract from the main meat dish. Its main purpose is to help soak the curry up and wipe the plate clean.

Sheermal is a bread imported into Mughlai cuisine from Persia and evolved in Awadh and Hyderabad. The bread is made by using maida, yeast and milk flavoured with saffron and a little sugar to prepare the dough. It can be cooked, like the naan, in the tandoor or baked in a regular oven. The use of saffron gives a reddish tinge to bread. It is a great accompaniment to galauti and kakori kababs.

In the previous chapter, I described various types of parathas. A special type of Mughlai paratha is **Lachcha paratha**, a sublimely flaky paratha. The dough is prepared no differently from other parathas, but the special trick lies in how the layers are created in the dough to result in the flakes in the cooked paratha. There are different techniques to achieve this: in one method, you first roll out the dough with a roti rolling pin to a circle of about 20 cm diameter, then roll up the flat circular dough by hand into a thin cylinder. Then the cylinder is folded in from one end, about five times. This resulting disc shaped dough is now flattened and rolled with the rolling pin back to a flat circle of about 20 cm diameter. The paratha is now ready to cook.

I used to find it difficult to decide what bread to have with what dish when eating Mughlai food. It would be great if there were some established protocol. Most restaurants are no help; if you are uncertain on what to choose, they just offer to bring you an assortment of naans, tandoori rotis, parathas and kulchas. Over the years, I've developed a rudimentary system.

Stuffed breads (stuffed paratha or kulcha) should be eaten on their own, perhaps with raita or some daal. In fact, it is best not to order a stuffed bread in a meal with other main dishes. The stuffing and main dish combination may not work together.

Plain whole wheat breads such as chapati and tandoori roti are best when there is daal or at least one liquid curry dish to go with. Being somewhat bland, they make a good accompaniment to most such dishes, especially the ones which are high on spiciness and heat. They are however not a good match with dry dishes like kababs and tandoori chicken.

Kababs are best with specially made breads, such as sheermal or lachcha paratha.

Tandoori dishes are best had with naan and kulcha.

The Mughlai curry dishes should be had with any of the breads described above – naan, kulcha, khameeri roti, sheermal and roomali roti – which all help soak up the curry quite well.

Mughlai meals are rounded up with an assortment of sweets and desserts. **Phirni** is often on restaurant menus. It is practically the same dish as kheer with one main difference: phirni is made with broken or crushed rice grains whereas kheer is made with full, long grained rice. Phirni is always flavoured, either with saffron and cardamom powder or other food fragrances and served with chopped nuts. It is not a light dessert but tops up a Mughlai feast beautifully.

Gulab Jamun, a sweet, is also very popular as a dessert with Mughlai food. Along with rasgulla and jalebi, it is one of the most popular of north Indian sweets. The name describes the sweet. 'Gulab' means rose and refers to the rose flavoured sugar syrup; 'jamun' is an Indian fruit, a dark coloured plum-like fruit, and the word describes the dark maroon coloured balls. The balls are made of khoya, described earlier as a key ingredient for many Indian sweets, mixed with a little bit of maida flour and shaped by hand into smooth balls. These balls are deep fried in oil or ghee and then soaked in sugar syrup for a few hours. The process is simple enough to describe but it is not always easy to get right. The balls need to have the right proportion of khoya and flour so as to not break during frying and be soft and spongy when cooked. The temperature of the oil or ghee when deep frying is crucial to get the outer skin of the balls of the right colour and texture while ensuring that the inside is properly cooked but not browned. Warm gulab jamun combined with ice cream or another chilled dessert makes for a delightfully decadent dessert.

Kulfi is a dessert very closely associated with Mughlai food. It is often called 'Indian ice cream', which is an apt enough description. The traditional method requires thickening flavoured and sugared milk over low heat. When sufficiently thick, this liquid is poured into serving-sized earthenware jars or moulds which are submerged in ice for freezing. The traditional flavours for kulfi are cream, saffron, cardamom and pistachio, though many different types of flavours are now available.

When I was a child, kulfi was sold by street side vendors during summer. They had to compete with ice cream vendors. Most of us considered ice cream as the better alternative, simply because there used to be many more flavours in ice cream. And ice cream looked more modern and cooler (in the figurative, not literal sense) compared to the kulfi servings in clay pots. I think it is fair to say that ice cream has won the war on the streets of Indian cities – it is rare to find specialist kulfi vendors on the streets these days. But, instead of dying, kulfi has been resurrected as an up-market restaurant dessert, sold at multiples of ice cream prices. There must be a life lesson in that.

Hyderabadi Mughlai food includes a couple of special sweet dishes. **Khubani Ka Meetha** is almonds cooked in sugar syrup till you get a dish of smooth consistency. It is served with malai (cream). Another Hyderabadi speciality is the beautifully named sweet dish **Gil-e-Firdaus**, which means 'clay of paradise'. With a name like this, the dish is bound to be a treat. It is a type of kheer made unusually with lauki (bottle gourd) cooked in ghee and then boiled in milk with ground rice and khoya. It looks like kheer but the cooked vegetable gives it a unique taste. Clay of paradise indeed.

Another unusual dessert in Mughlai cuisine is called **Shahi Tukra**. 'Shahi', as we have seen, means royal and 'tukra' means a piece. In this instance, the piece is sliced white bread. This dish is an Indian take on bread and butter pudding and seems to have resulted from the interactions of the British with the royals of Awadh and Hyderabad. In Hyderabad, it is known as 'double ka meetha'; baked white bread is sometimes called 'double roti' in Hindi/Urdu. The dish requires white bread slices, cut into smaller pieces or 'tukra', to be fried in ghee and then gently dipped in saffron flavoured sugar syrup. Rabri is then spooned over this sweet, fried bread and the dessert is ready to be enjoyed.

Mughlai food is now considered entirely Indian. But it remains a great example of intermingling of cuisines, drawing the best from various parts of the Indian sub-continent, the Middle East and Central Asia.

Chicken Korma

Naan

Gulab Jamun

Kulfi

5
Uttar Pradesh

More North Indian food including a deconstruction of Chaat

Routinely referred to as the largest state of India, Uttar Pradesh (UP) is the largest by population, about 200 million people, accounting for about 17% of the country's population. If it were a country, it would be the world's fifth most populous. In area, it is only India's fourth largest state, about 8% of the country's area. The numbers indicate its density of population. The region it covers has long been the heart of the country, covering the fertile plains of the Ganga and Yamuna rivers and their tributaries. Much of northern Indian history has centred around empires and kingdoms based in and around this region. Each political era has left an imprint on the culture. There are, hence, many layers of culture in the region and that is reflected in the cuisine as well.

Mughlai cuisine has been quite integral to the upper-class foods of UP. Awadhi cuisine is of course directly associated with UP because the kingdom of Awadh was a part of what is now UP. It is still the dominant speciality cuisine in the central part of the state, in and around Lucknow. But even without Awadhi food, there is a strong presence of Mughlai food in UP, especially in western UP. Agra after all was the capital city of the Mughal empire during its peak. In addition, the cuisine of western UP has also been influenced by the neighbouring regions of Punjab, Haryana and Rajasthan. There is in fact a strong continuity of Punjabi and Jat foods of Haryana in north west UP. Similarly, the robust food of

Rajasthan is also found in south west UP. On the other side, the food of east UP is quite similar to that of north Bihar. Then there are pockets of traditional Hindu foods centred around some of the main religious centres, especially Banaras (Varanasi), Mathura and Allahabad (now Prayagraj).

Among the various foods of India, I probably know UP food the best, almost on par with my own home food. It started in my school days when I spent some long holidays there. Then, as an adult, I had a few years in the state as a trainee and sales manager. That took me all over the state, to its cities, towns and villages. My wife is also from UP, with family roots both in the rural heartlands of east UP as well as the hills of Uttarakhand (formerly part of UP). So, my culinary experiences of UP have been not just through visiting the state but also, over the years, in my own kitchen.

In this chapter, I've described some of the foods of UP which either don't belong to the Mughlai genre or are popular in UP and have not been described elsewhere. Much of this food is vegetarian and, compared to the rich Mughlai dishes, simple. As I've said earlier, Mughlai food was, and to some extent still is, the food of the upper classes. UP is a poor state and the everyday food of people in UP while rich in heritage is not elaborate or expensive.

A good dish to start with is the ubiquitous **Kachori**. Found in many states, kachori is very popular all over UP. In eastern UP, it is usually eaten for breakfast with a vegetable curry. The eastern UP kachori looks like a poori and is a hybrid of poori and stuffed paratha. The flour generally used is maida, very finely milled wheat flour. A soft dough is prepared with a little bit of salt and water with some help from ghee, not dissimilar to the dough for poori, which is made with atta. The stuffing is cooked lentils, either moong or urad daal. Stuffed dough balls are rolled out for even distribution of the stuffing, very similar to the process for stuffed paratha, but to a size of a poori or smaller about 10 – 12 cm in diameter. Like poori, kachori is also deep fried, preferably in ghee. These kachoris come out puffed up like poori but are slightly thicker and heavier. The quantity of stuffing is less than a paratha and appears as a thin layer on the lower inside surface.

Kachori made the above way, with ground urad daal as the stuffing, is very popular in Banaras and is even called **Banarasi Kachori**. The confusing bit is that you also get a 'sada' or plain kachori, that is one without any stuffing, which looks like poori, tastes like poori and sometimes is called poori. As I've mentioned earlier, the labels poori and kachori are interchangeably used in eastern UP and Bihar, unlike in other parts of north India. A kachori similar to the Banarasi kachori is popular in west UP, especially in Agra, and is called **Bedai** or **Bedmi** (the 'd' is the same hard r sound as in vada) poori. Note that this dish has the suffix of poori rather than kachori, even though it has a stuffing.

The standard accompaniment to kachori for breakfast in UP is a dish simply called **Sabji** which means 'vegetable'. It is usually just a simple, lightly spiced curry of potatoes though sometimes pumpkin is also used. When served with a potato curry, kachori sabji looks, feels and tastes quite similar to poori aloo. Poori aloo is, in fact, also a popular breakfast and light meal alternative in UP and is also widely available. Kachori sabji and poori aloo are often substituted. It is not uncommon to ask for one and get the other at many restaurants and eateries.

To add to the name confusion, there is also a variant of kachori called **Aloo Kachori**, which is kachori with a stuffing of spicy, dry mashed potatoes. This can be shaped either as round balls or flat circles like poori. But they do not puff up as much as poori on deep frying because the crust is thicker, to hold the additional weight of the potato stuffing. The colour also tends to be a deeper brown rather than golden. That helps to identify the dish as a kachori rather than poori. This dish is normally served with a chutney and is more a snack than a meal.

Aloo kachori is the template for a wide variety of stuffed kachoris found all over north India, with many different types of stuffing. Other savoury stuffing include onions, paneer, besan, mashed peas, etc. A sweet version has a mawa or khoya stuffing.

As an aside, a full breakfast of kachori sabji or poori aloo in UP is often topped with warm, sweet jalebi. This is a practice that that I am familiar with from my childhood and was happy to rekindle in the time that I spent in east UP. It is quite common to find the jalebi being made in the same eatery as the kachori sabji, with a fixed price entitling you to both. The quantities are not large, but even so, this is breakfast done to a lifestyle of times past where such a carb heavy meal would be burnt down by extensive physical activity during the morning hours. This breakfast was a favourite of the salesmen that I used to work with. They had justification for a good breakfast, as their day would be spent walking from shop to shop making sales calls, with only a small break for a light lunch.

Another east UP speciality is **Bati Chokha** which is exactly the same as the more famous litti chokha from Bihar. **Bati**, like kachori, is a wheat ball, with a stuffing. The flour used is atta and the stuffing is of spicy sattu, flour of roasted chana (brown chickpea). Unlike kachori, bati is roasted, not deep fried, traditionally on open coal fires, and is always served with char marks on the surface. The bati crust can get quite hard when roasted, so visually it is very different from a kachori. The chokha is similar to what we have seen in the Bihari dish, with mashed brinjal or potatoes as the main ingredient.

We expect fancy dishes in Mughlai food. But there is sophistication in many everyday household dishes of UP as well. A good example of this is in the different types of daal dishes that can be found across the state.

The common daal is arhar or toor (pigeon pea), cooked in a standard way with turmeric and seasoning with a simple chhonk or tarka of cumin seeds. This daal has a variant called the **Awadhi** or **Lakhnavi daal**. The daal itself is made in the standard way with arhar daal and water boiled together with a little bit of turmeric, salt and perhaps some green chillies. The chhonk is a little bit more elaborate with asafoetida, cumin seeds, dried red chillies and garlic. Once the chhonk is added to the daal, a generous quantity of milk is added to the daal for added creaminess. This last bit is what makes the Awadhi daal different from other daals; the milk not only makes the colour paler than the regular yellow daal but also tends to make the daal taste softer. The milk alters the taste only subtly, so it is not the same effect as, for example, adding cream to daal. This daal variant has probably also originated from the kitchens of the nawabs of Awadh where softening of the taste of regular dishes was much in vogue.

Another type of daal dish found in UP and in other parts of north India is **Kali Masoor ki Daal** (daal of kali masoor). Kali masoor is the name for 'whole masoor' (red lentil), the lentil with its skin on. The skin is brown in colour, quite different from the pink grain inside. This is a daal more popular in west UP and especially common in the winter months. Like other daals, the lentil is cooked by boiling in water. The cooked lentils, in this case, get soft but retain their shape, so what you get is a mush of soft lentils rather than a consistent liquid as you would when cooking dehusked and polished pink masoor daal. The daal is brought alive with a complex chhonk of cumin seeds, onions, tomatoes, ginger garlic paste, green chillies, red chilli powder and turmeric powder. As a thick daal, kali masoor ki daal goes better with roti, chapati etc, compared to rice.

A very interesting daal dish, once again of unknown origin but popular in UP, is **Daal Panchratan**, also known by various other names such **Daal Lazeez** or **Mili Juli Daal**. Panchratan means five jewels and this dish takes the five common lentils used for making daal – arhar or toor, moong, chana daal, whole urad and whole masoor – and combines them in one jumbo daal dish. Arhar, moong and chana daal all lead to a yellow daal, so mixing them up combines the slightly different tastes into one hybrid yellow daal and the whole urad and masoor daals stay as soft grains in the dish, adding body and texture. The lentils are all cooked together in the standard way by boiling in water. The dish is then completed with a chhonk similar to the one in kali masoor ki daal. The chhonk can be varied but, to do justice to what is a special type of daal, it tends to be reasonably elaborate with onions, tomatoes, ginger, garlic and green chillies all being used in generous amounts of ghee.

I've described a dish called karhi badi in the earlier chapter on Bihar. This dish is also a regular part of UP food. **Karhi** is also often eaten as a stand-alone dish without the badi, as a substitute for daal. It is a key part of the cuisines of many other states in India. The cooking method is more or less the same everywhere. A mixture of besan flour, yoghurt, turmeric, chilli powder, salt and water is mixed into a thin gruel. This is then cooked in oil or ghee with a bunch of whole spices and more water till the dish is of uniform consistency. Due to the use of turmeric, karhi has a yellow colour like daal but is a much smoother liquid in appearance.

Rice in UP is generally cooked as plain bhaat or pulao or as biryani on special occasions. A type of vegetable pulao cooked in UP is called **Tahiri** or **Tehri**. The dish has a special place in my heart, if not necessarily on my taste buds. It is one of the first dishes that I learnt to cook in my own kitchen. I found the recipe in the instructions-cum-recipe book that came with the Hawkins pressure cooker and it looked like a simple dish to get started with. This is a one pot dish typically made with potatoes and cauliflower cooked with rice. Other vegetables such as peas, carrots and beans may also be added. The cooking process is similar to pulao with minor tweaks in the ingredients. First, some onions are fried with whole spices such as bay leaves, cardamoms, cloves, cinnamon, etc. and then the vegetables are added sequentially, potato first as it takes the longest to cook. Like most novice cooks, this is the bit that I got wrong the first few times, getting undercooked potatoes as the fruit of my labours. Once the vegetables are fried, powdered spices, chillies etc. are added to the mix, followed by rice and water. The dish takes time to cook unless cooked in a pressure cooker and, like pulao, once cooked looks and smells great. It is a hearty dish and can be eaten with just raita or daal for a complete meal.

Potato or aloo dishes have a special place in the everyday food of UP. I experienced this first-hand once while on a unique assignment.

Many years ago, during the training period in my first job, I had to go through a mandatory stint of eight weeks of a rural development program. This required the trainees to stay in a village in Etah district in UP and work with locals on infrastructure or social development programs. The ostensible goal was to give the trainees, most from cities, a direct experience of the India's villages as the rural market was an important target for the company. The program was run by a department of the company's dairy factory in Etah, so one also got to work with the supply chain network for milk in the district. It was a singularly unique program and such an unusual experience that the management recruits of the company of that time remember the Etah stint as one of the most memorable experiences of their working lives. I am not sure that memorable also translated to pleasurable though.

My stay in an Etah village was in the months of January and February. I stayed as a guest of a milkman in the village, who was also responsible for collecting the village's surplus milk for the company's dairy factory. My sleeping arrangements were in the local school, where one room had been kitted out with borrowed furniture and basic furnishing as a bedroom / living area. Just as well that it does not get very cold in UP. My meals, just two in a day, were cooked by my host's family. In the northern plains, potato is a winter crop and potatoes are plentiful in the period of January – March. So, without fail, every meal during my stay was a potato dish with chapati and a glass of hot, milky tea. Potatoes, as I said, have a special place in UP food. I remember finding regular excuses to go to the town to eat something other than potatoes, much as I love them.

The standard potato dish is called **Aloo Tarkari** in UP which is potato pieces in a mildly spicy, yellow curry. The dish that I had most often in Etah was very simply made. Boiled chunks of potatoes were first fried in oil with the standard powdered spices of turmeric, coriander, cumin and red chillies. Water was then added to the mix and the whole lot covered and simmered till the potatoes were nice and soft. A few of the cooked potato pieces would be mashed into the curry to give it thickness and the whole dish was garnished generously with hot ghee. The last bit was mainly because my host was a milkman and used to make ghee at home. The basic nature of the curry was due to the poor income levels of the hosts. We could have paid them, but tradition was that, as their guests, we ate what they ate and could only buy them gifts, not directly recompense them. This dish in a more complete version is made by frying onions and tomatoes with the spices for a thicker and more substantial curry.

A tastier potato dish, which I've mentioned earlier in the chapter on Bengal, is **Aloo Dum**. This dish is generally accepted to be from Kashmir originally, though variants are found all over north and east India. If you do a search online, you will find recipes for Kashmiri aloo dum, Punjabi aloo dum, Bengali aloor dom, etc. In all variants, baby or new potatoes are preferred and the potatoes and the curry are cooked independently and then brought together in the final stage. The differences are mainly in what gives body to the curry. In the original Kashmiri dish, the curry is mainly made of yoghurt with lots of Kashmiri red chillies. The aloo dum variant that you get in UP has a curry made from onions and tomatoes. It is customary to add yoghurt or cashew nut paste or even almond paste to the curry when the dish is being prepared for a special occasion which makes the dish richer and tastier, and far, far removed from the simple aloo tarkari that I ate in Etah.

A simpler dish in comparison is **Jeera Aloo** which I've eaten many times in my days in UP. This is a dry dish and gets its name from the relatively large amounts of whole cumin seeds used. The cooked, black cumin seeds visibly stick to the potato pieces when the dish is served, making this dish easily identifiable. Once the potatoes are boiled, peeled and cut into small pieces, the dish is fairly straight forward to prepare. The cumin seeds are first fried in oil with some green chillies, the potatoes are then added with a selection of powdered spices. The dish is fried till the potatoes are cooked and coated with the masala. As a dry dish, jeera aloo is normally served with daal, as one of the vegetable side dishes in a meal.

I've also tried a couple of uncommon vegetable dishes in UP. **Baingan ki Lonje** (or Lonji) is a UP brinjal speciality. The heart of this dish is a masala paste made from fried, caramelised onions mixed with roasted, whole spices. Caramelising the onions takes time and patience and is essential to getting the dish right. Each brinjal is cut into two halves and the masala paste is loaded onto the flat surface of each half. The loaded brinjals are then further fried on both sides till the brinjal is soft and the masala deep brown. This is not a particularly fancy dish but is quite unique and often found as a vegetable side dish even on restaurant menus.

A fancier vegetable dish from the kitchens of the nawabs is **Bhindi ka Salan**, okra in a curry. This dish, like many others, has both Awadhi and Hyderabadi versions. There isn't an obvious difference between the two versions, though the Awadhi version is probably less sour than the Hyderabadi one. A paste of roasted peanuts, coconut and sesame seeds is the special ingredient of the curry in this dish. The curry is made by frying onions with whole and powdered spices. The specially prepared paste is added to the mix with some water. Tamarind juice is added once the curry is cooked, with a bit of jaggery to balance the taste. Fried okra is added to the curry at the last stage. This is a complex vegetable dish of multiple tastes with the tastes of the spices mixing up with peanut, coconut, tamarind and jaggery. Okra is almost incidental to the curry in this dish. The template for this dish is used in a number of other similar vegetable dishes, all named with the suffix of salan. For example, Mirchi ka salan has red chilli in a curry, Karela ka salan is with bitter gourd, Kaddu ka salan is with pumpkin, etc.

During my stay in Etah, I tasted a unique dish called **Matar ka Nimona**, or green pea curry, for the first time. Unusually, this dish uses a coarse paste of ground green peas to give body to the curry, almost like a daal made of green peas. You start with frying whole and powdered spices and puréed tomatoes. Then the paste of coarsely ground green peas is added to this mix. It is also customary to add a few whole green peas along with the paste. Once the peas and the paste are cooked, water is added to make the curry and flavoured with a pinch of garam masala. This greenish curry dish is essentially matar ka nimona. But given the love in UP for potatoes, it is customary to add fried thin pieces of potatoes for a little bit of variety in taste. The dish can be eaten with both rice and chapati.

Another speciality dish found in UP is **Kofta**. Kofta or Kofte dishes are found all over the Middle East, Central Asia and the Indian sub-continent. The most common kofta dishes are balls of spiced, minced meat – lamb, beef, pork or chicken – fried in oil or roasted over a charcoal fire. In India, kofta dishes are generally served with a rich, creamy gravy. These dishes are not really specific to UP but I've included them in this chapter because one of the variants, the **Nargisi Kofta**, may be of Awadhi origin. I am not sure how the dish got its name. Nargis is a name for girls in Urdu and Persian with multiple meanings. It was the name of a famous Indian actress of the 1950s and 60s, most famously in the title role of the superhit *Mother India*. But the dish of course predates her by hundreds of years. The dish may simply have been named Nargisi to convey both feminism and nobility. The dish is very similar to the British Scotch Egg dish. If there is any connection between the two dishes, it is not firmly established.

The meatball in Nargisi kofta is actually a hard-boiled egg encased in spicy, minced lamb. These meatballs are deep fried. The gravy is separately prepared. The kofta gravies should be smooth and creamy and that means making pastes out of onions, tomatoes, ginger and garlic before frying them. Yoghurt is added to the fried mix and the gravy is mildly spiced. Once cooked, the meatballs are dropped in to soak in the gravy. It is customary to serve the meatballs cut into halves such that the egg inside is visible. Probably also to not mislead the diner into thinking that these are pure meatballs. As a rich and indulgent dish, it is best had with a similarly rich flatbread, a Mughlai paratha or naan, which soaks up the gravy.

The best known version of kofta in India is the vegetarian **Malai Kofta**, which is found all over in restaurants and homes and is a perennial favourite in wedding banquets and parties. It is a pan-north Indian dish with variants found in practically every state. Malai means cream and in this case refers to the cream used in the gravy. The kofta balls are typically made of potatoes and paneer (cottage cheese) mixed together with spices and sometimes dried fruits for an added feel of luxury. This mixture is shaped into balls and deep fried. The gravy needs to be smooth, as in the Nargisi kofta, and pastes of onions, tomatoes, ginger and garlic are fried and gently spiced. Cream is added to the mix which may be further enhanced with khoya or cashew nut paste or yoghurt or a mix. The gravy is cooked till it is quite smooth and creamy. The dish is served with additional lashings of cream and is visually very appealing, a dish well-suited for banquets.

No description of UP food is complete without describing **Chaat**. Chaat is found all over India with many local variations. The concept of chaat is believed to have originated in UP: small sized dishes sold by street-side hawkers and small eateries, practically always eaten outside the home when one is out and about. The word does not refer to a single dish but is a label for many dishes which are the mainstays of north Indian street food. The word means 'to lick' in Hindi and it could be the equivalent of 'finger licking good'. There is no formula to chaat dishes, but there are a few elements and ingredients that are common in many of the dishes. In the paragraphs below, I make the brave attempt to deconstruct chaat by listing the key ingredients and the roles they play in making chaat tick.

Most chaat dishes are a mixture or combination of multiple pre-cooked ingredients.

The most common ingredient is a spice blend called **Chaat Masala**. Chaat dishes are incomplete without chaat masala. There are many, many recipes for chaat masala; each street food seller has his own secret one. Most have amchoor (dried raw mango powder), rock salt and peppercorn mixed with other spices such as powdered cumin seeds, coriander seeds, carom seeds, etc. A bit of this spice blend gives a sharp and tangy taste to any dish and is commonly used in most chaat dishes.

A common element in chaat dishes is the use of a couple of chutneys mixed into the dish itself. The chutney most associated with chaat is the dark maroon coloured **Imli (tamarind) chutney**. The main ingredients of this chutney are tamarind and jaggery, giving it a distinctive and delightful sour and sweet taste.

The tamarind tree is cultivated in many places of India and is considered almost a native of the sub-continent though it may have come to India from Africa in in pre-historic times. The English (originally Latin) name is believed to be a combination of two Arabic words 'tamar' and 'hind', that is the 'date of India'. The ripe pulp extracted from the pod-like fruits is used as a souring agent in many dishes, chutneys and pickles. For the tamarind chutney, the traditional way is to first fry cumin seeds and asafoetida in oil, add water and boil the tamarind pulp and jaggery together. Once the mix thickens, powdered spices of red chilli, coriander and ginger are added. It is not difficult to make and can be had as an accompaniment to many dishes. In chaat dishes, its sweet and sour combination is considered essential and it is an ingredient rather than an optional accompaniment.

Another chutney used as an ingredient in chaat is **Hari (green) chutney** with coriander leaves and green chillies as the main ingredients. Mint leaves may also be used. The green colour of the chutney comes from the coriander and mint leaves. The chutney is a smoothly blended mix of lots of coriander leaves, green chillies, garlic, ginger, chaat masala, cumin seeds, lime juice and seasoning.

A third common element of traditional chaat dishes is a crispy ingredient, typically small pieces of deep-fried flour. This can be in the form of small, flat pooris made of wheat flour or crushed bits of crispy kachori or sev (fried strings of besan) or roasted puffed or flat rice or indeed a combination of any of these.

Giving volume and body to most chaat dishes is the final ingredient: some form of potatoes, boiled and cut into small pieces or mashed, or boiled or curried chickpeas.

Yoghurt, in small quantities, is added to many chaat dishes but is not an essential ingredient.

The combination of these ingredients means that chaat dishes tend to have multiple tastes, flavours and textures all mixed together. They have always been snacks, something to have in between meals, especially in the long gap between lunch and dinner. The dishes are not supposed to particularly filling; the draw is the taste and hence there is a premium on creativity. Experimentation is not only tolerated but expected.

The most common chaat that vendors in UP sell is a version of **Papri Chaat**. Papri is the name for small, about 5 – 6 cm in diameter, deep fried flatbreads made of wheat flour. Unlike the poori in gol gappa, these are not puffed up but flat and crisp. About half a dozen papri pieces form the base layer of the dish. The second layer is of mashed or chunks of boiled potatoes or boiled chickpeas or a mixture of the two, which are usually spiced with chaat masala and red chilli powder. Some vendors also add chopped onions and small bits of tomatoes to this layer, but it's not essential. The next layer is yoghurt. The yoghurt tends to be not very thick and is sprinkled with the vendor's special spice mix which has more chaat masala, red chilli powder, seasoning and other spices. The tamarind and green chutneys are added on top of the yoghurt and provide bright colour to the dish. Many vendors also additionally sprinkle sev, fried strings of besan, for added crunchiness, and chopped coriander, for added colour and flavour. In the traditional method of eating, you are supposed to dig out each papri and scoop up the rest of the ingredients with it. The idea is to get all the ingredients in each mouthful such that you get to taste and feel all the flavours and textures together; the magic of the dish is in the combination rather than the individual tastes.

Papri chaat can be modified in a number of ways to get other types of chaat. In a famous version found in Mumbai, **Sev Poori** (which is described later, in the chapter on Mumbai food), the yoghurt is omitted, but there is more of sev and chutney. In a version, often found in UP and other parts of north India, called **Sev Chaat**, there is no papri as the base layer. The base layer is formed of potatoes and chickpeas with yoghurt, chaat masala and couple of chutneys topped up with lots of sev. The crunchiness in this chaat comes entirely from sev. In another simplified version, both the papri and the yoghurt are removed and the chaat is essentially a mix of sev, potatoes, chickpeas, spices and chutneys. This version tends to be drier and not as delightful as the others.

Gol gappa is found everywhere in UP. It is not very different from puchka found in Bengal and described in the first chapter. However, there is a version of gol gappa called **Dahi Poori** which is found in UP and definitely worth a mention. Dahi poori is effectively gol gappa minus the spiced water but with spiced yoghurt. Now it must sound strange to remove what I've earlier called 'the heart and soul' of the dish but the yoghurt adds its own taste and body to the dish, making it quite different in taste but with similar effect. So, you have a small puffed up poori with a hole, into which a small quantity of boiled potatoes or chickpeas, a chutney or two and yoghurt, spiced with chaat masala, red chilli and other spices, is scooped. The loaded poori is even heavier than a gol gappa and quite liable to break, so the same care is needed when eating dahi poori as with gol gappa. The effect is similar to gol gappa or a mouthful of papri chaat, an indescribable explosion of flavours, textures and tastes, which intrigues, surprises and delights in turn.

Another popular chaat in UP is **Samosa Chaat**. I remember having this chaat many times when I was working in eastern UP. I had to travel to various towns by bus every day from my base in Gorakhpur. After a long day selling goods to small shops, I'd head back to the town's bus stop in the evening to catch a bus back to Gorakhpur. I'd be starving by that time since lunch would have been nothing more than a cup of tea and biscuits. In those towns, the bus stops were well served by street food hawkers and samosa chaat was one of the more easily available items. A bowl of this dish was often my sustenance till dinner back in Gorakhpur and, as a result, still holds a special place in my memories.

Samosa chaat is a combination of two well-known north Indian dishes, samosa and chhole, converted into a chaat. At its simplest, one or two samosas are crushed into small pieces and topped up with chhole, a spicy curry of white chickpeas. This in itself is a tasty dish but probably would not qualify as a chaat. What makes it a chaat is the addition of chaat masala and a couple of chutneys to the samosa and chhole mix. The chhole used in this dish is also relatively blander to allow the taste of chaat masala to come through. Once you do that, you get all the elements of a chaat in place in the dish. Some vendors also add yoghurt for a more elaborate form of samosa chaat.

A street food snack very common in UP and all over north India is **Aloo Tikki**. Aloo is potato and tikki, in this case, means a burger-shaped patty. Aloo tikki is sometimes called chaat though by itself it is a snack but not strictly a chaat. It is made by shallow frying patties of mashed potatoes lightly spiced with red chilli, cumin, coriander, chaat masala, etc. It is a simple dish and does not require a huge amount of skill to make. As a result, it is one of the easiest street foods to find in India. Freshly made, hot aloo tikki served with a chutney or ketchup is the easiest snack option if you feel peckish when out and about.

The plain aloo tikki is often modified with a variety of stuffing. One variant is aloo tikki with a stuffing of peas. Mashed peas are lightly cooked in spices and then stuffed into each patty of the aloo tikki. Similarly, the aloo tikki may be stuffed with cooked moong daal, chana daal or paneer. Sometimes the stuffing may be of grated coconut or dried fruits.

Aloo tikki is also the patty used in most vegetarian burgers that you get in India. Aloo tikki in a bun actually predates the vegetarian burger and has been eaten as a quick snack or on-the-go meal for many decades. In its traditional form, this dish called **Aloo Tikki Bun** or **Aloo Tikki Pav** is a piece of aloo tikki in between sliced halves of a bread bun, served with onion and tomato rings and a green chutney smeared on the inside surface of one bun half. So, an earlier avatar of the vegetable burger but also a cousin of the famous Vada Pav found in Mumbai.

Aloo tikki is also used as an ingredient in some chaat dishes where it replaces boiled potatoes. The simplest is **Aloo Tikki Chaat**. A couple of aloo tikki patties form the base layer of this dish. A bit of yoghurt with chaat masala and red chilli powder sprinkled on top forms the second layer. Tamarind and green chutneys go on top of the yoghurt as a third layer. The dish is served with a topping of some combination of sev, chopped onions and coriander. In another type of chaat with aloo tikki as an ingredient, aloo tikki is served with chhole and chaat masala with chutneys layered on top. This dish is called **Chhole Tikki** in the north and is similar to Ragda Pattice found in Mumbai.

Dahi Vada is another well-known snack dish in north India. It is not clear where this dish originated as it is found all over India and there are references of the dish in historic sources dating back many centuries. Vada is of course best known as a south Indian dish, described in more detail in later chapters. In this dish, the vadas can be either doughnut shaped, as the south Indian vada, or ball shaped as in the Mumbai vada. They are made by deep frying dollops of a spiced batter of urad daal. After frying, the vadas are soaked in warm water to soften them up. The vadas and yoghurt are then mixed together and seasoned for the plain variety of the dish. A single serving typically has two vadas with yoghurt. It is rare to serve the plain variety though. Usually, the dish has chaat masala, red chilli powder and tamarind and green chutneys added, making it quite a striking looking dish: the colours of the chutneys and spices in stark contrast to the white of the yoghurt. Apart from being eaten as a snack, dahi vada is also often a part of banquets and multi-course feasts, serving as a palate cleanser and coolant in between spicier dishes.

Many of the sweets described so far in the foods of other states are also available in UP. In fact, sweets like jalebi, laddu, barfi, gulab jamun, rasgulla, gujia, kheer, rabri, halwa, kulfi, etc. are as integral to UP food as they are to the foods of other states in north India. There is a degree of consistency in the naming of these sweets as well: most are called by the same name practically everywhere. One off-beat exception is the word rasgulla which in Allahabad (Prayagraj) and surrounding areas refers to both the dark brown gulab jamun and the white rasgulla.

As a state with a long and diverse culinary history, UP also contributes a few specialities to the mind-boggling array of sweets that you get in India.

A sweet many tourists are familiar with, because of its association with Agra, home of the Taj Mahal, is **Petha**, also called **Agra ka Petha**. This is a rare sweet made from a vegetable. The vegetable is from the family of kaddu (pumpkin) and lauki (bottle gourd) called petha kaddu or just petha, 'ash gourd' in English. It is a large cylindrical vegetable with ash like marks on its green skin from where it gets its English name. When cooked as a vegetable it is bland and tasteless and, hence, not very popular.

The cooking process for petha is quite tedious. The ripe vegetable is cut into rectangular chunks and needs to go through a few preparatory steps. The key step is to harden the vegetable pieces by soaking them in a solution of limestone water for about twelve hours. Then the vegetable pieces are thoroughly cleansed of the limestone water and boiled. The cooked pieces should come out looking almost translucent. A sugar syrup is separately prepared, often flavoured with cardamoms and sometimes saffron. The vegetable pieces are then boiled in the sugar syrup and left to soak in the thick syrup for a few hours. The next step is to dry the petha for a further few hours. The final sweet is translucent and has a thin crust of sugar. It is slightly squeezy to feel. Variants of the basic type are made by flavouring the sugar syrup with different ingredients. The whole cooking process seems to be a lot of trouble to go through for what is a fairly basic sweet, though it puts to good use an otherwise tasteless vegetable.

Petha belongs to a category of sweets called **Murabba**, which may have come to India from Central Asia. Usually, these are candies made from fruits, by boiling fruits in sugar syrup. When I was young, we would have murabba made from vegetables of the gourd family once in a while. When I first tasted the famous Agra ka petha, imagine my surprise in finding it to be the same as the humble sweet that I knew as murabba.

Another famous sweet from UP associated with a town is **Mathura ka Peda**. Peda is a sweet made from khoya or mawa, shaped like a small disc, similar to a milk barfi in texture but different in shape. The normal peda is white or cream coloured but the Mathura peda is brown in colour. This comes from roasting the khoya over low heat till it gets nicely browned. When made in large volumes in factory-like kitchens in Mathura, the khoya is prepared by boiling milk in large cauldrons and cooking till the khoya is brown. The browned khoya is mixed with ground sugar and cardamom powder and then shaped into its signature shape.

Mathura is associated with the Hindu deity Krishna and is an important religious centre. Peda is used as a religious offering in Mathura, especially during Janmashthami, the festival celebrating Krishna's birth. As a result, it is considered not just another sweet, but one with a somewhat elevated status. I personally prefer the taste and texture of milk barfi to any kind of peda. But one advantage of the Mathura peda is that, as a sweet blessed by the gods, you can eat it with no associated guilt!

Malpua is a sweet popular in many states including UP. There are multiple variants of this sweet and it is most commonly made during Holi, the festival of colours that celebrates the onset of spring. In many places, it is just called pua. There are historic references in ancient Hindu literature of a sweet sounding like pua, made of barley flour, fried in ghee and soaked in a sweet syrup. The basic recipe for malpua remains the same. First, a batter is made of flour, mixed with milk or milk products and sometimes mashed fruits. Dollops of the batter are poured into a deep karahi of hot ghee or oil, each spread to the size of a large poori. Each deep fried pua is then soaked in sugar syrup. The batter of the UP type of malpua is made of maida, semolina and sometimes khoya flavoured with cardamom and fennel seeds. Yoghurt and milk may also be used in the batter. In the eastern states, banana pulp is sometimes added, while in the south grated coconut is an ingredient.

Malpua as a sweet can be eaten on its own. When served as a dessert, it is quite common to top it with rabri and some chopped dried fruits. In this form, it has also become a favourite of north Indian restaurants and transformed from a sweet prepared during festivals to a dessert available all year round. It is by no means a light dish, either as a sweet or a dessert. Not something that you can pop casually, like a couple of rasgullas, and be on your way.

A not very common sweet dish found in UP (and also in surrounding states) is called **Rewari** or **Rewadi**. The name is similar sounding to rabri but the two are completely different sweets. Rewadi is made of jaggery and roasted til (sesame seeds) and identifiable by the coating of til seeds on each piece. Each piece is very small, about two cm in diameter. Many pieces are normally served in a large bowl to be shared. The dish is considered a winter sweet, as the jaggery and sesame seed combination are supposed to have a warming effect. In size and shape, it is quite similar to the savoury tilori made in Bihar, also with til as a key ingredient.

Most meals in UP end with **Paan**, described earlier in the Punjab and Delhi chapter. In east UP, it is almost a ritual and no meal is considered complete without paan. Banaras is famous for it paan. A hit song from a film called *Don*, first made with the superstar Amitabh Bachchan in the 1970s and then remade with the later superstar Shahrukh Khan in the 2000s, has immortalised the Banarasi paan. I am not a great fan of this concoction. I used to be offered paan regularly during my days in east UP and offended many people by not only refusing to have paan but also expressing my views about it in no uncertain terms. My primary objection is to the practice of spitting out the paan juice after you have chewed on it. If paan-eating becomes obsolete, I for one will not be mourning it.

When you travel around in UP, a common sight is the mobile sugarcane juice vending machine. **Ganne ka Ras** or sugarcane juice is one of the many interesting, non-alcoholic drinks to be found in India, most of which are supposed to help you keep cool in the hot weather, which is practically the whole year.

Sugarcane is one of the main crops of Uttar Pradesh. Most of the produce is converted to sugar in mills but some of the canes also make it to the market as is. One use is for the stalks to be cut into smaller pieces for people to chew and suck on for its juice. When we were young, we would sometimes try our teeth out on the hard bark of the canes, peeling them off with our teeth. It is also not uncommon to find peeled and cut stalks of sugar cane being served after a meal as a sweet dish.

A much more common use of the canes is by sugarcane juice vendors. This is a surprisingly popular drink across most of India. The vendors have large rudimentary machines where the canes are squeezed through rotating metal rollers to extract the juice. The rollers can be manual or powered. In the case of the former, the vendor is required to continuously work at the handles of the rollers while pushing the canes through. The fresh juice is green in colour and has a nice, frothy head. It can be drunk on its own. A masala variant has freshly chopped ginger, lime juice, black pepper and sometimes a bit of salt mixed with the juice. It makes for quite a refreshing, though very sweet, drink. One word of caution. The passage of the freshly squeezed juice, as it covers the distance from the rollers to the container, frequently attracts flies and their ilk. The drink, for all its popularity, is not always hygienic unless once can see everything to be clean and free of flies.

Similar in simplicity and massively popular is a simple drink made of freshly squeezed lemon juice mixed with water and sugar or salt or both. This drink, **Nimbu Paani** (lemon water), can be found everywhere in India, at homes, on the streets and even in fancy restaurants. Made with cool or cold water, this drink is a life saver in the summer months. The fact that it can be made with juice squeezed from a freshly cut lemon and bottled water makes it suitable for stomachs of different levels of sensitivity. In UP, apart from the plain variety, it is often found flavoured with flower essences, e.g. rose, for a slightly more complex tasting drink. I call it the Nawabi nimbu paani.

A number of variants are created from the basic recipe of nimbu paani with small additions. One well-known variant is called **Jal Jeera** (water and cumin). This drink is a basic salted nimbu paani with a spice combination of roasted ground cumin, ginger, black pepper, rock salt, tamarind, etc. It is considered a digestif and even recommended for upset tummies.

Another variant found in Punjab is called **Shikanji**. The basic shikanji is just nimbu paani with both sugar and salt, with rock salt preferred. But this is a versatile drink and it can be modified in a number of ways. One version which I personally like has chaat masala in addition to roasted ground cumin, black pepper, rock salt, etc. Refreshing and with a slight kick. Variants of shikanji or nimbu paani are often the base for some innovative cocktails found in upscale bars of the bigger cities. I came across another variant when I was in Kolkata. The canteen there used to serve a warm version, with a bit of honey. This was a drink had in lieu of tea and coffee and was called garam nimbu paani, helpfully shortened to 'GNP' by students fresh out of Economics 101.

A cooling drink offered during the hot summer months is **Sharbat**. This label is applied to drinks made from concentrated flower and fruit juices. The name itself is Persian in origin and the drink came to India probably with the Mughals. The label now applies to all kinds of drinks, including many which predate the Mughals. While concentrates must have been made in home kitchens in the past, in modern times, concentrates are bought in mass produced bottles. The most popular varieties are orange, mango, rose and lime. Orange, mango and lime are straight-forward fruit concentrates. Rose sharbat or squash used to be the interesting one for us when we were young. This was a thick, sweet pink or red coloured syrup and was then synonymous with sharbat.

Making sharbat is simple, so simple that even the children of the household can be trusted to make them for guests when required. This must have been the first 'food' item that I prepared as a child. If I remember right, the formula was: pour out a small measure of the syrup in a glass; if the drink is for an adult, add one spoon of sugar and if for a child, two or even three; add some ice cubes and then top the glass with cold water; stir and serve. Simples!

A special type of sharbat brand was created in UP in the early twentieth century called **Rooh Afza**. 'Rooh' means soul in Urdu and the name is often translated to mean 'refreshment for the soul'. It is a red coloured syrup with many herbal ingredients, considered especially good as a coolant. It has roots in Unani medicine and the ingredients include flowers, fruits, vegetables, herbs and roots. As a sharbat, it is simply mixed with water and ice. It is also had with milk especially as a welcoming drink during Iftar meals in Id. It used to be quite popular in the 70s and 80s. With the western fizzy drinks capturing the market since the 1990s, it is now very much a niche and somewhat old-fashioned drink.

A more elaborate cool drink for summers is called **Thandai** (from the Hindi word 'thanda' which means cold). The drink is traditionally had during the festival of Holi where adults drink it spiked with **Bhang**, an edible preparation of cannabis. Drinking bhang-spiked thandai during Holi has been an accepted practice for a long time. So, even though public intoxication is frowned upon generally in popular culture, it's considered acceptable during Holi. Bollywood films, over the years, have had a number of song and dance sequences based on drinking bhang during Holi. One of the more famous ones, 'Rang barse', has the superstar Amitabh Bachchan singing a Holi and bhang themed UP folk song in the movie *Silsila*. The song celebrates not only drinking but also adultery and has been a perennial favourite at Holi parties since it first appeared in the 1980s.

The non-bhang variant is a delightful drink in its own right. It has a long list of dried fruits and seeds which are ground and added with sugar to boiling milk. The milk is further flavoured with rose water and saffron, the latter giving the drink a yellow colour. The main variety is called **Badami Thandai** or almond thandai. Almonds, pistachios, poppy seeds, watermelon seeds, peppercorns, fennel seeds and green cardamoms are some of the ingredients which are used in the drink. The drink is served chilled. It is not as common as the other drinks described earlier and tends to be found in specialist sweet shops and restaurants rather than at street side vendors.

In UP, one has to be careful when buying this drink as there is a risk of getting the bhang thandai instead of the plain thandai, if you don't specify clearly. A couple of drinks and you may have personal experience of the Hindi expression associated with bhang – 'din me taare dikhne lage' (seeing stars in daylight).

Kachori

Jeera Aloo

Papri Chaat

Dahi Poori

6
Tamil Nadu

Idli, Dosa, Sambar and beyond

It is a cliché to say that Tamil cuisine is 'not just idli, dosa, vada and sambar'. Yet, most non-Tamilians will experience Tamil cuisine first, and sometimes only, through these iconic dishes. My first exposure to Tamil food, or 'South Indian food' as it is universally known, was also through these dishes. Even in the 1970s, idli and dosa were widely available all over India. My first taste of these dishes was in fact at home. There were a number of families from the southern states in the townships that we lived in. My mother must have picked up the recipes from one of them. By the time I was old enough to remember, idli and dosa were made as occasional treats at home.

As I was growing up and discovering different types of foods in restaurants and food shops, I found idli and dosa were easily available in local restaurants and eateries. Some of these were not even specialists in south Indian food, but general purpose restaurants, happily serving idli and dosa along with chhole bhature, aloo poori, samosa, pakora, etc. The quality of idli and dosa was not necessarily very good in these small restaurants, but even when of average quality, these dishes taste great. I've been a fan ever since.

Dosa is part of the cuisines of all the south Indian states: Tamil Nadu, Karnataka, Kerala and Andhra. In describing the dish in this chapter, I am not implying exclusivity to Tamil Nadu but simply giving the dish pride of place in the first chapter covering south Indian food.

Dosa, also spelt dosai or dose, is a made from a fermented batter of rice and urad daal (black gram or lentil). The batter takes time to prepare and ferment; the rice and daal need to be soaked before being ground into a thick paste and then the paste needs to be left to ferment for at least eight to twelve hours. So, dosa is definitely not an 'on-demand' dish at home. When the batter is ready, a scoopful is evenly spread into a thin circular shape over a hot tawa or griddle and cooked in oil or ghee. The cooked dish is like a crepe in appearance, cooked to a semi-crisp and golden finish. The finish is a key element of quality in dosa. It should be in between a roti and a papad in crispiness. If it cracks off like a papad, it's not good; nor should it feel too soft and rubbery.

The basic dosa, without any stuffing inside, is called a **Plain dosa**. The most common stuffed dosa is called **Masala dosa**. It is stuffed with a spicy potato and onion mix, which is prepared separately and added to the dosa in the final stages of cooking. Here 'masala' refers to the potato stuffing, which can be misleading as the word masala generally refers to a mix of spices. Dosa is served folded over in halves or thirds, sometimes in cones, with the stuffing inside. It is always served with at least a coconut chutney and, in Tamil Nadu, with Sambar, another staple of south Indian food, which is described later.

One of my good friends in Barauni, Mohan, was from the south. He let slip, at some point early in our friendship, that his mother made great dosa. There were four of us who used to hang out together then and we managed to convince him to invite us for a dosa meal at his home. His mother liked us enough to accede to the request. While dosa is eaten for breakfast or lunch in most households, school timings and parental permissions meant that we had this feast organised for an evening. It couldn't have been easy for Mohan's mother. Feeding four boys with healthy appetites is not an easy task, especially if they come with the intent to eat big. If you have eaten a masala dosa, you will know that a single masala dosa is normally enough for a meal. Even granting for those home-made dosas being slightly smaller, we must have eaten three or four dosas each. This thankfully did not put off Mohan's mother. We had many of these dosa meals there over our school years. Only on a couple of occasions did she say 'Enough!' before we did.

There are many different types of dosas. You can add almost any fried food as a stuffing inside the dosa. The traditional varieties are all vegetarian and include onion dosa, paneer dosa, ghee dosa, ghee masala dosa, rava dosa, paper dosa, podi dosa, Mysore masala dosa, set dosa, neer dosa, etc. Most are named after the stuffing, but some need a bit more description.

Rava dosa is made of a batter of rava (another name for sooji or semolina) with rice and maida. Unlike the rice and lentil batter, the rava dosa batter does not need to be fermented; this makes it the go-to-choice when dosa needs to be made on a short notice. Rava dosa looks different from the regular dosa. It is not as smooth and golden in appearance and has minute holes. It can be made plain or with stuffing. When the stuffing is similar to the mix used for masala dosa, you get rava masala dosa.

A visually striking type is **Paper dosa**. Its name denotes its thinness and, as if to compensate, it is spread into a very large size, 50 – 60 cm in diameter. It is always a sight when brought to the table from the kitchen, at home or in a restaurant. I always feel a bit embarrassed when I order a paper dosa as it invariably draws everyone's attention to what you are eating. A plus point is that it is easily shared. In my college days, it was not uncommon to see courting couples sharing a paper dosa by eating from each end. You do strange things when you are young.

Podi dosa is somewhat less well known outside the southern states. It gets its name from podi chutney which is applied to the dosa as it is being cooked. This chutney, also called idli podi, is often served as a separate chutney with idli. Its main ingredient is red chilli, though coconut and tamarind give it a more complex taste than a plain red chilli paste. But make no mistake, it can be sharp and this dosa mostly appeals to people who can handle the heat.

One of the best known dosa variants is the Mysore masala dosa, originating from, as you would expect, the erstwhile kingdom of Mysore in Karnataka. Set dosa and Neer dosa are also special types of dosa originating in Karnataka. I've described them in the chapter on Karnataka later on in this book.

There are dosa fanatics all over India. I am one of them, even if an unlikely one, given that I was born and brought up in the east of the country. As a true fan, I've never eaten a bad dosa: in my experience, all dosas are either good or excellent. In a restaurant review a few years ago, I read masala dosa being described as 'this is what heaven looks like when fashioned from carbohydrate'. My feelings exactly! It is one dish that I get cravings for regularly. The great thing is that because of its popularity, it has not been difficult to find a dosa restaurant near home in the cities that I've lived in, in India and outside India. In fact, for a number of years, our home in London was a short driving distance to not one but three south Indian restaurants, each serving multiple varieties of dosa. Bliss! One of those even did home delivery. This was the same south Indian restaurant that I had convinced to make aloo parathas for me, on the sound principle that I could get both my food fixes from one place. My current vendor is a Keralan restaurant. When I call to place a takeaway order for lunch, on hearing my voice the manager straightaway responds, "One masala dosa, sir?".

Idli is so often mentioned along with dosa that you would be excused if you thought 'idli dosa' is one dish. Idli is actually a more widely available breakfast dish in Tamil Nadu. Each idli is a small, spongy circular rice cake, convex shaped on top and bottom. It uses the same but slightly thicker batter as dosa. The batter is poured into idli-shaped moulds on a special idli pan and steamed. Many idlis are cooked at one go. Idlis, like dosa, are also served with coconut chutney and sambar. Sometimes, an idli dish may be served as a couple of idli pieces soaked in a bowl of sambar. While ultimately that is how idli is eaten, I think the practice of pre-soaking it in sambar is done to soften idlis which have gone dry. Well-made idlis get the firmness right; firm enough to hold shape and not break at a touch but soft enough to break when spooned up with sambar.

Idli and sambar make for a very good breakfast. There are many eateries in south Indian cities and towns which provide idli and sambar for breakfast, for those who don't want to or can't cook at home. The really good ones have queues in front of them all morning. Idlis are also quite common in the breakfast buffets of more expensive hotels. They are touted as a light and healthy breakfast but that is relative to some of the other Indian breakfast options, for example aloo paratha with ghee. Idli itself is quite light but bland. Eaten only with chutney, it is indeed a light breakfast (but you need to restrict yourself to a couple, not always easy to do).

There was a period, in my first job, when I was in Mumbai (then Bombay) for a few months. I was a bachelor, staying in a shared apartment in Andheri. Work was in south Bombay, a good one hour or more of commute every morning. To save on commute time, I had signed up to a commuter mini-bus which would pick me up from outside the apartment and drop me off very close to the office. On the first day of the commute, I was looking for something to eat before going to the office. My nose led me to the canteen of a college near the office, from where the aroma of freshly made idli and sambar was wafting out. A plate of two idlis with chutney and sambar was on offer for two rupees. Breakfast ceased to be a problem during that stay in Bombay, at least on weekdays.

I'd take the commuter train back to Andheri in the evening. Right outside the Andheri train station was a typical Bombay restaurant, serving all kinds of things and, yes, dosa. So, breakfast of idli used to be often topped with dinner of masala dosa. I used to have a glow on my face those days. Many friends and family members who saw me then commented that 'Bombay seemed to have agreed with you', euphemism for 'you have put on weight'.

Vada or **vadai** is a dish had as tiffin or snack. Each piece is a doughnut-shaped, circular disc with a hole in the centre, and about the same size as idli. The Tamil vada, called **Medu vada**, is made by deep frying vada shapes made from a spiced batter of urad daal, a lentil. The deep frying gives vada a very crisp and golden surface while the inside remains soft and white in colour. Vada is also served with chutney and sambar. Like idli sambar, it may also be served soaking in a bowl of sambar. A combined dish, idli vada sambar, is a piece each of idli and vada served together in a bowl of sambar.

Another type of vada is called **Masala vada**. The batter for this vada is made of another type of lentil, toor daal. The batter is shaped into a thin patty, not a doughnut, and deep fried. The addition of stronger spices and sometimes a little bit of spinach give this a different taste to medu vada. The masala in the name in this case does refer to its spiciness. This type of vada is mainly had as an evening snack, not for breakfast.

Uttapam completes the quartet of well-known south Indian dishes. It is routinely referred to as an Indian pizza, a somewhat misleading description. It is better described as a flat dosa with vegetable topping. The most common uttapam is the onion uttapam which has onions and green chillies sprinkled over the batter during cooking. So instead of dosa with stuffing, you have a slightly thicker dosa with onions and chillies as a topping. Uttapam is not folded like masala dosa but served flat and open, hence the resemblance to pizza. The toppings can be varied, with other vegetables such as tomatoes, bell peppers, carrots, etc. also used.

All the dishes mentioned so far are almost always served with **Sambar**, often called the 'South Indian daal'. It is, more correctly, a strongly spiced lentil and vegetable stew. That is why, paired with one of the famous quartet of dishes described above, it makes for a complete meal.

The lentil used in sambar is normally toor daal (pigeon pea). The daal is cooked separately and mashed to mushy consistency. Two or more vegetables are cooked in parallel. The vegetables can be some combination of drumsticks, beans, carrots, pumpkins, potatoes, tomatoes and onions. The daal and vegetables are then brought together with some tamarind solution, a key ingredient, and further cooked. A number of spices are used at each stage of cooking, with a special spice combination, called sambar powder, added when the daal and the vegetables are being cooked together. The popularity of sambar means that this masala powder is easily available in packaged form from shops, making sambar cooking a little bit easier. Once fully cooked, the dish is further topped up with an additional spiced tarka. Once you know how complicated sambar is to make, or have attempted to make it yourself, you stop calling it a daal – it is so much more.

I've never lived anywhere in Tamil Nadu, but have been there on holidays, college trips and many work trips. The first time I went to Tamil Nadu was in the late 1970s when I was still in school. This was a fantastic family holiday, on a multi-city package tour organised by the Tamil Nadu state tourist agency. Checking up their web site now, they still have an eight-day package tour of Tamil Nadu covering a number of towns including Pondicherry, Chidambaram, Tanjore, Rameswaram, Kanyakumari, Madurai and Trichy. We must have taken something similar, with a few days spent in Chennai on both sides of the package tour.

We travelled in a well-equipped bus, on a fixed itinerary, with nights in hotels run by the agency. These package tours can be a bit of a lottery depending on the kind of fellow travellers you get. Luckily for us, the people in our group were mostly families from other parts of India, so there was no shortage of company at all age groups and lots to talk about. We also ate well on that trip. The places we ate in were not fancy, either dining rooms in the hotels that we stayed in or small restaurants near tourist attractions, but the food was consistently good to great.

Breakfast was in the hotels, generally a buffet with idli, vada and sometimes plain dosa on offer. I am reasonably sure that toast, butter, jam, porridge etc. were also available, but don't recall eating them at all. Lunch would be somewhere in the vicinity of a tourist attraction and on the guide's recommendation. With limited amount of time, lunches were not elaborate, though even a simple lunch had rice, sambar, yoghurt (called curd in Tamil Nadu) and a couple of vegetables.

Dinner was when we had a bit more time to try out a more elaborate meal. Most dinners were multi-course meals, which I will describe in a bit. First, an incident from that trip.

That winter Tamil Nadu had had more than average rainfall. On one stretch, after Tanjore, we passed a village with a temple whose gopuram, the tall gateway of temples, was clearly visible from the highway. It was not a well known tourist attraction, so we drove right past. Immediately after the village, we ran into a vast flooded field with a stretch of the road covered with a few inches of water. Since the road was vaguely visible, the driver decided to drive on. Almost immediately, one rear wheel got stuck on a bit of muddy shoulder. A fellow passenger, a Bengali gentleman, insisted on all of us evacuating the bus and walking back to the dry bit of road, before the driver tried to pull out the bus. A timely intervention, it may have saved us from injuries or worse. We found out later that the bus had got stuck on the edge of a ditch and could have toppled. In the time that it took for all of us to get off the bus, the rear wheel sank into the ditch. The bus was stuck. There was nothing that the bus staff could do to get it out. One of them had to find a way back to town to arrange for a tow-crane to be brought to pull the bus out.

Meanwhile, all of us were stranded. The guide and a few of the adults made their way to the village to see if arrangements could be made for sleeping and feeding a bus load of people. In the village they were told a legend – every tourist vehicle that passed the village without stopping, even if for a few minutes, to pay respects to the temple deity met with a mishap. The guide was duly berated for not knowing this bit of essential legend, among all the fancy stories that he had been telling us.

We ended up spending two nights and a bit in that village. Accommodation was somehow arranged in the temple precincts. It must have been very uncomfortable though I've no memory of discomfort, just of a wonderful adventure. My lasting memory, and the point of telling this story, is the food. The first night was a problem. We shared out whatever food we were carrying with us but that was clearly not enough to feed all of us. The morning brought succour. The same Bengali gentleman, a resourceful chap in hindsight, found a couple in the village who ran a small eatery. With some cash advance from the passengers, they agreed to cook meals for all of us: Idli for breakfast, dosa for lunch and a 'thali' (platter) for dinner, all served with sambar, chutney and pickles. I still remember the prices: ten paisa for a plate of idli, forty paisa for masala dosa and a rupee for dinner.

After almost forty years, the idli and dosa that we had in that small eatery are still part of our family folklore, 'the best idli and dosa ever'. Part of the magic was in the setting. We sat on the clay floor of the porch of the shop, the temple visible in the background, with a banana leaf for a plate and waited for our turn to be served. Then a piping hot idli or dosa, with a steaming sambar in a clay bowl was served. There is of course no objective measure to whether it was the best idli and dosa that I've had. But it is a memory best kept that way.

Dosa

Idli

Back to the tour. The dinners that we had were typical Tamilian multi-course meals. These are called **Sappadu** and are meant to satisfy the six taste senses in one meal. This is a concept inherited from Ayurveda. The Sanskrit and Tamil words for the six senses translate as sweet, sour, salty, bitter, pungent or tart and astringent; the last two don't have precise translations. Intriguingly, the word sappadu sounds very similar to the word supper though there is no evidence of any etymological connection as far as I am aware.

A proper sappadu meal could have up to twenty dishes. And it is still not considered a feast, which has a separate word, **Virundhu**. It is not the number of dishes but the occasion which determines whether you are having a sappadu or a virundhu, the latter being the feast organised for more ceremonial occasions and religious festivals. Either term on a restaurant menu indicates a multi-course meal.

The most obvious thing about a Tamil meal is the importance of rice. Not only is rice used as an ingredient in many dishes, most meals have multiple rice preparations for the vegetable and meat dishes to be eaten with. There is some similarity with Bengali food in this respect. But rice is far more important in Tamil cuisine with many different preparations of rice, captured in the multiple words that you can find to denote rice and its dishes. Raw rice is called **Arisi**, also spelt Arici. The word 'rice' may actually be derived from this word via Greek and Latin. Different rice preparations have compound names, the main additional ingredient's name is added as a prefix to the word **Sadham**, also spelt Sadam or Satham, which means cooked rice. Thus, lemon rice, one of the most common rice preparations in Tamil cuisine, is called **Elumichai Sadham**, that is lemon cooked rice. Confusingly, the name for plain boiled rice is not sadham, as one would expect, especially because sadham also means plain. Plain boiled rice is instead called **Choru**. Even more confusingly, a few rice dishes will have choru as the suffix instead of sadham. Languages as old as Tamil tend not to be systematic about these things.

The Sanskrit word for a religious food offering is 'prasad' (which is also my family name). The Tamil equivalent is 'prasadam' or 'prasadham' which can be taken to mean a religious offering 'of sadham'. This meaning is often accepted because cooked rice is the most common food offering to the deities in Tamil Nadu temples.

Lemon rice, elumichai sadham, is one of the best-known rice preparations in Tamil cuisine. It gets its yellow colour from turmeric and unique taste from lemon juice added to the cooked rice. The rice is first cooked by boiling in the usual way. A small quantity of mustard seeds, lentils, onions, chillies, curry leaves and turmeric are fried in a pan and the boiled rice is added to this fried mixture. Lemon juice is added after the spices are thoroughly mixed with the rice. Fried peanuts and cashew nuts may be added for garnishing. The resultant dish has a distinctive yellow colour and a tangy taste from the lemon juice. It can be eaten on its own, though in a big Tamil meal it will be one of the many varieties of rice served.

With minor variations in ingredients and cooking method, one finds the following other preparations of rice: Thengai sadham (coconut rice), Paruppu sadham (lentil rice), Pasi Paruppu sadham (moong daal rice), Thakkali sadham (tomato rice), Puli sadham (tamarind rice), Milagu sadham (pepper rice), Thayir sadham (curd or yoghurt rice), etc.

Thayir Sadham or **Curd rice** is a Tamil innovation. Yoghurt, a bit of milk, and seasoning is added to cooked rice. To this mix, you add a tarka of fried mustard seeds, lentils, chillies, ginger paste and curry leaves. The tarka makes the curd in the dish come alive, otherwise it would be quite bland. In some multi-course meals, you may be given a bowl of yoghurt tempered with spices to add to plain rice for a self-made curd rice. Whichever way it is served, curd rice is an essential part of a multi-course Tamil meal, eaten towards the end as a coolant and digestive aid.

Paruppu Sadham or **Lentil rice** can be of different types depending on the lentil used. Rice with moong daal is called pasi paruppu sadham and with toor daal, it is called arisiyam paruppu sadham. These dishes are similar to khichri found in other states of India. The main difference is that rice and lentil are added to a fried mixture of onions and spices and then cooked in water. The rice and lentil may also be fried a little bit before the water is added, so that the final dish is not a gruel. Hot ghee may be added as a final flourish.

Lentil rice once came in very handy when I was on a trip to Chennai (then Madras) with a group of friends.

This was in December 1987. We were on a trip organised by the students' organisation AIESEC for a conference in Coonoor in the Nilgiri Hills of Tamil Nadu. We travelled by train from Delhi to Madras, stayed there for a day and then went by train to Coimbatore and then bus to Coonoor. A long journey. We stayed for three days in Coonoor. We pretended to be grown-ups in meetings and seminars during the day and, much more enjoyably, partied in the evenings. We then retraced our way back on the return journey. Having arrived in Madras train station early in the morning of 24th December, we were scheduled to take a train later in the day to Delhi. The Chief Minister of Tamil Nadu, M. G. Ramachandran (MGR), a much-loved politician and former film star, died that morning. His death led to an immediate public outpouring of grief which somehow transformed into rioting and looting all over. A curfew was imposed in the city. The sequence of events, even after all these years, still sounds baffling. Why should grief over a politician, even if much-loved, lead to rioting?

A couple of trains leaving Madras had also been damaged and so all trains, including ours, were suspended. There were a large number of people stuck in Madras station. The waiting rooms and the platforms were overflowing with passengers and their baggage. The station had police protection, so there was no risk to the people inside, or at least that is what we were told. From the waiting room windows, we could clearly see evidence of the rioting that had taken place outside. There was no choice but to wait at the station for the train services to resume.

Food and drink inevitably started to run out. This could have led to unrest in the station. Someone among the Indian Railways staff must have had both initiative and culinary skills. I am not sure how this was managed but as evening approached, it was announced that lentil rice would be served from a few distribution points. Lentil rice or khichri, as I've said earlier, is eaten all over India, and is easy to cook. In this case, it had the added benefit of being easy to distribute. All in all, a good dish for such a situation. That single serving of lentil rice kept most of the passengers going till the train services resumed in the early hours of the next day. I remember all of us awake and hungry on our train to Delhi, waiting desperately for the next station where we could get some more food.

There are two other popular Tamil rice preparations that I've enjoyed in my travels around the state. **Pongal** is a dish mainly had for breakfast. The dish shares its name with the famous Tamil festival of Pongal, celebrating the winter harvest in January. The dish is distributed as prasadam during the festival. The savoury version, which is called **Ven** or **Khara pongal**, is quite popular and is made from a mix of rice and moong daal. The difference from khichri or lentil rice is that there are no spices added to the rice and lentil mix during cooking. Since no turmeric is added, Pongal is not yellow like khichri and lentil rice. Rice and lentils are cooked together with a little more water than would be used for lentil rice. The mix is cooked till it froths over (that's where it gets its name from). A tarka of cumin seeds, curry leaves and peppercorn in hot ghee is added to the rice and lentil mix. Like other Tamil breakfast dishes, Pongal is eaten with coconut chutney and sambar. The sweet version of Pongal, called **Sakkarai pongal**, can be eaten as a dessert, though it is most commonly used as prasadam.

Another rice-based dish is **Appam**, which looks like dosa and does the job of roti in a meal, that is as the carb accompaniment to curried dishes. Appam is made from a batter of rice only, not a batter of rice and urad daal as in idli and dosa. It is cooked in a special appam pan which is shaped like a small, shallow karahi or wok. This gives the cooked appam a bowl shape and it has a thick and spongy centre where a little bit of extra batter settles. The batter may also have coconut milk or grated coconut added. Appams are common in Tamil Nadu, Kerala and Sri Lanka. In Sri Lanka, they are better known by their English name, Hoppers, which is also the name of a hip restaurant chain in London.

A Tamil multi-course meal is traditionally served on a banana leaf. A large banana leaf, with its spine running parallel to the edge of the table or the diner's mat if sitting on the ground, is placed with a glass or bowl of water to hold it down. Each diner is expected to do a ritual cleaning of the banana leaf before food is served. Since the leaves are washed before being placed in front of the diner, a little bit of sprinkling completes the ritual. If the banana leaf is not clean, you are better off asking for a properly washed one, rather than trying to clean it at the table. The various dishes are then all served at one go. A large serving of rice, either a big mound of plain rice or smaller heaps of different types of rice, takes up the centre space of the lower half. Various dry or mostly dry dishes are served directly on the upper half of the leaf, while the liquid and curried dishes are served in bowls arranged on the top of the leaf.

You are expected to fold the banana leaf when finished eating. It is polite to fold the leaf towards yourself to indicate satisfaction with the meal. I am not sure if the opposite also holds true: do you fold the leaf away from you if not satisfied with the meal? The banana leaf and the left-over food tend to be collected and fed to animals, so there is little food wasted and of course the practice minimises water required to do the washing up.

Among the many dishes served in bowls, a bowl of **Rasam** is quite common along with sambar and curd. The word rasam means juice. But rasam, the dish, is not really a juice. It is a thin soup with a base of tamarind, tomatoes and lots of spices, especially black pepper. The resultant dish is very sharp and sour, with a strong taste of cooked tamarind. The combination of tamarind and black pepper can be quite soothing for a throat infection or a cold. It is not, of course, a cure, even though you will find many people vouching for its therapeutic properties for flu and common cold. Medicinal properties aside, rasam is had either as a soup or mixed with plain rice as a first course in the meal.

The next course is normally rice and sambar, eaten with vegetable dishes. **Poriyal** is the equivalent of tarkari or torkari, seen in northern and eastern states. Poriyal is the label for a dry vegetable dish in which a single vegetable is shallow fried or lightly fried with spices. Most such vegetable dishes in Tamil Nadu may also have coconut. They taste different from tarkari mainly due to the different spices used. One interesting practice is to use whole urad daal, a lentil, as a whole spice for flavouring. Poriyal can be made of practically any vegetable. The common ones are beans, cabbage, cauliflower, carrots, okra and potatoes. A multi-course vegetarian sappadu will have at least a couple of vegetable poriyal dishes.

A Tamil meal will also include a number of curry dishes called **Kuzhambu**, also spelt Kozhambu or Kulambu. A vegetable sambar and kuzhambu dish are similar. It is possible to see the difference when a kuzhambu dish does not have the curry made predominantly from lentils. In such dishes, the curry has a base of onions and tomatoes. But this is not a hard rule. Kuzhambu dishes can sometimes have lentils as the base for the curry. The main ingredient of a kuzhambu dish can be vegetables, but unlike sambar, also meat or fish.

The prefix to the word kuzhambu in a dish's name describes the main ingredient in the curry. Any dish which has 'paruppu' in the prefix to kuzhambu will also have lentils. Some recipes will by default use lentils, rather than onions and tomatoes, and still call the dish kuzhambu. Unfortunately, the nomenclature is not a precise science.

Some examples of kuzhambu dishes are Puli kuzhambu with tamarind, Vendakkai puli kuzhambu with okra and tamarind, Keerai kuzhambu with spinach, Poricha or poritha kuzhambu with coconut, Meen kuzhambu, a fish curry with chillies and tamarind, Kozhi milagu kuzhambu, a chicken curry with extra pepper and Moar kuzhambu, a variant with a yoghurt base rather than tamarind.

Vendakkai puli kuzhambu is an okra curry. There are two distinctive elements that this dish has, in common with many other vegetable kuzhambu dishes. First, whole spices, such as mustard seeds, fenugreek seeds, cumin seeds, red chillies and urad daal, are roasted and ground to a paste with a bit of water. This masala paste is added to the curry at an intermediate stage of the cooking. Grated coconut may also be added to the spice mix but it is not essential. The curry in this dish is made by frying onions and tomatoes with spices to which okra is added. The second key element is the addition of tamarind solution at the finishing stages of the cooking for that distinctive sour taste.

Keerai kuzhambu is a good example of a lentil based kuzhambu, made by combining spinach with toor daal. A milder version is available as spinach daal elsewhere (even, in packaged form, in my supermarket). The preparation is quite similar to a vegetable sambar, with toor daal and spinach being separately cooked and then brought together with fried spices and tamarind solution. It is spicier and more complex in taste than a plain spinach daal.

Non-vegetarian kuzhambu dishes mostly don't have tamarind as a key ingredient. These dishes will, however, have a freshly prepared paste of roasted whole spices added to the curry for each dish's distinctive taste.

Kozhi Milagu kuzhambu, or pepper chicken curry, is a special dish with strong use of black pepper. Pepper is used in a couple of different ways in this dish. Roasted peppercorn is ground with other whole spices for the masala paste. Whole peppercorn is fried with the curry base of onions and tomatoes to give the curry an extra kick of pepper. In some recipes, the chicken will be marinated beforehand with black pepper powder in the marinade. As long as the proportions are kept right, this ensures a very hot but great tasting dish.

A widely available chicken dish is **Kozhi Varutha kuzhambu**. This is a chicken curry which comes in many avatars. I've eaten kozhi varutha kuzhambu in a number of restaurants, some with specific geographic prefixes, e.g. Thanjavaur kozhi varutha kuzhambu, Chettinad kozhi varutha kuzhambu, Madurai kozhi varutha kuzhambu, etc. I assume there are some differences in the recipes, but the basic formula seems to be the same. First, the chicken is marinated in ginger and garlic paste, turmeric and red chilli powder. Second, a special masala paste of many whole roasted spices is prepared. Grated coconut is added to this mix. The specific spices used and the proportions vary for each variant of the dish. Then the dish is cooked, starting with the curry base, frying onions and tomatoes with spices. Into this mix goes the chicken, the special masala paste and water. The final dish is a spicy and fragrant chicken curry, which can be eaten with both rice and Parotta, the Tamil version of plain paratha.

One of the variations of the chicken curry above is the **Chettinad kozhi varutha kuzhambu**. This dish, with perhaps a few tweaks in the spice masala, is the famous **Chicken Chettinad curry**. Chicken Chettinad curry is the flagbearer dish for the Chettinad region, which is the best-known of the three or four subregional cuisines of Tamil Nadu. The region is named after Chettiars, a community of traders. This community has had an over-sized impact on trade in history. Among other things, they were spice merchants, importing whole spices from south-east Asia for use in India and further export to the Middle East, Africa and Europe. Many men of the community were widely travelled and brought back not just new food ingredients but also new methods of preparations and recipes from foreign lands. The region's own cuisine has evolved into a large variety of dishes, including meat, fish and vegetables, rich in spices for both taste and aroma.

Chicken Chettinad is a popular dish in south Indian restaurants and for cooking at home. However, there are as many recipes as there are cooks. It is difficult to tell what exactly is authentic Chicken Chettinad curry. I haven't managed as yet to visit Karaikudi, the town in Tamil Nadu known as the home of the Chettiars, to get a taste of original Chettinad food. On the premise that Chennai should be a good second-best, I've tried a few restaurants touting Chettinad cuisine on my trips there.

A chain of restaurants, called Anjappar, have been purveying Chettinad cuisine for more than fifty years. Their menu does not inspire confidence, with all kinds of dishes, including north Indian kababs and Indian Chinese, on offer. The signature chicken dish is called Chettinad Chicken Masala, which is a delicious dish but quite hot. I had not expected a Chettinad dish to be quite as fiery. The restaurant serves a number of other chicken curries, including Karaikudi Kozhi Kuzhambu and Nattu Kozhi Kuzhambu. So, instead of one, there are many different types of Chettinad chicken curries in this restaurant.

A meal in the Southern Spice restaurant in Chennai is on the other end of the price scale, with taste, ambience and service befitting the price. The restaurant serves dishes from all over south India and the Chettinad speciality on offer, in non-vegetarian curries, is Kozhi Melagu curry. This is pepper chicken curry as described earlier, a fantastic dish without any caveats. But it is not Chettinad chicken curry as one has been led to believe. So, I am not sure if I've as yet eaten an authentic Chettinad chicken curry.

A close relative of the chicken curry is **Kozhi Varuval**. If kuzhambu is a generic label for curries, varuval is a similar label for dry and fried, mostly non-vegetarian dishes. So, Kozhi Chettinadu varuval is Chicken Chettinad made without the tomato and water, such that you get a dry chicken dish with a thick masala gravy.

A dry, fried fish preparation called **Meen varuval** can be found all over the state. Different types of fish can be used for this dish, including king fish, seer, pomfret, swordfish, etc. Fish pieces are marinated in a thick paste of garlic, red chillies, turmeric, coriander, pepper, curry leaves, salt, etc. The pieces are then shallow fried, or even deep fried, till the outer surface becomes red and crisp. There is no curry in this dish. It can be eaten by itself with a chutney or mixed with rice and sambar. It is one of the more easily available dishes on the streets of Chennai, especially from the stalls near Marina beach.

Sometimes you will see a dish called **Chicken 65** in restaurant menus. This was created by a restaurant in 1965, hence the name, though you have other myths associated with the name, including the false claim that it has 65 ingredients. Small, boneless pieces of chicken are coated with a masala paste, with a little bit of flour, and deep fried. The cooked chicken pieces are then further coated with fried spices. These are chicken nuggets south Indian style. Chicken 65 is also eaten as a snack and, like chicken tikka, is a popular party snack.

It would be negligent to not mention a few more fish and seafood dishes native to Tamil cuisine. They are quite common in Tamil Nadu, as you would expect with its long coast. In Chennai, a dish called **Madras prawn curry** can be found in many small eateries especially near the beach. The dish has not been renamed Chennai prawn curry (should it be? Refer to my earlier question about Kolkata biryani in the Mughlai food chapter). Madras prawn curry is made in a manner similar to other kuzhambu dishes with roasted ground spices and coconut added to the curry base of fried onions and tomatoes and finished with tamarind.

A similar dish is the **Madras fish curry**. The fish pieces are marinated with lime juice and salt. Otherwise, the dish is cooked with similar ingredients as the Madras prawn curry, with ground roasted spices, coconut and tamarind. The small eateries in Chennai start serving a fish curry from mid-morning onwards.

My abiding memory of this dish is not the fish, but the quantity of rice served along with it. If I remember right (this was many years ago), the rice served was almost enough for two people. The fish curry is spicy and fiery hot, it needs a cool drink or coconut water to wash it down.

A different type of fish curry is **Meen Manga kuzhambu**. The dish has raw mango pulped and added to the curry. I've only eaten this dish in one restaurant, so can't be sure if this is a popular dish. The combination of raw mango and tamarind in the dish gives a distinctive sour edge to the curry.

Speciality seafood restaurants generally carry many different types of seafood dishes, but apart from fish and prawns, the most commonly available seafood is crab. I've eaten crab meat dishes only in some of the higher end restaurants in Chennai. The most common crab dish is the crab masala, similar to a varuval dish, crab meat cooked in a thick gravy of onions and tomatoes fried in spices. In the crab masala and curry dishes available in most restaurants, the crab meat is completely out of the shell or the shell and claws are only decorative. This makes eating crab quite easy, like eating fish, with none of the struggles one has to go through with a crab dish in which the meat is cooked in the shell.

A Tamil meal is never complete without **Payasam**, a sweet dish similar to kheer found in north India. Apart from being a popular dessert, payasam is also used as prasadam. To do justice to the many types of payasam that exist in the southern states, I'd need an entire chapter. Instead I will describe a couple.

Plain rice payasam is made by adding small-grained rice and sugar to boiling full fat milk and cooking on low heat till the mix becomes thick and viscous in consistency. The rice gets cooked during this process. The dish is flavoured with cardamom and then finally tempered with cashew nuts roasted in ghee.

Rice can be substituted with other ingredients, for example vermicelli or coconut, to create different types of payasam. A speciality payasam is called **Elaneer Payasam**, which uses coconut. A plain payasam is likely to be on the menu of most south Indian restaurants, but if you also find elaneer payasam, you know that the restaurant is trying just a little bit harder for authenticity. This dish uses a paste made of coconut pulp from tender coconut and coconut milk, instead of rice. The cooking process is otherwise more or less the same.

Most Tamil meals end with coffee and a description of **filter coffee**, also called kaapi or kafi, is an apt way to end this chapter. Coffee was brought to the southern states by Arab traders many centuries ago. But it remained a premium drink as long as it was an imported item. The legend is that the Arab traders used to export only roasted beans to prevent cultivation elsewhere, just as the Chinese guarded their tea plants. Some seeds must have made their way through, either via the traders or smuggled, as there is evidence of coffee cultivation in south India from the sixteenth century onwards. The British are credited with expanding coffee cultivation in Tamil Nadu in the nineteenth century. With cheaper coffee available, it quickly grew in popularity.

Coffee is now by far the most popular beverage in Tamil Nadu. When we used to go on trips to the state by train, we knew we were in Tamil Nadu when the vendors on the train stations started calling out coffee rather than tea. In those days, it was a delight to be woken up, as you arrived by an overnight train journey, by calls of 'kaapi, kaapi … Neskaapi' on the train stations. Nescafe is a well known instant coffee brand and was the largest selling coffee brand in India at that time. While the vendors were not selling the instant coffee brand, they had taken to advertising their wares under the brand to make sure that people coming from other parts of the country understood what they were selling.

Tamil coffee is also called south Indian filter coffee. Coffee beans are roasted and powdered, then placed in a filtering utensil and pressed down upon by a plunger. Boiling water is slowly passed through this pressed coffee. The brew thus prepared is quite strong. A little bit of this brew is served with hot and frothed milk and sugar in a steel tumbler. The convention is to place the steel tumbler in a steel bowl called a 'dabra' or 'dabara'. Its primary purpose is to help the drinker cool the coffee by repeatedly pouring the drink from the tumbler to the dabra and back.

Many vendors will create a head of froth on the coffee and cool it to the right temperature before serving the coffee. To do this, they pour the coffee from the tumbler to the dabra or another tumbler a few times. This offers scope for spectacle. So, sometimes you will have coffee vendors performing tricks while serving coffee, just as some bartenders do. The commonest trick is to start by pouring coffee from one tumbler to another held a couple of inches apart and then increasing the distance between the two with each pour. The final pour may be with the two utensils a couple of feet or even a metre apart. Apart from the fun of watching them do this without spilling a drop, you also get a drink with a nice head of froth and cooled to a perfectly drinkable temperature.

Meal on a Banana Leaf

Chicken Chettinad

Payasam

Filter Coffee

7

Kerala

God's own food

The ads run by the Kerala tourism agency market the state as 'God's Own Country'. The state's food justifies the label.

Kerala shares a number of dishes with Tamil Nadu, especially rice based dishes which have a strong heritage across south India. But its cuisine is quite distinctive, shaped by its geography and history. Apart from having a long coastline, the state has many short monsoon-fed rivers, most flowing westwards from the Western Ghats hills to the Arabian sea. This results in an abundance of freshwater and seawater fish, which form a major part of the cuisine. The land is very fertile and grows plenty of rice and a wide variety of vegetables, fruits and spices, all finding their way into the cuisine. Kerala is also quite diverse religion-wise: only about half the population is Hindu, with the rest being Muslims and Christians. Both religions took root in Kerala earlier than in other parts of the country due to the region's historic trade links with the Middle East. As a result, there is a strong influence of specific Muslim and Christian communities on Keralan cuisine.

Most of my personal experience with Keralan food has been outside Kerala, mainly in restaurants, though I've been there on holidays. It is an incomplete experience, much to my regret as what I've tasted has always, quite literally, whetted my appetite. I did have a direct personal experience with Keralan food for a brief period of time though. For a few years, when I was living in Delhi in the 1990s, we had a cook from Kerala. She had been living in Delhi for some time and most of her cooking was adapted to north Indian tastes. But every once in a while, especially when cooking fish, she would bring in glimpses of Keralan recipes. More recently, my local south Indian restaurant, Nivedyam (recently renamed Cochin) near Hampton Court, is a Keralan restaurant. For survival, it also serves British curry house must-haves such as chicken tikka masala, biryani and tarka daal. But true to its roots, it has many Keralan dishes on its menu.

There are many varieties of fish dishes in Keralan cuisine. Fish dishes are made from any of the widely available fish varieties: pomfret, mullet, seer and king fish. The most sought-after local fish is Karimeen or Pearl spot, a fish found in the backwaters of the state. The word for fish in Malayalam, the local language, is meen, so a dish with meen in the name will use any popular fish, but a dish with karimeen in the name will only use this pearl spot fish. It is a fine distinction of words for the non-Malayalam speaker and I must confess I often confuse karimeen and meen kari.

As an aside, the observant reader may have noted that the way Malayalam is spelt in English, makes it a palindrome. It used to be the answer to a standard quiz question in schools when we were young.

The best known fish curry from the state, **Meen Moilee** or **Molly**, combines the two most plentiful food items of the state, fish and coconut. The dish is believed to have originated from the Christian community in the state and is now widely available. Fish pieces are first marinated and then fried lightly. Separately, onions and tomatoes are fried with spices in coconut oil which is a distinctive feature of Keralan cooking. The dish gets its characteristic taste and appearance from the addition of coconut milk extracts to the curry at two or three stages of the cooking. The thinner extracts (the second or third extract of coconut milk) are added at earlier stages of cooking and the thicker extract (the first extract of coconut milk) is added right at the end along with the fried fish. The coconut milk gives the dish a pale, creamy appearance. In taste, it has a strong coconut flavour and is not particularly hot.

For a state famous for its spices, meen moilee makes surprisingly limited use of spices. The legend is that this was a curry adapted to the tastes of the Portuguese, the first Europeans in India. The dish is supposedly named after the lady who first added coconut milk to a fish curry. The story could be true, because there is otherwise no connection that the word 'moilee' has with either fish or curry in Malayalam. The closest sounding word is the word for 'daughter' or 'girl'.

Another popular fish dish is called **Fish Mappas**. This is a hotter and spicier fish curry, with red chilli powder added to curry base of onions and tomatoes. The quantity of coconut milk added to this dish is also proportionately less compared to meen moilee. The curry may be topped with a little bit of tamarind solution to make it tangier. In appearance, the addition of red chilli powder gives the curry of this dish a more conventional reddish tinge.

A regional speciality, **Alleppey fish curry** or **Allapuzha Meen curry**, is named after a historic town in Kerala. The key differentiating ingredient in this dish is raw mango which gives the curry a very distinctive sour or tangy taste. There are a couple of different ways of making this dish. In some recipes, the curry has a base of onions and tomatoes, fried in coconut oil with spices, and raw mango and coconut milk are added at different stages of cooking. Others use a paste of coconut, raw mango, onions and tomatoes as the base for the curry. The fish, most commonly seer, is not separately fried but is cooked directly in the curry. While some red chilli powder may be used, the dish is not supposed to be very hot, such that the combined and distinctive tastes of coconut and raw mango stand out.

Many restaurants, especially outside the state, list a dish called **Kerala Meen curry** or Kerala fish curry. This can be misleading. There is no standard fish curry in Kerala, so a Kerala fish curry generally implies that the dish uses one or more of the standard ingredients used in the cooking of the various types of Keralan fish curries. The most common is the use of coconut milk. A souring agent may also be added. Depending on the restaurant, you can get a fish moilee or a fish mappas or a combination. I once asked a waiter in a south Indian restaurant if the Keralan fish curry listed on the menu was a fish moilee or a fish mappas. "Yes", he answered. I think he was being honest.

Dry, fried fish, as you would expect, is also widely available in Keralan food. Generally, a thick, spicy paste is applied to fish pieces which are shallow fried in coconut oil. The paste can have a number of ingredients including ginger and garlic paste, turmeric powder, red chilli powder, black pepper, curry leaves and lime juice. The amount of red chilli powder calibrates the heat, though you should expect the dish to be fiery in appearance and taste.

I am told that in many places in the state, there are eateries close to fishermen's wharfs where you can take freshly bought fish and get them fried, to eat on the spot or take home. This is a practice I've seen in other places as well, especially places with a strong tradition of fishing in India and abroad. In a variant of this practice, you can also find beach-side shacks, where you pick the fish that you want to eat, from a displayed selection of uncooked fish and seafood, and it is prepared with a masala paste and fried or grilled right in front of you.

An extravagant fish dish is **Meen Pollichathu**, fish in banana leaves. This dish can be prepared in a few different ways. The initial preparation of the dish is not dissimilar to the dry, fried fish described above. The fish is marinated to start with. A thick paste, of ginger, garlic, red chilli, lime juice, and sometimes cooked onions and tomatoes also, is applied. The fish is then wrapped and tied in a banana leaf like a parcel. These parcels can be cooked in a couple of different ways. The easier way is to grill the fish by cooking the parcels over a heated tawa or griddle. The parcels may also be cooked in oil, taking care not to burn the banana leaves. The fish is served in the banana leaves, so when you unwrap the parcel, the flavours captured within it burst out at one go, like a treasure chest of aromas popping open.

A more complex variant of the above dish is **Karimeen Pollichathu**, karimeen fish in banana leaves. This dish is prepared in three steps. First, whole, cleaned karimeen fish is covered with a paste of turmeric powder, red chilli powder and salt and shallow fried. Second, a thick masala paste of onions, tomatoes, lots of spices, chillies and a little bit of coconut milk is separately prepared. Each fried fish is smothered in the masala paste and wrapped in a banana leaf. Finally, these banana leaf parcels are either grilled over a hot tawa or lightly cooked in oil in a pan. The last step doesn't take long as it is mainly to infuse the dish with the aroma of the leaves.

Karimeen pollichathu is a luxuriously rich and spicy dish. Cooking in banana leaves gives meen or karimeen pollichathu a unique flavour and taste, very different from a regular fried fish. These dishes can be had as a starter course or as a main course with accompaniments. I prefer appam as an accompaniment as the masala can be a bit too hot and spicy on its own. Eating this dish is a delightful experience. There is intrinsic mystery in a dish which is served wrapped up in a leaf. Not only can you not see the food, even the flavours tend to be camouflaged.

When you open the string tying the parcel and unwrap the leaf, it is the aromas that hit you first. In my case, sometimes I can only smell the dish and not see it, as the steaming dish mists up my spectacles. As the mist clears, nirvana follows. You get to see the dish inside the leaf, not neatly laid out but a jumbled-up mass of thick red gravy with the fish hidden somewhere inside. The urge to dig in is quite irresistible.

A few observations on the ingredients used in Keralan fish dishes which make the dishes distinctive. I've already mentioned the use of coconut milk in fish curries. It is also extensively used in meat and vegetable curries. Coconut oil is also the preferred cooking oil. It is a strong-tasting oil which is one reason why Keralan food tastes quite different from other south Indian foods even when the dish is the same, as in the Keralan sambar.

While tamarind is sometimes used as souring agent, it is more common to use a solution made from a local fruit called Kudampuli, called Cambodge in English and sometimes referred to as the Malabar tamarind. This fruit and another called Kokam or Cocum are native to south west India, both used as souring agents and as pickles. They belong to the same biological family and can be substituted for each other. The kudampuli fruit is dark purple or nearly black in colour when dried for storage. When soaked in water, it produces a solution used as a souring agent in cooking, with a taste which is sour with undertones of sweetness. It is considered especially good for fish curries.

Curry leaves, kariveppela in Malayalam and karipatta in many parts of India, are a common flavouring agent in Keralan food, either used right at the beginning, fried in oil with mustard seeds, before the curry is cooked, or added right at the end as part of tarka or tempering.

Black pepper is also very common in Keralan food, used both as a whole spice and in powdered form, sometimes both in the same dish. This is not surprising. Pepper has grown in south west India since ancient times and has been used in cooking for as long. Its use in cooked food has been tried out in every possible way and it continues to be an important ingredient for imparting a distinctive sharpness to dishes.

When studying history in school, one of the first things we learnt was that pepper was one of India's main exports in ancient and medieval times. I used to find it amazing that a simple spice, something that was often not even an essential ingredient in cooking and was added only as an optional seasoning, could be so important in the cuisines of historic times. It was much later that I found out that red and green chillies, used so liberally in Indian cuisine only came to India and the rest of the Old World, after the discovery of the Americas in the late fifteenth century. Before that black pepper and another spice, rarely used now, called long pepper, were the main ingredients to spice up bland food.

A short detour on pepper and its historic role in global trade is quite interesting.

Pepper, along with cinnamon from Sri Lanka, was exported from Kerala to ancient Egypt for religious purposes – cinnamon was used for embalming mummies and pepper in religious offerings. Pepper grows naturally in Kerala and some other parts of south India; the cinnamon tree similarly grows wild in Sri Lanka. How the trade links between India's south west coast and the Arabian Peninsula were first established is not clear, but by the time Augustus became emperor in Rome, just before the start of the Christian Era, trade links between ports in south west India and ports in Arabia were very well-established. The links between the Arabian ports and Alexandria and other Mediterranean ports, passing through the Red Sea and overland through Egypt and the eastern Mediterranean regions, had been active for even longer. Greek, Arabian and Indian merchants were all active participants on these trade routes.

Pepper was exported in large volumes to the Roman empire. It was used mainly as an ingredient in cooked food. The only known surviving cookbook from that era, by Apicius, had pepper as an ingredient in 349 out of 468 recipes; it was used not just in main dishes but also in sweets and wines. In addition, it was also used in medicines. Traders made huge profits out of pepper – it was called the 'black gold' long before that label was applied to petroleum. Not all saw pepper as useful: The elder Pliny has a paragraph full of rant against pepper in his collected works on Natural History, quoted every time the history of pepper is retold.

The southern ports of India also had trade links towards the east, starting in the centuries before the Christian Era and getting well established during the first millennium CE, with active trade links with ports in modern Myanmar, Malaysia, Thailand and Indonesia. These ports in turn had trade links with south east ports in China. So, pepper was exported not only to the west but also to the east, including ancient China.

The volume of trade with the west came down as the Roman empire declined but the export of pepper only reduced, never disappeared. It slowly became an exotic and, consequently, an expensive spice. As most of Arabia converted to Islam in the second half of the first millennium CE, Europeans were shut off from the trade route connecting India and Arabia. Arabian merchants were responsible for creating many myths about products from the East, including about pepper. Pepper was supposed to grow in places guarded by deadly dragons and poisonous snakes which needed to be slayed to get to the pepper. These myths were useful marketing tactics, helping create a cachet for the product and keeping prices high.

In medieval times, the merchants of Venice and Genoa controlled the Mediterranean trade and used their monopoly to sell-on pepper and other spices at huge mark-ups. It is believed that the Portuguese and Spanish maritime expeditions of the fifteenth century were to break these monopolies, leading famously to not only the discovery of the alternate route to India and the East around South Africa but also, the much more historic discovery of the Americas.

The small peppercorn carries a heavy weight of history.

One side effect of this history continues to impact pepper directly. As is well-known, Christopher Columbus had set out to discover India through a westward route. The knowledge that the earth is round was slowly gaining general acceptance: it was hence a reasonable proposition that if you travelled far enough westward across what was believed to be one big ocean between Europe and Asia, you would eventually get to India. When he landed in the Caribbean islands and central America, he believed he had found India. He called the people 'Indians' and as a result Native Americans are still sometimes called Indians. He also thought that a sharp-tasting vegetable that he found in central America was pepper. The name unfortunately stuck. The vegetable from the capsicum plant is still referred to as pepper or bell pepper in America and the west. The original pepper has to be called peppercorn or black pepper to differentiate.

There used to be a restaurant called Coconut Grove in Delhi which was probably the first specialist Keralan restaurant that I ate in. It was good, if not exceptional, but did have a number of Keralan, not just generic south Indian, dishes on the menu. This was the place where I first tasted appam. Appam is much more a Keralan dish than Tamil; it is far more common to find appam as the carb accompaniment to curry dishes in Kerala. If you like dosa, you will like appam. I love dosa, ergo I also love appam.

Soon after we found Coconut Grove, we were told that a chef from the restaurant had set up a Keralan restaurant near our home in south Delhi. This was a really small restaurant, not more than half a dozen tables. The menu was limited but on it were some great tasting dishes: fish moilee, fish wrapped in banana leaves, Keralan chicken curry and dry lamb fry, all served with really soft and spongy appams. Between Coconut Grove and this small restaurant, both now closed, I started my personal discovery of Keralan cuisine.

So far, I've only described the fish dishes of Kerala. There are, of course, a number of other seafood dishes as well.

Prawn is the most easily available seafood and the most common dish is prawn curry. The Keralan version is called **Chemmeen Kari**, which just means prawn curry. The dish is prepared along expected lines, with dry spices such as fenugreek, mustard seeds and curry leaves tempered in oil, with a curry base of onions to which coconut milk is added at the finishing stages. This dish does not use a lot of chillies and is, hence, quite a mild dish. Depending on the amount of coconut milk used and if both the thin and thick extracts of coconut milk are used, the dish is also called **Chemmeen Moilee**. Keralan prawn curry does not have tamarind or kokam. The taste of coconut dominates.

Nivedyam, my local south Indian, used to do a dish called **Chemmeen Asadh**. I am not sure if this is a common dish in Kerala itself. It is a prawn curry with raw mango and green chillies added to the standard Keralan prawn curry ingredients, the prawn equivalent of the Alleppey fish curry. The quantity of coconut milk used is also somewhat reduced. The resultant dish has added notes of sourness and heat, which make it quite different from the standard chemmeen kari.

Prawn is also cooked in a drier form as a **prawn masala**. The prawns in this dish are cooked separately, with turmeric, coriander and red chilli powder. The thick masala gravy is made by frying onions, tomatoes with ginger, green chillies and curry leaves to which coconut milk is added. The prawns and the thick masala gravy are brought together right at the end.

A simpler dry prawn dish is called **Chemmeen Varuthatu**, or prawn fry. Shelled prawns are marinated in a paste made of lime juice, red chilli powder, turmeric powder, cumin powder, ginger and garlic. After marinating for about 30 minutes, the prawns are shallow fried in coconut oil. This is a completely dry dish and can also be served as snacks. Like other snacks, it is often served with onions and chutney. It is a remarkably simple dish to cook and one which I sometimes make at home as a starter (with the red chillies dialled down to suit my children's tastes).

Similar to the prawn masala is **crab masala**. Mud crabs are very common in the Kerala backwaters, so this is not a difficult dish to find. The crab meat is taken out of the shells and diced into small pieces for easy cooking. The masala gravy has more or less the same ingredients as in prawn masala. The crab meat is added to it when it is almost cooked, with thick coconut milk added at the end. Crab meat is naturally soft and juicy and this dish lets that come through. It is common to find the dish served in a crab shell. I am sceptical whether this adds anything to the appeal of the dish, unless some of the claws served still have crab meat inside them. Otherwise, in my experience, the shells unnecessarily clutter up the plate.

Most fish and seafood dishes in Kerala are eaten with appam, rice or parotta (similar to paratha). A very different combination in Keralan cuisine is fish curry eaten with cooked tapioca, called **Kappa**. This combination is so popular that **Kappa Meen Kari**, that is tapioca and fish curry, is often listed as a dish on its own. Tapioca is the starchy flesh extracted from the roots of the cassava plant. It used to be a cheap substitute for rice but over the years has become a very accepted accompaniment to fish curries. The simplest kappa preparation involves boiling pieces of tapioca flesh with seasoning and then steaming with a paste of grated coconut and chillies. The cooked dish is often also tempered with fried shallots, mustard seeds and curry leaves.

While Kerala does not have the equivalent of the many sadham (rice) dishes found in Tamil Nadu, there are many other interesting rice preparations. In these dishes, rice flour (ground rice rather than full rice grains) is often used. I've listed a few rice dishes that I've had a chance to try and, while not comprehensive, it does give an idea of how Keralan cuisine is as versatile as Tamil where rice is concerned.

Appam, mentioned earlier, is the best known rice dish from Kerala. The authentic Keralan appam, called Palappam, is made of rice flour, coconut milk and toddy, a mildly alcoholic drink made from the sap of the coconut tree. The toddy helps to ferment the rice flour batter and may be substituted with yeast. Once the batter is fermented, appam is made in a special wok shaped cooking pan. The shape of the pan results in extra batter settling in the centre for a soft and spongy middle and thin crispy edges. Appam goes well with pretty much all Keralan meat, fish and vegetable dishes, though it is not usually eaten by itself as dosa is.

An unusual Keralan speciality rice dish is **Puttu**. This is routinely eaten for breakfast with a curry made of chana (brown chickpea) called **Kadala Kari**. To make puttu, coarsely ground rice flour is mixed with water and little bit of salt. The idea is to create a mix which is not as soft as dough but crumbly and similar to breadcrumbs. Puttu is made by layering this rice with grated coconut in a perforated, cylindrical tube and then steaming the tubes in a pan of boiling water (an unusual way of cooking, if ever there was one). Traditionally these tubes used to be made of bamboo but are now made of metal. Once cooked, the rice and coconut mix is pushed out of the tube and comes out as a cylindrical roll.

Puttu and kadala curry are as commonly paired in Kerala for breakfast as chhole and bhature are in Delhi and Punjab. And it is as common for the combined dish to be called **puttu kadala**, just as chhole bhature is. Kadala curry is a thin curry of chana, made by frying onions or shallots in coconut oil with whole spices such as mustard seeds, dried red chillies and curry leaves. This curry base is further spiced with a masala paste of many spices and grated coconut. Boiled chana is added to this mix with water. The curry is generally made thin such that it can be mixed with puttu for ease of eating.

Yet another rice-based preparation is called **Pathiri**. This is a dish from the Muslim community of Kerala. There are many varieties of pathiri, but the basic one can be described as a roti made of rice. The dough for pathiri is made by boiling rice flour and then kneading it. The process after that is similar to making roti but requires greater care as rice dough does not hold as well as wheat flour dough. Like roti, pathiri is also cooked over a hot tawa. It may be served brushed with coconut milk. Just in case there isn't enough coconut in whatever dish you are eating the pathiri with.

A distinctive looking rice dish, also eaten for breakfast, is called **Idiappam** or **Idiyappam**, also known as 'string hoppers' in Sri Lanka. These are noodle shaped, steamed strings of rice. You have to go through a few hoops to make these string hoppers. Rice flour is first mixed with hot water to create a mix which can be kneaded into a soft dough. The dough is then pushed through a perforated mould to make strings, which are collected in a special steaming utensil or an idli pan. If steamed in an idli pan, you get each mound of strings in the size and approximate shape of an idli. Idiappam and egg curry are a popular breakfast combination.

Plain roti or chapati is not common in Kerala. But a special type of paratha, called **Malabar Parotta**, can be found in restaurants especially as a side to meat or chicken dishes. This paratha is similar to the north Indian lachcha paratha in flakiness and softness and is as complicated to make. Malabar parotta is made from maida. The trick is in preparing a dough which is just right for the required softness and can be worked with to get the layers. Once the dough is ready, the individual parotta pieces are prepared by rolling out a bit of the dough, stretching it, folding it back into a thin cylinder, twisting the cylinder into a spiral shape and then finally rolling it out into a circular shape of about 20 cm diameter. This piece is then cooked on a tawa with a bit of oil on both sides. Like appam, Malabar parotta is very absorbent and goes really well with the spicy curries of Keralan cuisine.

When I was in school in Barauni, a number of our teachers were from Kerala. There is a long tradition of people from Kerala becoming teachers and nurses, working in other parts of the country. Our English teacher, Mr. Abishai, was from Kerala. In my final years in school, a group of us were on very friendly terms with him and would often go over to his home for coffee and general chit-chat – a bit about school but also about books, politics, sports, etc. We probably learnt as much over coffee as in the classroom. There were a few occasions on which he invited us over for dinner as well. I remember the first quite well. That is my earliest memory of a Keralan chicken stew with rice.

Chicken stew, also called **Kozhi Ishtu**, is a mild, coconut-based, curried chicken dish. The local name ishtu is of course a mispronunciation of the word stew, but so widely practised that it is quite common to find the dish labelled as such even in high-end restaurants. Mr. Abishai, as an English teacher, would have none of this mispronunciation and I've known the dish only as chicken stew.

In preparation, kozhi ishtu has similarities with meen moilee. Not surprising, as both dishes originate from the Christian community of Kerala. The curry base is prepared by frying whole spices and then onions, ginger, garlic, green chillies and curry leaves in coconut oil. Chicken pieces are added with carrots and potatoes to the fried curry base and cooked. Thin and thick coconut milk are added at a middle and final stage respectively for the Keralan signature on the dish. The dish is normally eaten with rice or appam.

The chicken may be substituted with mutton for a **Mutton Ishtu**, a similarly mild and coconutty dish.

Kerala is the only state in India where beef is easily available and widely eaten. This is partly due to the fact that about half the population is Muslim or Christian, but also due to greater tolerance and acceptance of differences in eating practices. A dry, rich in spices dish called **Erachi Ularthiyathu** is the best known beef dish. The word erachi means meat and sometimes the dish may be made of lamb rather than beef. Nivedyam, the Keralan restaurant near my home, served a lamb version of this dish. The dish is considered properly cooked only when the meat has turned practically black, so it is an easy dish to visually identify.

This dish is also a great example of the use of spices in Keralan cuisine: more or less every tropical spice known to mankind finds its way into this dish. There are various 'authentic' ways of cooking this dish. Most involve three steps. The meat is boiled to softness with salt, pepper and a spice combination called meat masala. This spice mix is made of roasted whole spices including cinnamon, cardamom, cloves, aniseed, fenugreek, mustard seeds, star anise and nutmeg. Separately, the gravy base is cooked by frying onions, ginger, garlic, green chillies and coconut with a number of powdered spices. The gravy base and meat are then fried together till the meat turns black. The dish is finally further garnished with curry leaves and mustard seeds fried in oil.

A dish which is so elaborately prepared deserves to be a main course. So, erachi ularthiyathu is typically listed as a main course in most Keralan restaurant menus. However, you also get a spicy lamb or beef fry as a starter dish, which is also cooked till the meat is almost black. The main course is spicier than the starter, but the difference in taste is difficult to make out because both the dishes are quite hot. The starter dish is a family favourite and practically always one of the dishes ordered when we eat at Nivedyam.

There are two chicken dishes that I used to regularly eat at or order from Nivedyam. One is **Nadan Kozhi Kari**. Nadan kozhi is supposed to be country chicken or fowl. I doubt if the chicken used was actually a free ranging country fowl, so this is really just the standard Keralan chicken curry. Chicken cubes are marinated in lime juice with red chilli, turmeric, garam masala, salt and pepper. The curry base is made of onions, ginger and garlic paste fried in coconut oil, but without tomatoes. The chicken is cooked with the curry base and a mix of whole spices, separately roasted and powdered, is also added at this stage. Coconut milk is added at the final stage.

The other dish that I regularly got from Nivedyam is Pepper Chicken, called **Kurumulaku Kozhi** in Malayalam. This is a dry dish with a thick gravy. Most of the heat in this dish comes from black pepper. Probably what a Keralan meat dish would have tasted like before chilli came to India. Chicken pieces are marinated with turmeric, pepper and salt. The gravy base is made of onions, curry leaves and ginger garlic paste fried in coconut oil. To this is added crushed black pepper, fenugreek powder and garam masala. The marinated chicken is then added and the whole mix cooked till the chicken is of a dark colour. Fried coconut may be added at the final stages. Green chillies are also sometimes added to this dish. That makes an already hot dish really fiery. I regularly eat this dish with appam or Malabar parotta. Lots of yoghurt or raita on the side helps.

The Hindu contribution to Keralan cuisine is in the many vegetarian dishes. While most Hindus in the state, except brahmins, eat non-vegetarian food especially fish, their meals on religious occasions and festivals tend to be fully vegetarian.

The equivalent of the sappadu of Tamil Nadu in Kerala is the **Sadhya** or **Sadya**. Like the Tamil feast, sadhya is also served on a banana leaf and has many dishes. The dishes that are served for sadhya are also what a Keralan vegetarian would eat on a regular basis. It is the number and the variety that is the characteristic of the sadhya. Including the chutneys and pickles, the number of dishes in total can be more than two dozen. The dishes are all served at one go and the diner is expected to make their way through the meal at their own pace.

Rice is central to the meal. Many of the dishes are expected to be eaten with rice. There are a number of varieties of rice grown locally in Kerala. These tend to be of smaller grain than some of the varieties found in the north of India, especially basmati, but fluff up more when cooked with water. So, short and fat works perfectly well for rice. A unique type of rice, served for sadhya meals, is Red Rice or **Kerala Matta rice**. This is a special type of rice grown only in Kerala and south Karnataka. The type grown in the Palakkad region of Kerala has a Geographical Indication and hence sells for a premium. The grains have a red coloured pericarp covering. Unlike white rice, red rice is not polished and, hence, when cooked the red covering gives the cooked rice a pinkish hue.

A proper sadhya platter will have at least three or four curried dishes and a similar number of dry dishes. These are served with a range of chutneys, pickles and poppadum.

A yoghurt-based dish called **Kichadi** is one of the likely dishes in a sadhya platter. This is not the same as khichri found in other parts of the country. This dish is like a north Indian raita, yoghurt with cooked coconut, vegetables and spices added to it. It is eaten mixed with rice, in a close approximation of the curd rice found in Tamil Nadu.

Sambar is another curried dish which is regularly a part of a sadhya meal. A simple **Keralan sambar** used to have only shallots and coconut added to cooked daal. It is now, however, customary to cook sambar with more vegetables such as drumsticks, carrots, brinjal, okra, just as in Tamil Nadu.

Rasam and Parippu, a daal tempered with curry leaves, are also regularly present in a sadhya meal.

A fixture of vegetarian meals in Kerala is a mixed vegetable dish called **Aviyal** or **Avial**. Aviyal is a thick mixture of many vegetables coated with coconut paste, cooked in coconut oil. Some of the vegetables used in the dish are drumstick, brinjal, yam, pumpkin, beans, carrots, raw banana, raw mango, etc. Quite a long list of vegetables for one dish. There are not too many dishes like this generally in Indian cuisine – vegetables are typically cooked solo or paired with another. There isn't any great technique to cooking aviyal either. The vegetables are chopped up and all cooked together over low heat in water with turmeric and salt. A coconut paste, made of grated coconut, cumin seeds, green chillies and a souring agent or yoghurt, is added to the vegetables at an intermediate stage and the dish is also tempered with coconut oil and curry leaves at the end.

There are a couple of myths associated with the origins of aviyal. The one I like best is from the *Mahabharat*. In the epic, the five Pandav brothers have to be incognito for the final year of their twelve year exile. The second brother, Bheem, the strong one, took up employment as a cook in the kitchens of one of the regional kings. His decision to become a cook was on a somewhat tenuous premise that he could do the job because he was fond of eating. He was not the first and certainly not the last to make that mistake. When the head cook asked him to prepare something as a test, he came up with aviyal, essentially a whole bunch of chopped vegetables thrown into the cooking pot and boiled together.

The Keralan equivalent of tarkari and poriyal is **Thoran**. This is a generic label for a dry vegetable dish. The dish is made from one or two vegetables such as cabbage, beans, beetroot, spinach, etc. While these are the commonly used ones, practically any vegetable can be used. This is also a reasonably simple dish. Mustard seeds, curry leaves, onions and chillies are stir-fried in a small quantity of oil. The chopped vegetables are added to this mix with seasoning, covered and cooked in their own steam. Coconut, either as paste or grated, is added at the finishing stage. A couple of thoran dishes are always part of a sadhya meal.

There are quite a few types of vegetarian curry dishes that may be part of a sadhya meal such as Erisseri or Elliseri, Kurukku, Kalan and Olan. These are all different types of dishes with the only common element being the use of grated coconut or coconut milk as an ingredient along with the main vegetable. Subtle variations lead to a different type of dish and, unless you have grown up eating these dishes, it is difficult to tell the difference. I personally recommend looking at the main vegetable rather than the type of curry to decide if you want to try it (when given the choice).

Payasam is the label for many desserts in Keralan food. The basic formula is to boil a cereal or lentil in full fat milk or coconut milk with sugar or jaggery. The dish is flavoured with cardamom and may be garnished with cashew nuts. It can be eaten warm or cold. This basic formula allows for a number of different types of payasam. It is customary to serve at least two in a sadhya meal.

Rice payasam, called **Pal payasam**, is the simplest and is also commonly used as a religious offering. It is made by boiling red rice and sugar with full fat milk and then cooking on low heat till the mix becomes thick.

A variant of this dish is called the **Pal Ada payasam** or **Pal Ada Pradhaman**. Instead of rice grains, this dish uses rice flakes. Otherwise, the method of cooking is similar. The dish can also be made with jaggery and coconut milk, in which case it is called Ada payasam or Ada pradhaman.

A different type of payasam, in taste and appearance, is **Gothambu payasam**. This dish uses broken wheat or couscous as the cereal, jaggery as the sweetener and coconut milk as the liquid. The broken wheat needs to be first boiled to a point where it is almost cooked. Then the usual process is followed: wheat, melted jaggery and coconut milk are cooked on low heat till the coconut milk reduces and becomes thick. The use of jaggery makes this dish brown in colour. The combination of jaggery and coconut milk also makes this very different in taste from a sugar and milk based payasam. A fitting way to finish off an elaborate sadhya meal.

Meen Moilee

Karimeen Pollichathu

Appam

Puttu with Meat Curry

8

Karnataka

More Dosa and many lesser known gems

My best friend from school days, Ashok, is from Karnataka. I've had a few fantastic meals at his home when young but there are not many dishes that I remember, after all these years, as specialities from Karnataka. The one dish that I remember was a very delicious egg bhujia for breakfast. The closest dish that I've found in taste to that is actually a Parsi dish called Akuri which I describe later in the chapter on Mumbai. My personal experiences of Karnataka food came much later, first in restaurants, especially the Udupi chain of restaurants, and then in work trips to Bangalore (renamed Bengaluru in 2006 but Bangalore is still widely used). Apart from Bangalore, I've had only a few trips elsewhere in the state, so my personal experience of Karnataka food is not extensive. As a result, the description of Karnataka cuisine in this chapter is like a highlights reel rather than full coverage, but should provide enough by way of an introduction to someone not familiar with the foods of the state.

Karnataka is a state in the south west of India. It shares borders with every state in south India: Maharashtra to the north, Goa to the north west, Telangana to the north east, Andhra Pradesh to the east, Tamil Nadu to the south east and Kerala to the south, with the Arabian sea to the west. The coastal regions between the Western Ghats and the sea are the southern part of the Konkan coast. Kannada is the main local language. The region is very fertile with two main rivers, Krishna and Kaveri, and many smaller rivers. The region covered by the state has been hence well populated from ancient times and has been the centre of many kingdoms and empires over the years.

Karnataka has a strong culinary tradition of its own and also shares cooking methods and dishes with its neighbouring states. It is more vegetarian than the other south Indian states. North and South Karnataka have some differences in food. South Karnataka is, in some respects, similar to Tamil Nadu and Kerala, with rice as a dominant grain. Meals are elaborate and there is a variety of dishes of all types, reflecting a mature and rich tradition in food. North Karnataka, apart from rice, also has jowar (sorghum) as a common grain, similar to Maharashtra to its north. The food there was traditionally simpler and hardier than in the southern parts. The Konkan coast has a strong culinary tradition of its own with seafood an important part of the diet. Mangalore, on the coast and Karnataka's second largest city, has over the years gained fame for its cuisine, enriched by its various coastal communities. A pocket of regional cuisine has also developed in the Coorg or Kodagu region of the state, based on a tradition of eating game from the nearby forests. Finally, Mysore used to be the capital of the most recent kingdom in the state. As we have seen in other states, affluent kingdoms have historically contributed to the creation of speciality dishes, which is true for Mysore as well. I've described some of the most commonly found dishes in Karnataka in this chapter, attributing them to specific regional cuisines where necessary.

I came across Udupi branded restaurants when in school. These restaurants, found in many cities in the country, take their name from a temple town in Karnataka. The restaurants were not under common ownership but operated on a loose affiliation to the town and its cuisine, with the chefs or at least the head chef from Udupi. These restaurants played a significant role in popularising the iconic idli-dosa-vada-sambar dishes in the cities of north, east and west India. The town Udupi itself is claimed to be the birthplace of masala dosa. There is not enough evidence for me to support or dispute this rather sensitive point of food history. According to K.T. Achaya, the eminent Indian food historian, dosa is mentioned in ancient Tamil Sangam literature, making Tamil Nadu the likely place of its origin. The Udupi claim, however, is specific to masala dosa, not plain dosa. Suffice to say that dosa and idli are as integral to Karnataka cuisine as they are to Tamil Nadu.

A few specific types of dosa, such as Mysore masala dosa, Set dosa and Neer dosa have been created in Karnataka. I've already mentioned these earlier in my ode to dosa in the chapter on Tamil foods. Each deserves a proper description.

Mysore masala dosa has a red coloured chutney made of garlic and red chillies applied to the dosa when it is being cooked. It also has a masala of potatoes, called palya locally, as the stuffing. If you flip a Mysore masala dosa open, you can see the red chutney on the inside surface. A hotter version of the masala dosa in summary. It is probably the best known regional variety of masala dosa.

Eating Mysore masala dosa in Mysore had been one of my bucket list items. I finally had the chance a few years ago. The first time we were just passing through Mysore for a holiday elsewhere. We stopped over for lunch. You can imagine my disappointment when we discovered that the restaurant didn't serve dosa for lunch. It was strictly for tiffin, that is breakfast or early evening. That was such a disappointment. I was luckier the next time when we stayed in Mysore for a couple of days. The funny thing was that the hotel we stayed in had dosa on the breakfast menu, but it was not called Mysore masala dosa. I had to specifically ask for one, just to make sure. Mysore itself is full of places where you can get the eponymous dosa. As in other cities in India, a bit of local help can help find the best ones. But one has to be careful to take recommendations from taxi drivers etc. with a pinch of salt. I remember when we were on our way to dinner recently when on holiday, the driver enthusiastically endorsed the restaurant as his 'favourite restaurant'. A bit later, he sheepishly admitted that he had never eaten there himself, only heard good reviews from tourists.

Set dosa, a Karnataka speciality, uses a somewhat different combination of ingredients for the batter compared to a regular dosa. Rice is mixed with a type of flattened rice called poha and a reduced quantity of urad daal. The batter is fermented and then cooked like a regular dosa. Set dosa is spongier and thicker than the regular dosa and often smaller. When bought from specialist dosa shops, you will often find set dosas stacked like pancakes, ready to be served. It is often served with a chilli podi, a dry spice condiment, sprinkled on it and eaten plain or with a curried vegetable dish.

Neer dosa is also a Karnataka speciality and not very easy to find outside the state. Its name translates to 'water dosa'. Unlike the regular dosa, the rice batter is not fermented and is thinner, that is it has more water. When spread over the cooking tawa, the thinness of the batter results in tiny air holes, giving the cooked dish a lacy appearance. It is a soft and light dosa. It can be eaten on its own with chutney and sambar (but beware, one is unlikely to be enough) or, more often, as the carb accompaniment to curried dishes. For example, when eating Mangalorean non-vegetarian curries, it is quite common to have neer dosa on the side, similar to the way appam is often eaten in Keralan meals.

A less well-known dosa is **Davangere Benne dosa**, supposed to have originated from the town of Davangere in north Karnataka. Benne means butter, so this is dosa made with extra butter, liberally spread on the inside during the cooking. In most restaurants, you will find something similar listed either as butter dosa or ghee dosa, the latter using ghee rather than butter.

In Karnataka, dosa is usually eaten with just a coconut chutney. Sambar is not a necessary side dish to dosa, especially at breakfast. Most restaurants and eateries will now serve sambar but mainly due to popular expectation. The **Udupi sambar** is different from the sambar that one gets in Tamil and Keralan cuisines. The key difference is the mild sweetness of the sambar which results from adding a small quantity of jaggery. Coconut is also an ingredient, with grated coconut roasted and ground along with other spices that make the sambar masala. The sweetness is not to everyone's liking and now even in Udupi restaurants, the sambar served is not always the traditional Udupi sambar.

Sometimes a vegetable dish called **Saagu** may be served with plain dosa or set dosa. It may even be used as a stuffing to make a saagu masala dosa. A north Indian may mistakenly think that saagu is the same as saag, a dish of cooked leafy vegetables such as spinach. It is actually a mixed vegetables curry where a selection of vegetables, from beans, peas, carrots, cauliflower, potatoes, brinjal etc., get cooked and boiled with lots of spices and coconut. The vegetables become almost a mash in the cooked dish. It is a thick curry and is also served with poori or chapati for breakfast.

There was an Udupi restaurant in Munirka in south Delhi that I used to go to regularly during my college days. Apart from idli, dosa, etc., it also used to serve a south Indian 'thali'. The word 'thali' means a large plate and is a label for a complete meal. In this case, it used to include boiled rice, rasam, sambar, curd (yoghurt is always curd in south Indian food), a couple of vegetable dishes, poppadum, chutneys, pickles and a sweet dish. The vegetables were made to Udupi recipes and would include both dry and curried dishes.

A specialist rice dish called **Bisi Bele Bhaat** or **Bhath** was on the Udupi menu and is one of the better known speciality dishes from Karnataka. Bhaat, as we have seen earlier, is the name for cooked rice. Bele means daal or lentil. The name of the dish translates to hot lentil and rice. So, this is another variant of khichri or lentil rice that is found all over India. But it is one of the more complicated khichri variants. First, rice and daal are cooked separately. Then a medley of vegetables, such as beans, peas, carrots etc., are boiled in water. The rice, daal and vegetables are then brought together in a single pot with the vegetable stock. To this mix, tamarind solution and a special spice combination, called bisi bele bhaat masala, are added. The spice combination is the special ingredient of this dish and is made by roasting and grinding a range of spices such as red chilli, urad daal, chana daal, cumin seeds, coriander seeds, cloves, cinnamon, fenugreek seeds, peppercorn, grated coconut, etc. An uncommon spice called Moggu, dried buds from kapok tree, may also be used. Bisi bele bhaat is so popular in Karnataka that you can get its spice combination pre-prepared as a packaged product. The rice, daal, vegetables and spice mixture is cooked till the water has mostly boiled off and the dish has a thick consistency. The dish is then further tempered with a tarka in ghee. Roasted peanuts and cashew nuts may be added for garnishing.

Bisi bele bhaat is a complete meal in itself and you really need nothing more apart from perhaps a pickle or two and some poppadum to crush into the dish. Like khichri, it is great comfort food but, unlike plain khichri, it can hardly be considered food for the sick; it is way too spicy and rich for that.

When I was living and working in Delhi, the Karnataka Sangh in R.K. Puram was not far from home. Its canteen was one of the places that I'd go regularly for my fix of dosa. The menu had a long list of dosas, a smaller list of idlis and vadas and a similar list of speciality rice dishes, including bisi bele bhaat. There were no separate vegetable dishes and no question of non-vegetarian dishes as this was a strictly vegetarian restaurant. As a result, I had some idea of the state's food but didn't experience the full range till I visited Bangalore.

Bangalore has over the years grown into a foodie city with restaurants and eateries of all types and budgets. When I first visited it in the late 80s, it was not a big city and most visitors headed to a few well-known restaurants and eateries. In my first couple of trips to the city, I remember going only to the well-known idli dosa places. The first place that I went to was the famous Mavalli Tiffin Rooms or MTR. For a dosa devotee, going to MTR in Bangalore is almost on the same scale as going to St. Peter's in the Vatican is for a Catholic (perhaps not, but I am sure you get what I mean). MTR has been operating in Bangalore since 1920, first as Brahmin Coffee Club and since the 1950s as Mavalli Tiffin Rooms. It moved into its primary location in Lalbagh Road in 1960 where it continues to operate. The masala dosa here has a well-deserved fame. It is served in triangular shape rather than the cylindrical or semi-circular shape seen in most places. It is also a much darker brown in colour, due to the generous amounts of ghee used during the cooking. The MTR dosa is always served with an additional pot of ghee in a small bowl placed on top of the dosa. Pouring some of it over the dosa is part of the ritual. As is customary in Karnataka, the dosa is served with a coconut chutney but no sambar. It is probably as close to dosa perfection as you can get. The continued popularity of the restaurant probably means that they have done a decent job of maintaining the quality in spite of the increase in volumes. The restaurant is also famous for its rava idli, idli made of semolina, which it claims to have invented during the Second World War, when there was a shortage of rice in the region.

Once my idli-dosa pilgrimages were done, I started exploring and discovered other foods of Karnataka in subsequent trips to Bangalore. First a description of some more of the vegetarian specialities of Karnataka.

Upma, or **Uppittu** in Kannada, is a popular breakfast dish all over south India and now across India. One test of popularity, at least with the affluent, is when a dish is available in the breakfast buffets of more upscale hotels. Upma meets that test and is routinely available in hotel buffets. Its main ingredient is rava or semolina. It is made in three easy steps. First, rava is dry roasted. Then, a tarka of mustard seeds, cumin seeds, lentils, chillies, curry leaves and onions is fried in oil. Cashew nuts are also often used. Finally, the right amount of water is added to the fried tarka, brought to a boil and the rava gently mixed in. The dish is ready when the water is fully absorbed.

Khara Bhat or **Bhath**, a speciality of Karnataka, is a more substantial variant of upma. The name can mislead you into thinking this is a rice dish but it is not. It is rava upma made with mixed vegetables. The vegetables, a selection of capsicum, carrots, peas and tomatoes, are fried with onions and spices as in the second step described above. A special dry spice combination called vangi bhat masala is added to the mix and makes it taste spicier than plain upma. A bit of extra ghee, added at the end, also makes this a much heavier dish than upma.

Khara bhat is often served in a small portion along with a similar sized portion of **Kesari bhat**. This is a sweet version of upma. Khara and kesari bhat is such a common combination for breakfast that it has its own name, **Chow Chow Bhat**. Kesari bhat is made by adding roasted rava to a proportionate quantity of boiling, sugared water. Saffron and food colour give the kesari bhat a distinctive yellow colour. As the rava cooks, ghee is added to it along with cardamom powder. Roasted cashew nuts and raisins are added at the end for a bit more pampering. Even though it is most commonly eaten for breakfast, it can also be served in small portions as a dessert or as part of a thali.

Around the early 90s, I read rave reviews of a recently opened restaurant in Bangalore called Karavalli. Karavalli is now a legendary restaurant, almost an institution. It was making waves in the early 1990s and I remember booking myself in the Taj hotel, on a work trip to Bangalore, specifically to eat in the restaurant. The food in the restaurant was of course as good as the hype, but as interesting was the menu itself. Karavalli not only served great food but also informed and educated its diners about the foods of the south west coast of India. Reading about the provenance of the dishes and the historic notes on the menu kindled in me an interest in those foods beyond just eating it. It was also the first time that I realised how rich and diverse the cuisines of the south west coast were.

Kori Gassi is a dish from the regional cuisine originating in Mangalore. Kori means 'chicken' and gassi is 'curry', so a literal translation does not tell us much about the dish. However, the gassi curry of Mangalorean cooking is made in a special way. There is extensive use of a local variety of red chilli called Byadgi which gives the curry a strong red colour but is only medium hot. This chilli is the main spice used, along with a few others, and onions, grated coconut and tamarind, to prepare a special gassi paste which gives the curry its distinctive taste. The dish is prepared otherwise in a manner similar to other chicken curries. The chicken is first marinated, then cooked in a fried curry base of onions, garlic paste and curry leaves. The special paste is added to the mix with the chicken pieces and fried. Coconut milk and water give volume to the curry. The resultant dish is a great blend of tastes of chillies, coconut and tamarind.

Kori gassi is one part of the combined dish from Mangalore called **Kori Rotti**. The chicken curry is served with '**rotti**', a rice roti quite different from the better known wheat-based roti (it is spelt with a double t mainly to differentiate the two, otherwise the words are pronounced exactly the same). Rotti is made from circular pieces of rice flour paste rolled out and dried till they become quite hard and crispy. When the chicken curry is poured on it, the rotti becomes soft and soggy, with crispy edges. You then use it just as a piece of roti or appam to eat the chicken curry with.

A Mangalorean dish deservingly popular across the state is **Ghee Roast Chicken**. It is a dish with a thick, fiery red gravy. It is believed to have been created by an eatery in Kundapura, a coastal town just north of Mangalore, but is now served in practically every restaurant and eatery serving Mangalorean dishes. If there is an authentic recipe, it is probably lost in the many different types of ghee roast chicken found in restaurants and cooked at home. There are a few elements that are consistent. The first is of course the generous use of ghee in the cooking. Ghee is used in both roasting the spices for the special masala and also in cooking the chicken with the masala. The second is the use of lots of red chillies, a mix of byadgi, Guntur chillies (among the hottest used in cooking, described in the next chapter) and sometimes also Kashmiri. This ensures both a fiery red colour as well as heat. The recipes vary in the proportion of chillies used. The milder ones use mostly byadgi or Kashmiri chillies for colour. Most recipes also recommend to marinate the chicken in a base of curd with other ingredients.

Finally, a bit of tamarind and jaggery is added to the dish to for some added notes in the taste. The special spice combination used for this dish is made by roasting red chillies and a number of spices in ghee and then grinding them into a paste. This paste can be added either to the marinade or to the chicken when it is being cooked. This is a hot but delicious dish, best had as a main course in a meal. Restaurants in Karnataka usually serve it with neer dosa or rice but a paratha is also very suitable.

Mangalore is also famous for its seafood. A Mangalorean speciality is **Kane Rava Fry**. Kane is the name for lady fish and rava is semolina, so this is fried lady fish with a coating of semolina. The fish is marinated in a red chilli paste. The paste has lots of red chilli powder and a few other ingredients such as lime juice, coriander powder, ginger garlic paste and corn or rice flour. The marinated fish is then coated with semolina and deep or shallow fried in coconut oil till the crust becomes golden. It is a fairly standard fried fish preparation with the red chilli giving it a strong bite. It can be eaten as a starter or with rice and daal or sambar.

Another Mangalorean fish speciality is **Bangude Puli Munchi**, which translates to 'mackerel sour and hot'. This type of hot and sour curry is found in other regions of the Konkan coast. The strong tastes of the curry are especially suited for strong tasting fish such as mackerel, sardine, shark, etc. The recipe is not complicated. A masala paste is made with lots of red chillies (a combination of byadgi and regular chillies ensures both colour and heat), a range of spices, ginger, garlic and onions. This masala paste and tamarind pulp, which gives the curry its sourness, are boiled in water till you get a curry of the desired consistency. The cleaned and lightly marinated fish is then cooked in this curry. While quite easily available in Mangalore and the coastal areas, this dish is not as widely available elsewhere in the state.

As in Tamil Nadu and Kerala, thin soup-like curries, called **Saaru**, are usually part of full meals in Karnataka. They are thicker than the Tamil rasam due to the addition of lentils. The simplest type is **Bele saaru** or **lentil saaru**. First the lentil, usually toor, is boiled in water with turmeric. Tomatoes are separately fried and added to the lentil along with tamarind water, jaggery and coconut. Then a special spice combination, rasam powder, which can be freshly prepared but is also available pre-prepared, is added. The whole mix is then boiled with some more water and further tempered with curry leaves in hot oil. The dish is usually eaten with rice as a course in a full meal. Even though it looks like a soup, it is rarely eaten on its own.

One can also find both meat and vegetable curries with the label saaru. The curries in these dishes are thin and meant to be eaten with rice. **Koli saaru** is the name for chicken curry made in this style. There are a number of regional or town specific prefixes to the name to differentiate dishes with minor variations in the recipes. Kundapura Koli Saaru is, thus, the chicken curry from Kundapura. The preparation follows a standard template. A special saaru spice combination is made first by roasting and grinding whole spices, red chillies and grated coconut. The curry base is of onions and tomatoes, fried in coconut oil. The chicken is fried in this curry base with the special spice mix. Water is then added to complete the dish.

The people of Coorg or Kadagu, a district in Karnataka, are known for their fondness of food and liquor, kari and kudi in the local language. The food has a higher proportion of non-vegetarian dishes, compared to other south Indian regional cuisines, attributed to the easy availability of game in the nearby jungles. There are not many speciality Coorgi restaurants, so the dishes are not as well-known or widely available in other parts of India. But most restaurants specialising in foods of Karnataka or the south west of India will include a couple of Coorgi dishes in the menu.

A pork curry called Coorg **Pandi curry** is often presented as the signature Coorgi dish. This is probably because pork dishes are not common in other south Indian regional cuisines. It may not be the dish that Coorgis would necessarily pick to represent their food. The dish is prepared in a method similar to other meat dishes in the south. The curry base is of onions fried with ginger, garlic, green chillies, etc. A dry spice of combination of whole spices is added to the meat being fried with the curry base. The meat is fried till it gets a dark colour and then slow cooked with water till it is soft and tender. A souring agent, traditionally made from the local cambodge fruit, is added at the final stage.

Coorg pandi curry is best eaten with **Akki rotti** which is roti made from rice, similar to plain pathiri found in Keralan cuisine. Cooked rice and rice flour are mixed with water and kneaded to make the dough. Once the dough is ready, the process is the same as for a wheat flour roti. Akki roti is more absorbent than regular roti and makes for a great side with hot and spicy meat curries.

An uncommon and not easily found speciality of Karnataka is **Chigli Chutney**. This chutney's main ingredient is ants, specifically red fire ants found in the hills of the Western Ghats. The ants are collected by trained locals and are roasted after being harvested. Once cleaned and dried, they are mixed with salt and can be stored for quite some time. The chutney is prepared by grinding the dried ants with coconut, onions, garlic, chillies and spices with water. The chutney has a distinctive sour and sharp taste. It is protein rich and believed to have other medicinal properties. It is served as an accompaniment to other dishes in a meal and you may not notice anything special unless you are told that it is made from ants. So, if you happen to find a red coloured chutney which has a very different sour and sharp taste, do ask. It may be chigli chutney. Or it may just be a red chilli chutney with tamarind.

Ants are eaten in other cuisines of the world. I experienced it in an unexpected place a few years ago. The Copenhagen-based Noma, at that time ranked the best restaurant in the world, had a pop-up in London in the summer of 2012. It was an opportunity not to be missed. I managed to get a table for lunch. I had deliberately not read any reviews before going for the meal, wanting to be surprised and delighted. The meal turned out to be as good as the hype. One of the surprises came early in the meal: a dish of live red ants served with crème fraîche and cabbage leaves in a glass jar. You needed to eat the dish quickly otherwise the ants would run away. Your food running away is not a risk that you normally have while eating! From what I remember, the dish mainly tasted of crème fraîche and the leaves, with a bit of sourness and occasional crunch coming from the ants. Not at all difficult to eat, as long as you got over your squeamishness.

I'd like to mention one other dish while on the topic of strange dishes. One of the best historical sources about foods of south India is a book called *Manasolassa*, a composition in Sanskrit verse. It was written by king Somesvara III of the Western Chalukya dynasty in the twelfth century. The Western Chalukya ruled over most of modern Karnataka and parts of surrounding states from the tenth to the twelfth century CE. The book was written by Somesvara to demonstrate his scholarship and covers many topics. From a food history perspective, it is a goldmine, as it describes about a hundred dishes in a section on food. Many of these dishes are similar to what is still found in the region. But there are a few unusual ones as well. The one which caught my attention is Barbecued River Rats. The practice of eating rats must have been quite widespread as there are mentions of rats being sold in the markets of the Vijayanagar kingdom a couple of centuries later as well. The book describes how the dish was cooked which I will refrain from repeating as the dish has died off.

A sub-regional cuisine of Karnataka comes from Mysore. The erstwhile kingdom already gives its name to the dosa described earlier but has two other famous dishes with its name. **Mysore Bonda** are table tennis ball-sized savoury snacks.

They are made of a batter of maida, mixed with onions, chillies and coriander leaves. The individual balls usually have a stuffing of potatoes or vegetables. Once the batter is shaped into balls, they are deep fried till the outer crust becomes brown and crisp. The bondas are eaten as a snack with chutney.

Mysore Pak is a well-known sweet from the region. It looks like barfi or fudge and is made of besan and sugar. Besan is mixed into a sugar syrup solution and then cooked in generous amounts of ghee and flavoured with cardamom. Once cooked, the mix feels and looks like halwa and needs to be transferred quickly to a flat pan or tray where it is pressed and flattened into a rectangular shape, ready to be cut into barfi sized rectangles or squares. Mysore pak, like so many other Indian sweets, can be eaten as a dessert or as a snack.

Set Dosa

Bisi Bele Bhaat

Ghee Roast Chicken

Mysore Pak

9
Andhra Pradesh & Telangana

Where gunpowder is food

The state of Andhra Pradesh was split into two, Telangana and Andhra Pradesh, in 2014. There is a convoluted history behind this. Before Independence, the Telugu speaking regions of coastal Andhra and Rayalseema used to be a part of the large Madras Presidency, which also included modern Tamil Nadu and parts of modern Kerala and Karnataka. The region of Telangana, with a majority of Telugu speaking people, was a part of the State of Hyderabad, a kingdom ruled by the Nizam of Hyderabad under British protection. After Independence and the annexation of the Hyderabad state into the Indian Union, these administrative arrangements continued with coastal Andhra and Rayalseema continuing as part of the Madras state and Hyderabad constituted as a separate state. Following popular demand and aggressive agitation, the state of Andhra was first created in 1953, hiving off coastal Andhra and Rayalseema from the Madras state (which was later renamed Tamil Nadu). Further agitations resulted in merging Andhra with the Telangana region of the state of Hyderabad, including Hyderabad, to create the state of Andhra Pradesh in 1956. This arrangement lasted for about six decades but was unstable, with demands for a separate state of Telangana popping up at various times. After decades of simmering demands and agitations, the state of Telangana was again separated from Andhra Pradesh in 2014. Hyderabad is the capital of Telangana and Amaravati, near Vijaywada, will be the new capital of Andhra Pradesh.

From a cuisine perspective, the three regions, Rayalseema, coastal Andhra and Telangana, are traditionally identified as having separate cuisines, though there is much that is shared. Telangana is probably the most different among the three. Rayalseema shares borders and thousands of years of cultural bonds with Tamil Nadu to the south and Karnataka to its west. That is reflected in its food. Coastal Andhra on the east coast of the Deccan shares many culinary features with Rayalseema and Telangana but has also been influenced by Odisha to its north. It must also be repeated that Hyderabad city itself has a strong identity in food, as we have seen earlier in the chapter on Mughlai food. As in other chapters, I've not described each sub-cuisine separately but grouped the common dishes under a broad Andhra label.

Andhra food is known to be one of the hottest, in terms of chilli, in the country. That is saying something in a country where chilli is a common feature in foods all over. One reason is easy availability. Andhra is the largest producer of red chilli in the country. **Guntur Red Chilli**, a label for red chilli varieties grown in the district of Guntur, are justifiably famous and considered among the most potent red chillies used in cooking. A specific type called **Guntur Sannam** has a Geographical Indication. The Guntur red chillies have high potency and deep red colour. When a Guntur red chilli is used in a dish, it cries out its presence visually and in taste. As they say, you cannot miss it.

It is somewhat of a mystery as to why Andhra food, on average, has a much higher chilli content than food from other states of India. Chilli, as I've mentioned before, is not native to India and was brought from the New World by the Portuguese in the sixteenth century. Andhra Pradesh and Telangana were not even the first regions in India to be introduced to the chilli plant. Colleen Taylor Sen, in her book *Feasts and Fasts: A History of Food in India*, mentions a legend that 'there was once a severe famine in the area and all that grew were red chillies, which then became a staple of the local diet.' This is a little hard to believe. Even if red chillies were the only thing to grow, people could hardly have survived on a diet of red chillies. It is plausible though that red chilli cultivation could have spread in the region during the famine when other crops failed. Wider cultivation would have made chilli more easily and cheaply available leading, in time, to higher consumption. On a more frivolous note, it could be that the use of chilli spiked during the famine to make people eat less!

The other thing to note is that chilli is not dialled up to high levels in every dish in Andhra cuisine. In a not very rigorous analysis, my evaluation shows that non-vegetarian Andhra dishes tend to be much hotter (chillier? that word would mean the opposite of what is intended) than the vegetarian dishes. This could be for a very practical reason. The use of spices in hot climates was meant to prevent the food from going bad, especially for non-vegetarian dishes. The high chilli content may have been for just this reason, facilitated by the easy availability of chilli in the state.

Andhra food is also characterised by the importance of pickles and chutneys as accompaniments to meals. It is not an exaggeration to say that pickles and chutneys have been elevated to the status of dishes. Most meals are accompanied by a number of pickles and chutneys and much care is given to the preparation of these accompaniments.

My introduction to Andhra food was unusually through a condiment. It is known all over the country colloquially as '**Gunpowder**' and called **Kandi Podi** locally. The colloquial name denotes its high chilli content. The name is like a red flag to the kind of people who have the strange need to prove their virility through tolerance of chilli. I've come across many such, especially young men, not just in India but in other countries as well. Gunpowder as a result is widely available in restaurants serving south Indian food. In spite of its dreaded reputation, it is not necessarily the hottest preparation you will find in Andhra cuisine. It is actually a reasonably complex condiment, prepared by roasting and blending together a number of ingredients: lentils such as toor, urad and chana daal, garlic, cumin seeds, sesame seeds, curry leaves, asafoetida, etc. and lots of dried red chillies of course. The dry, orange or reddish masala powder is often sprinkled on idli and dosa. It is also sometimes sprinkled on plain boiled rice with ghee for a simple meal, with a very powerful kick.

As you would expect from a south Indian state, idli and dosa are popular for breakfast in Andhra. While the idli is the same as found elsewhere, Andhra has a few different types of dosa. The best known Andhra dosa is **Pesarattu** or **Pesara Attu**, a dosa made from a batter of moong dal. Whole moong daal (green gram) is soaked for a few hours and then ground into a smooth batter with some ginger, green chillies, etc. Unlike the rice and urad daal batter of the standard south Indian dosa, this batter does not need to be fermented overnight, making this dosa less onerous in preparation and less sour in taste. Once the batter is ready, it is cooked just as the standard dosa on a griddle and may have a topping of chopped onions and green chilli. When made from whole moong daal, it has a greenish tinge and is visually quite different from the standard, golden plain dosa. If the batter is made from split moong daal (yellow gram), it is still called pesarattu but is quite different in appearance and taste. Either way, it is best eaten with a chutney and is regularly also paired with a ginger pickle.

While pesarattu is not normally served with a stuffing, there is a variant of it found in Hyderabad intriguingly called **'MLA' Pesarattu**, which is pesarattu with a stuffing of savoury upma, made of rava. The word MLA has nothing to do with upma but is an abbreviation for Member of Legislative Assembly. One story behind the name is that it was first created in the canteen of the state legislative assembly at Hyderabad, as a special order for those MLAs needing a somewhat more substantial breakfast than a plain pesarattu. The story sounds credible enough and has the benefit of being the only story behind the name.

The Andhra dosa, also called **Minapattu** or **Minapa Attu**, is similar to the standard plain dosa and is made from a fermented batter of rice and urad daal. The proportion of urad daal in the Andhra dosa may be more than what you find in the standard plain dosa in Tamil Nadu or Karnataka. Some recipes also suggest adding chana daal along with rice and urad daal. The net result is a stronger lentil-flavoured dosa.

Urad daal and rice are also used to make **Dibba Rotti**. The word 'dibba' may refer to its thickness. The dish is also called minapa rotti. This is a thick flatbread made from a batter of urad daal mixed with rice ground to a coarse powder. The batter is poured into a heavy-bottomed deep pan coated with lots of oil. Once the lower side is cooked and crusty, the bread is flipped over to make the other side similarly crusty. It can be eaten on its own but also makes a great side for absorbing curried dishes.

The urad daal and rice batter is put to good use in Andhra food. Left over batter is often made into a teatime snack called **Punugulu**. These are spicy fried balls, the size of small laddus, with a crispy brown exterior. The batter is thickened with dry, flattened rice or rice flour, chopped onions and green chillies. Balls of the thickened batter are then deep fried in oil till the outside turns brown and crisp. This is also a popular street food in coastal Andhra. This snack is somewhat similar to **Paniyaram**, cooked balls of rice and urad daal batter, found further south, though paniyaram is cooked, lightly brushed in oil, in special pans and not deep fried.

Uppudu Pindi or **Uppindi**, a rice-based dish similar to upma in name and appearance, is also a popular breakfast dish. The dish is made of 'rice rava', which is coarsely ground rice. Grinding rice is not an easy task and, in the past, Andhra households used to grind large quantities at one go and store. It is now possible to get factory-made rice rava in packaged form, making the dish somewhat easier to cook at home. Like rava upma, the recipe is simple. Onions and a few whole spices are first fried in oil and then the rice rava and a small quantity of moong daal are added with water and boiled together. Note that the whole spices include red chillies and if you have this dish for breakfast, it will not be a mild start to the day.

As I've mentioned earlier, chutneys and pickles have an important place in Andhra cuisine. So much so that some of the special chutneys and pickles are as well-known as the dishes. In Andhra food, **Pachadi** is the label used generally for chutneys, with the key ingredient's name added as a prefix.

Tamati (tomato) Pachadi is made by frying tomato with garlic, turmeric and seasoning till it becomes mushy, as one would expect for a chutney. To this mush is added a roasted and powdered masala combination (or podi) of urad daal, chana daal, sesame seeds and inevitably red chillies. The pachadi is further tempered with small quantities of mustard seeds, cumin seeds, curry leaves, asafoetida and perhaps some more red chillies (just in case you like it hotter!) fried in oil. This is a reasonably easy dish to prepare and is one of the most widely used chutneys in Andhra meals.

Allam Pachadi has allam or ginger as its main ingredient. It is one of the more complex chutneys that you will find across cuisines in India. It is made by lightly frying fresh ginger with small quantities of lentils and red chillies and then making a paste. This paste is mixed with tamarind pulp, turmeric, salt, some red chilli powder and at the end some jaggery. It may also be further tempered with whole spices fried in oil. The resultant paste is simultaneously sharp, sour, hot and sweet. It takes a little bit more effort to make but is often found as accompaniment in main meals and also with single dishes like idli and dosa.

A chutney unique to Andhra is **Gongura Pachadi**. This is a chutney made of the leaves of the Gongura plant, a type of hibiscus grown extensively in Andhra Pradesh and Telangana. Apart from Andhra, gongura dishes are also found in surrounding states but are not as popular as in Andhra. The leaves taste quite sour and are used in a number of dishes in combination with other ingredients. For the chutney, the most common method of cooking requires frying the leaves in oil with mustard seeds, urad daal, red chillies, garlic, salt, etc. till the leaves are soft and mushy. The dish is considered an essential part of a proper Andhra meal, so it is widely available in restaurants serving Andhra food.

Pickles are as important as chutneys. A broad label of **Uragaya** or **Ooragaya** is used as a suffix to denote pickles. Pickles are made of many different fruits and vegetables. A generous amount of red chillies is de rigueur with the other main pickling spices being powdered mustard, fenugreek and salt in groundnut oil.

Among the popular pickles is **Avakaya** or **Avakai**, a mango pickle. This is normally prepared in the early part of summer when green, raw mangoes are plentiful. The best pickles are made from hard and sour mangoes. In traditional Andhra households, making Avakaya is a summer ritual and the pickle is prepared in large quantities, such that it can last for a year till the next mango season. Cutting the raw mangoes is hard work. Extra care needs to be taken to make sure that everything is dry during the preparation as moisture makes the pickle go bad when stored. To prepare, mango pieces are individually soaked in oil and dipped in a spice mix of powdered mustard seeds, fenugreek seeds, salt and red chilli. The pieces are then stored in dry jars with more oil and allowed to pickle. This step takes about three to four days. The pickle is then ready to be enjoyed for the next 12 months, used as an accompaniment in practically every meal.

Nimmakaya Urugaya is a pickle made from lemons. To make this pickle, small pieces of lemons are soaked in lemon juice, salt and turmeric in jars till the pieces become soft. Powdered mustard seeds, fenugreek seeds and red chilli are then added directly to the pickle jar and mixed. Compared to the avakaya, this is a simpler pickle to prepare and is made two or three times a year.

A typical Andhra meal is similar to the thali that we have seen in other south Indian states. It has plain boiled rice, called **Annam**, as the main carb. The etymology of the name is revealing. The word in Sanskrit and in many other Indian languages means 'food' and shows the importance of rice in Andhra cuisine. Andhra Pradesh and Telangana grow a lot of rice and one variety called **Sona Masoori** (or Sona Masuri) is quite famous. It may be the second most famous type of rice in India after basmati. It has medium length grains, unlike the long-grained basmati, but is very aromatic. It also has lower calories and starch than basmati. It is a sought after and expensive rice variety, so not necessarily what you will find in every meal in Andhra.

Rice, as in other parts of south India, is eaten as multiple variants when cooked with other ingredients. **Pulihora** is the name for tamarind rice in Andhra cuisine. It is made by combining boiled rice with a fried mix of lentils, red and green chillies, curry leaves, turmeric, peanuts and tamarind. The turmeric gives the rice a yellow colour and the tamarind a tangy taste. Pulihora is regularly used as prasadam or religious offering. It can be served as one of the rice dishes in an elaborate meal or eaten by itself with chutneys and pickles. One reason for its popularity is the use of tamarind which is considered an important ingredient in Andhra cuisine, supposedly as a counter to the high content of fluorine found in the water of the region.

Curd rice, also called **Daddojanam**, is also eaten widely especially during the summer months. It is a simple preparation where cooked rice is mixed with curd (yoghurt) and topped with a tarka of cumin seeds, mustard seeds, urad dal, chana daal, red chilli, etc. in oil. Curd rice is also used as a religious offering, in which form it tends to be cooked without chillies. The Gods don't like their food too hot it seems.

Apart from rice, a proper meal will also include at least one daal dish, either plain or with vegetables. Daal dishes are called **Pappu** in Telugu. The prefix tells us either the type of lentil used or the vegetable in the pappu. Thus, **Mudda Pappu** is a daal made of toor (pigeon pea), **Palakura Pappu** is daal with spinach and **Gongura Pappu** is daal with gongura leaves. Simple, as long as you know what the prefixes mean in Telugu.

The main dishes to be eaten with rice can be both vegetarian and non-vegetarian. Andhra is mostly non-vegetarian but not all meals have meat or fish dishes. Most dishes with a liquid gravy or curry have the label of Kura or Koora, though special types of preparations have specific names: Charu is the name for a rasam like soup; Pulusu for a thin curry which has tamarind; Iguru is the name for a thick curry; and Vepudu is a dry, fried dish. A word of caution. I've listed these as if there is a fixed nomenclature but, as we have seen in other states, there are always exceptions. Having said that, more often than not you can tell what you are going to get by the name of the dish. Which is helpful.

Rasam is typically always a part of a full Andhra meal. A plain rasam dish is called **Charu**. The label is also applied to a number of different types of rasam and rasam-like dishes. A typical plain charu has whole spices and tomatoes fried together and then boiled in water with tamarind, a little bit of jaggery and a special rasam powder. The rasam powder ingredients include lots of black peppercorn, coriander, cumin seeds, fenugreek seeds and red chillies. Charu, like rasam elsewhere, is quite watery and light. It is usually had mixed with rice as a course in a full meal.

Pappu Charu, or lentil rasam, is the name of a dish similar to sambar. The difference with the Tamil sambar is that the pappu charu has only a couple of vegetables, if at all, added to the soup. The dish is otherwise prepared in a similar manner where the lentil, usually toor, is boiled with turmeric and salt and mashed for smoothness. Onions and tomatoes are fried separately in oil with some whole spices and chillies. Vegetables, if used, are cooked along with this mix. Tamarind is added for sourness, as in other charu dishes. The cooked lentils are mixed in at the final stage. The dish looks like daal, if without vegetables, and like sambar, if with vegetables, and is in between the two in terms of spiciness.

Ulava charu is another Andhra speciality likely to be served in an elaborate Andhra meal nowadays. It used to be poor man's dish till being discovered as a health food. Ulava is horse gram, a lentil grown in the Deccan region. Its name comes from being used as horse feed. The dish is cooked similarly to the pappu charu described above.

Kodi Kura is a generic label for chicken curry. There are many different types of Andhra style chicken curries. One special type is **Konaseema Kodi Kura**. This is an elaborate chicken dish and surprisingly not widely known. The chicken is added to onions fried with green chillies, curry leaves and ginger garlic paste. The spices added include the standard powdered spices (turmeric, cumin, coriander and red chilli) along with a special masala paste of roasted peanuts, red chillies and seeds of poppy, sesame, cumin and coriander. Coconut milk is added to the curry at the finishing stage. It is, as you would expect from an Andhra dish, quite hot – it has green chillies, red chilli powder and dry red chillies going into it. The coconut milk helps balance the heat. This is actually quite a tasty dish if you can handle the heat and I find it surprising that it is not as well known as other regional chicken curries.

A better known Andhra style chicken curry is **Rayalseema Natu Kodi Pulusu**. Natu kodi is country chicken or fowl. This is also a fairly complex chicken curry with a number of steps and ingredients. The chicken itself is richly marinated in spices and may even be lightly fried or grilled separately before being added to the curry. The curry is prepared in the standard way with onions fried with ginger garlic paste, green chillies, powdered spices and tomatoes. Being an Andhra dish, generous amounts of red chilli powder are used. A further mix of dried coconut, cashew nuts, poppy seeds, etc. is also added to the curry in the final stages. A little bit of tamarind water may also be added for a note of sourness to the dish.

There are similarly multiple types of Andhra-style mutton curries, most are simply called **mutton kura**. There is no standard recipe to these mutton curries. The only thing that you can be certain of is the use of lots of red chillies resulting in a dish with plenty of heat. Camellia Panjabi in her best-selling recipe book, *50 great curries of India*, lists a mutton curry (Andhra style) from Nellore. The mutton in this recipe is marinated in yoghurt with red chilli powder, turmeric and ginger and garlic paste. The base of the curry is fried onions and tomatoes with cardamoms and cloves. The mutton and marinade is fried in this base, seasoned and then water is added for the curry. A nice tasting dish but it could be from anywhere in the country.

One definite speciality of Andhra food is **Gongura Maans** or **Mamsam**, that is mutton with gongura leaves. This is a sour and sharp mutton curry and not to everyone's taste. In the first bite the sour taste of the gongura comes through quite strongly especially if you are not familiar with it. But it is a taste that quickly grows on you as you go through the dish. It is not a difficult dish to cook but does require time as both mutton and gongura take time to cook. The standard cooking method usually requires the mutton and gongura to be cooked separately and then be brought together in the final stage. The preferred way is to boil the mutton somewhat blandly and fry the gongura with onions, ginger garlic paste, chillies and lots of spices. The cooked mutton is added to the fried gongura mix and simmered with water till you get the dish with a gravy. The dish looks like mutton with spinach but of course is very different in taste.

A typical Andhra fish curry is **Chepala Pulusu**, freshwater fish in a sour, tamarind-based curry. There are multiple ways of making this dish, all require tamarind to be added to a curry of onions and tomatoes fried in lots of spices. The fish used for this dish is often murrel, locally called koramenu. It is considered a special fish in Andhra and can be quite expensive. So, while the dish itself is not complex, the cost of the fish elevates it to a special occasion dish.

Prawns are called Royyala in Telugu. The first time I saw a dish with royyala in a menu I mistook it to be a corrupted version of 'royal', a prefix like 'shahi' in Mughlai dishes. Prawns dishes are now quite easily and widely available in Andhra Pradesh. This is because of the growth of shrimp farming in the last three decades. Andhra Pradesh is in fact the largest producer of farmed shrimps in the country.

Royyala Vepudu, stir fried prawns, is a simple dish to cook. The first step is to marinate the cleaned prawns in lemon juice, red chilli powder, turmeric and salt. Then onions are fried in oil with a couple of whole spices, curry leaves and green chillies and the marinated prawns are added to the mix. The mix is further spiced with powdered spices and cooked till the masala coats the prawns. This is a dish eaten with rice and may need a pappu (daal) to lubricate the meal. **Royyala Iguru** is the same dish with a thick gravy which is achieved by frying tomatoes with the onion mix and adding a little bit of water for the curry.

One of my secret pleasures is watching food related videos. Some of these are straight-forward dishes being cooked but many are food travelogues. Most of the videos are produced by enthusiasts but there are a few made by foodies who do this for a living. I wonder if it is as good a job as it looks. The pleasure of eating may be diluted if you have to try out all types of foods even those that personally don't appeal to you. One particular video specific to Andhra food is worth recounting. This is a video produced by a gentleman from Bangalore,

Kripal Amanna, who has a series under the brand *Gourmet on the Road*. His focus is mostly on restaurants in Bangalore but he has also produced videos on foods of other parts of south India. He has an engaging style and clearly loves the food of the region, which comes through in his videos.

In this particular video, Mr. Amanna tries out Andhra food in a restaurant in Hyderabad called Spicy Venue. In a single sitting, he works his way through a biryani, a vegetarian thali and multiple non-vegetarian dishes. After eating about half of a decent sized plate of the restaurant's special biryani, he manages to eat quite a bit of a thali which includes charu, ulava charu, vegetable pappu, pappu charu, many vegetarian dishes, pachadi, pickles and podi served with poori and multiple helpings of rice. In between he also samples a number of non-vegetarian dishes: a kodi (chicken) iguru, Rayalseema natu kodi pulusu, chepala (fish) vepudu, chepala pulusu, fried royyala (prawn), and a peethala (crab) iguru. Though a bit dazed at the end, he still seems to be enjoying every mouthful and even manages to taste a dessert. The list of dishes that he covers in one sitting probably covers the whole list of main dishes that I've described above. I've eaten tasting menus running up to a dozen dishes, but the dishes are small to allow you to taste many dishes. It is rare to see someone able to pull off so many full-sized dishes in one go. Full marks to Mr. Amanna for enthusiasm, commitment and stomach capacity.

Andhra cuisine has many sweet dishes similar to what is found in the other south Indian states. These include different types of payasam, sweet rava dishes and many different types of laddus. A sweet dish from the state with worldwide fame is the **Tirupati Laddu**.

One of the best known temples of India, the Tirumala Venkateshwara temple, is in Tirupati in south Andhra Pradesh. The temple is dedicated to Sri Venkateshwara, believed to be one of the incarnations of Vishnu. It is an old temple, probably first built in the fourth century CE though it became pre-eminent probably during the medieval time under the patronage of the kings of the Vijayanagar kingdom. It is one of the most visited holy sites in the world with an estimated 30 to 40 million visitors every year. I've visited this temple only once and remember being quite impressed with how well organised it was to manage the visitor numbers, in comparison to some of the other temples in India. It remains a well-endowed and well organised temple. Among other things, the temple is one of the largest global suppliers of human hair for wigs, etc. The supply comes from the ritual of tonsuring of hair that many devotees undertake. The temple management smartly collects the hair, grades and auctions it. This commercial smartness has also led to the branding and legal protection of the Tirupati Laddu.

The laddu is the traditional religious offering made to the deities in the temple. The laddus are carried back by devotees as prasadam, often to be distributed among family members and local communities back home. Imagine 30 million visitors buying large quantities of laddus every year. The temple management has got a Geographical Indication on the Tirupati Laddu and manages the entire process of cooking the laddu in-house. Hundreds of cooks in a special workshop-like kitchen make the laddus to a defined recipe. The recipe itself is not special or secret: essentially this is a besan laddu cooked in ghee with sugar, cardamoms, cashew nuts and raisins. You can make it at home, but you cannot call it Tirupati Laddu.

The other speciality sweets from Andhra pale a little against the spiritual weight of the Tirupati Laddu.

Poornam Booleru or **Poornalu** is a sweet dish where rice balls are filled with a sweet stuffing. The poornam (stuffing) has boiled and mashed chana daal mixed with jaggery or sugar, coconut and cardamom before being lightly roasted in ghee. The stuffing is shaped into small balls by hand. These balls taste somewhat like laddus though it is not common to eat them as they are. They are dipped into a batter of rice and urad daal and deep fried till the crust is crisp. Booleru is not an everyday sweet and is mostly made during religious festivals and special occasions. One useful by-product is that if any of the rice and urad daal batter is left over, it can be used to make punugulu, the savoury snack that was described earlier. So at the end the cooks have both a savoury snack and a sweet dish to show for their efforts.

A speciality sweet dish of the state, originating in the East Godavari district, is called **Pootharekulu**. It is also called **Paper Sweet** as its main element is a thin rice sheet which holds a sweet stuffing. The rice sheet is difficult to make and requires specialist skills. Hence this is a sweet mostly bought from sweet shops who themselves source it from specialist makers. The rice sheet is made from a very thin batter of rice. This batter is spread over a convex surface, usually an upturned clay pot, heated from below. The spreading process requires skill and is done by soaking a thin cloth in the rice batter and spreading it in one quick motion on the heated convex surface. The rice sheet forms reasonably quickly and has to be removed at the right time. For the sweet, a couple of these sheets are coated with warm ghee and filled with jaggery or sugar powder. The sheets are folded and then rolled. They are sold as rolls wrapped in paper or plastic. The fancier versions have nuts and other flavourings also in the stuffing. Some modern variants even use sweet chocolate instead of jaggery.

Pootharekulu doesn't have a religious identity like the Tirupati laddu. Without some other form of market pull, it is a justified concern that the skill of making the rice sheets and the sweet may disappear eventually.

Pesarattu

Different Types of Chutneys

10
Mumbai

Food that inspires Bollywood masala films

Mumbai, formerly Bombay, has a rich and historic food culture of its own. The city has been a major port since the sixteenth century, when it came under the control of the Portuguese. Before that it was a minor outpost of the Gujarat and Deccan kingdoms mainly comprising of fishing villages. In 1661 CE it was famously transferred to the British by the Portuguese as a part of a royal dowry. Its ascendance as a port and a city started during the British rule in India. As the British power in the country expanded, so did the importance of Bombay. During the eighteenth and nineteenth century, it became the most important port and the administrative headquarters of the British in western India. Since then, it has been the business capital of India and a magnet for economic migrants from all over India. It is also the city where the Hindi filmmaking industry, referred to as Bollywood (Bombay + Hollywood), is based. Dreams of stardom serve as another attraction for immigrants from the rest of the country.

Mumbai's food reflects the melting pot nature of the city. One of the major influences on its food is obviously the adjoining regions and coastal areas of the state of Maharashtra, of which it is the state capital. It has also always had close connections culturally and economically with Gujarat to its north, and Gujarati food is both a strong presence on its own and an influence on the city's food. The hundreds of years of Portuguese and British rule have also left a lasting impact on the food and eating habits. Migrants from other parts of India have brought their foods along with them and these have been adapted and modified in Mumbai. This is especially seen in food from south India, available in thousands of south Indian restaurants and small eateries, and a variety of street food originally from north Indian states. One unique type of food in Mumbai is Parsi food, of the eponymous community, found in many Irani cafes, as speciality dishes in restaurants and, of course, in Parsi homes. Mumbai's cuisine also retains its fishing heritage with many fish and seafood dishes.

I first visited Mumbai (then Bombay) in the 1970s, in one of the 'discovery of India' holidays that my parents took the family on when we were young. That holiday was quickly followed by a combined Bombay and Goa holiday the year after. In those two trips, I had my first experience of the foods of Bombay and Goa. I've since been to Bombay many times on college and work trips and also lived there a couple of times.

In one of my brief stays in Bombay, during my post-graduate summer internship, I was lodging in the hostel of Wilson College. I've no idea how good a college Wilson College is, but its hostel couldn't be better located. It is right on Chowpatty Seaface Road. This was at that time as close to the beating heart of Bombay as you could be. Chowpatty beach is right across the road. If you have been to Mumbai, you will know that this wide expanse of sand is less a beach for sunbathing and water activities and more a public park for recreation and many types of street food. The food arrangements in the hostel were quite limited and, out of necessity but not reluctantly, I ended up trying a lot of the fare available in the Chowpatty food stalls across the road.

You can find many of the street food dishes that you find in Mumbai elsewhere in India. But nowhere else will you find the variety, easy availability and consistent quality as in Mumbai. This is best seen in Chowpatty. Going to the beach for a stroll and a snack has been a well-established social practice in the city for years, so there is no dearth of business for the street food shops. These shops are not mobile street hawkers as you find in most other cities and towns, but proper shops with permanent fixtures, brightly lit with colourful display boards and great quality food.

Many street foods of Mumbai, but not all, are adapted from north Indian street food with a generic label of **Chaat**. In an earlier chapter, on the foods of

Uttar Pradesh (UP), I've described how a chaat dish is constructed from multiple pre-cooked ingredients. It is widely believed that chaat was brought to Mumbai by immigrants from UP and, hence, the dishes follow mostly the same formula though with modifications specific to the city.

One of the best examples of Mumbai chaat is **Bhel Poori**, a Chowpatty speciality. The term bhel is almost used as a synonym for chaat in Mumbai. It is made of kurmura or murhi (puffed rice) and sev (fried savoury strings of besan) and has some similarities with jhaal murhi, the street food described in the Bengal chapter. The bhel mix also has boiled potato, fried chana (brown chickpea), onions, peanuts and sometimes raw mango, topped with fresh coriander. The magic in this dish is created by adding chaat masala to this mix and layering in two or three chutneys. Each chutney brings in a different taste: sweet, sour and hot. A single crispy small poori is stuck into the dish, giving the dish its full name. This poori can be used to eat the bhel with, though most vendors now provide a spoon as well.

Bhel poori is deceptive in appearance. Its magic is in its combination of multiple tastes and textures in one dish and you realise that only when you taste it. Murhi and sev provide different types of crunchiness, boiled potatoes softness and chana, onion, etc. something to chew on. Depending on whether the chutneys are fully mixed or layered, each spoonful of the dish can sometimes taste different and there is an element of surprise in each bite. Like a good Bollywood blockbuster, the dish has everything in one package ('this film has song, dance, action, emotion, romance, comedy, tragedy.....', as the advert for the stereotypical Bollywood film from the 1970s and 80s would go). The servings are not too big and, with puffed rice giving it most of its body, it is a fairly light dish. An evening snack of bhel poori should leave you absolutely fine for a proper dinner afterwards.

Another similar and equally popular chaat dish is **Sev Poori**. This dish has multiple, four to six, small crispy fried flat pooris, also called papri, on a plate. Each is loaded with a mixture of boiled potatoes, onions, may be chopped cucumbers, two or three chutneys and topped with lots of sev. The mix is not very different from bhel but without the puffed rice. Each poori with all the toppings is supposed to be eaten as a single bite. The effect is a magnified version of eating a spoonful of bhel poori or almost like a solid version of gol gappa. Each bite fills up the mouth and the different tastes and textures burst through as you slowly chew away.

Gol gappa is called **Paani Poori** in Mumbai. The basic elements are the same as the dish in other parts of the country: a puffed up small poori perforated at the top; a teaspoon of filling; and spicy water of tamarind or mint base. The filling in paani poori is most commonly chickpeas or white peas but a number of vendors use potatoes and some use both. The other difference in the Mumbai paani poori is that the spicy water is more commonly of mint base and you may be offered a choice between spicy and sweet water. Some of the shops that get lots of tourist traffic have started using bottled water to make the paani poori water, bringing much needed hygiene to this delightful dish.

There are many videos on the internet on Mumbai street food, presented by Indians and foreign tourists. It is wonderful to watch their expressions as they eat paani poori. For the first timers, there is almost an element of disbelief about what they are experiencing. Most describe it as an explosion of tastes. I've absolutely no doubt that whatever name it is called by, gol gappa/paani poori, etc., this is among the best street food dishes that you can have anywhere. If you haven't tried it yet, put it on your bucket list and don't miss it the next time you get the opportunity.

A street food which is unique to Mumbai is **Pav Bhaji**. **Pav** or **pao** is the name for a squarish, soft bread bun. Pav came to Bombay with the Portuguese but has become a mainstay of the local cuisine. For pav bhaji, the pav is cut open like a clam shell and toasted on a pan with lots of melted butter. So much butter is used that the inside of the pav when served is yellow, rather than white. **Bhaji**, in this case, is a thick slurry of mashed potatoes, vegetables, tomatoes and spices, also cooked in lots of butter. The red colour is due to the tomatoes and the dish looks fierier than it actually is. The dish is served in specially moulded plates with spaces to hold the bhaji, a couple of pavs and some raw onions, a slice of lemon, etc. It is far more filling than some of the other street foods and is best eaten as a meal, not a snack.

Pav bhaji has been a part of Mumbai street food for a long time. Some say that it was first created in the nineteenth century during one of the trading booms in the city, caused by a shortage of cotton in Europe due to the American civil war. The dish was the late-night meal for traders finishing off work and on the way home. Others say that the dish was created for cotton mill workers as a quick-to-eat lunch. Whatever the origin, the dish seems to have been a part of the city's street food culture for a long time.

Pav is part of another iconic Mumbai street food, **Vada Pav**. The vada in this dish is not the south Indian doughnut shaped vada that I've described previously but a dish made from potatoes called **Batata Vada**. Batata is the word for potato in Marathi, the local language. A similar dish is called potato bonda in south India. Boiled potato is mashed and tempered with spices. Medium sized balls of this mashed potato are coated with a spiced batter of besan and deep fried. The balls come out looking golden and are soft inside. In vada pav, the batata vada is served in a pav, like a burger, with chutney applied to the insides of the pav. It is customary to serve the vada pav with a red chilli chutney and a fried green chilli. It is eaten as a snack rather than a meal. For Mumbaikars, this dish is comfort food, something for the times when you feel peckish in between meals or as a very light substitute for a full meal. It is not a dish that will make you go wow, like a bhel poori or paani poori, but is more filling and quite satisfying.

That summer when I was in Bombay and staying in Wilson College, one of my friends, also interning and from out of town, was very fond of chaat. This is not uncommon. In Hindi, there is even a word for such people: 'chatora' (male) or 'chatori' (female). She made it a personal mission to find the best chaat places in the city. This was before we had the internet, so there were no online web sites or guides to look up. You relied on word-of-mouth and newspaper/magazine articles. I was a willing accomplice in this endeavour which meant that a number of my evenings and weekends that summer were devoted to street food. In the process I ate not only the chaats that I had eaten on earlier trips to Bombay but also discovered a few I had not tried before.

A somewhat less well-known street food is called **Ragda Pattice**. The name includes two of the three parts in the dish. Ragda is a mild curry of white peas, made by boiling the peas in water with a bit of turmeric and salt. It is similar in appearance to chhole. Pattice, a misspelling of the word patties, are mildly spiced, fried potato patties. Boiled and mashed potatoes, with salt and sometimes green chillies, are shaped into discs and fried till browned on both sides, very similar to aloo tikki found in northern states. Both the ragda and the patties are quite mildly spiced and the dish would be boring without the third part: chaat mix of a couple of chutneys, chaat masala, sev, chopped onions, coriander etc. which is scooped on to some ragda curry and two potato patties to make the full dish. The chaat mix transforms the dish, making it part of the pantheon of street food delights found in Mumbai. This is a reasonably substantial dish and can be eaten as a meal on the go. The peas also make this a slightly more complete meal nutritionally than the carb heavy pav bhaji or vada pav.

A variant of the pav bhaji, called **Misal Pav**, can also be found in many places in Mumbai. This is a traditional Marathi dish and more common than pav bhaji in other parts of Maharashtra. The difference is in the bhaji. The missal pav has a curried dish made of moth bean sprouts, though other bean sprouts or a combination of beans may also be used, with potatoes, onions, tomatoes, etc. It is served topped up with raw onions, tomatoes and sev. Some variants of this dish have a lot of red chillies and can be very hot, definitely more than the pav bhaji.

A non-vegetarian variant of the pav bhaji is **Keema Pav**. Instead of a vegetable based bhaji, it has a spicy minced mutton curry served with pav. Keema means 'minced meat' and can be beef or mutton, though in most parts of the country it is likely to be mutton. It is cooked similarly across the country with lots of spices. The simplest version requires cooking minced meat in a curry base of fried onions and tomatoes with ginger garlic paste. A spice blend of toasted and powdered whole spices including coriander seeds, cumin seeds, cinnamon, cloves, cardamom, peppercorn and red chillies is added to the mix. Green chillies may be used for additional heat. A small amount of water is added to give the dish a thick gravy. Served with pav in Mumbai, it is interestingly a dish often eaten for breakfast, though it can easily be eaten as a light lunch or as a main course in a more elaborate meal. The pav, served warm, is used to scoop up the meat and soak up the gravy, so keema pav can also be had as a quick meal on the go, requiring no cutlery.

Mumbai also has its own special kind of sandwich as part of its street food offerings, called **Chutney Sandwich** or **Bombay Sandwich**. The concept of sandwich is clearly an import but it has been modified to suit local tastes. The sandwich has the inside of the bread smeared with a green chutney made from coriander leaves, garlic and green chillies. The sandwich filling has boiled potatoes, tomatoes, cucumber and perhaps a few additional ingredients such as onions, bell peppers, cottage cheese, etc. The vegetables are sprinkled with chaat masala and some spices. The sandwich is then grilled in a portable toaster and served with a chutney or ketchup. The chutney and spices give it a very Indian taste. No wonder that Mumbaikars, brought up on the chutney sandwich, tend to be somewhat disappointed by the bland vegetarian sandwiches found in the west.

Like other cities in India, Mumbai also has a number of street food shops and eateries selling **seekh kabab** and **chicken tikka rolls**. The best non-vegetarian street food shops are not always found in the same places as the vegetarian ones. The non-vegetarian eateries have traditionally been owned and run by Muslims. One of the better known ones is Bademiyan (which should be correctly written as Bade Miyan, 'the elder or elderly Muslim gentleman'), near the Taj Mahal Hotel, which was set up by a migrant from Uttar Pradesh, presumably the elderly gentleman in its name. Most of these types of eateries serve a variety of Mughlai kababs with different types of bread. Some have larger menus including various Mughlai curries and biryanis.

Seekh kabab and chicken tikka rolls are most popular as on-the-go food. Typically, the meat is freshly cooked and placed straight off the skewer in a roomali roti. Some chopped onions and a chutney are added to the meat. The roti is then folded up a couple of times and rolled up into a cylindrical shape. The roll is wrapped up in a soft paper, with one end nicely tucked into one end of the roti roll to prevent the stuffing from squeezing out when you bite into the roll at the other end. The popularity of these places is best seen late at night when they have large numbers of hungry customers lining up in person and in cars, many after an evening of boozy entertainment.

On hot days, which is pretty much all year round in the city, cool drinks and ice creams are naturally quite in demand. In Mumbai, you get a type of ice lolly that is surprisingly more popular than ice cream at street food places. It is called **Gola** in common usage, though the original name was Barf ka Gola (ice lolly). It is also called **Chuski** in other parts of India. The vendor starts by making a plain ice lolly by moulding lots of shaved ice around a stick. The ice lolly is then dipped into a glass of fruit flavoured syrup of the customer's choice. The syrup soaks into the ice. Gola is served with the ice lolly in the syrup glass. It is eaten by licking or sucking the ice and you can simultaneously also sip the juice which is cooled by the ice lolly. The fun in buying a gola is mostly in deciding what syrup to have from the fantastic range of choices available. The syrups are displayed in glass bottles and there may be a dozen or more of these, in all kinds of colours. The vendors not only serve basic juices but also combinations, some quite difficult to imagine.

One of the signature gola variants of Mumbai is the **Kala Khatta Gola** (black and sour gola) with an unusual taste for an ice lolly. The key ingredients of this syrup are an Indian fruit called jamun (black plum or Indian blackberry) and kala namak or black mineral salt. These tastes are balanced with lime juice and a little bit of sugar. Some vendors will also add black pepper or even chilli (!) powder to the syrup. This gola in description sounds like creativeness gone mad but its enduring popularity means that there is something that clearly works in this concoction of unusual and unexpected tastes.

A few years ago, a restaurant called Dishoom opened in London, modelled on the Irani cafes of Bombay. It has a version of this kala khatta gola on its menu. It must be difficult to source jamun fruit in London, so the restaurant uses a combination of blueberries for the colour and kokam, the fruit which is used as a souring agent in many dishes in Karnataka and Maharashtra. The dish is quite nicely described on the menu: 'fluffy ice flakes steeped in kokam fruit syrup, blueberries, chilli, lime, white and black salt. The first spoonful tastes bizarre. The second spoonful is captivating'.

Bhel Poori

Paani Poori

Vada Pav

Akuri

Dishoom does a good, if posh, imitation of the traditional Irani cafes of Bombay. These were restaurants and bakeries set up by the Zoroastrian Iranis, who emigrated from Iran to British India during the nineteenth and early twentieth century CE. They settled in cities along the western coast of the Indian sub-continent, with a sizeable population in Bombay. They are often confused with the Parsi community already living in India.

Parsis, who are also Zoroastrians from Persia (modern Iran), arrived in India sometime between the eighth and fourteenth century in small groups to escape religious persecution. They settled along the western coast of India, mainly in Gujarat. They have managed to keep their distinct identity by following strict rules on religious practice. When the British established Bombay as their main port and administrative headquarters in western India, many Parsis moved there to support the new rulers, both in building the city and supporting trade. They were also among the first communities in west India to master English. As a result, the community has thrived especially in business, even though its numbers have been shrinking in recent years. Because of their close association with the British, the Parsis adopted a number of British practices, especially in matters of food and dress.

One well-known and visible consequence of the close association with the British was in the creation of Parsi surnames. The British wanted everyone to have names like theirs, so the Parsis who used to have a single name needed to create surnames. Many took the names of the village or town that they had settled in. Some decided to use the name of their occupation or trade with a suffix of 'wala' added. Thus, we have surnames like Daruwala (seller of liquor), Bottlewala, Screwwala, etc. and also the apocryphal 'Sodabottleopenerwala'.

The more recent Irani and older Parsi communities had been given separate legal status, but they have integrated well. The Irani cafes are a good example of this integration. They were set up by the Irani immigrants but serve dishes with both recent Irani heritage as well as dishes from Parsi cuisine. Many were initially set up as cafes serving tea and snacks or as bakeries and became restaurants in a natural evolution due to market demand. They continue be called cafes but most are restaurants in all but name. Parsi cuisine is best experienced at a Parsi home or during their festivals but the Irani cafes are good alternatives.

The most traditional item on the menu is a simple breakfast combination called **Bun Maska** had with Iranian tea. Maska means butter. So, bun maska is a bun, a special type with raisins, and a slab of fresh butter between its two halves. This is not butter just smeared onto the surface as you would on a toast but a thick slab, visible as a separate layer between the two halves of the bun. You dunk the bun into the tea and bite it off. The dish is the very definition of simple and satisfying. The Iranian tea itself has lots of milk and sugar, so it is not to everyone's taste. Unlike masala chai, found in other parts of the country, it does not have any spices but may be flavoured with vanilla.

A Parsi dish commonly found in these Irani cafes is **Akuri** or **Ekuri**. This is a spicy scrambled egg dish, made by frying eggs with onions, tomatoes, green chillies, ginger garlic paste and some spices, such as turmeric, cumin and coriander powders. Its ingredients are not dissimilar to the egg bhujia or bhurji found in other parts of the country, though the akuri tends to be wetter. This is achieved in various ways, such as by slightly undercooking the eggs or by adding a bit of milk at the final stage. It is not complicated to cook though it does require a little bit of care to ensure that the consistency of the dish comes out exactly the way one wants. Akuri is best eaten with pav, treating it like a curry, but it also works perfectly well with toast.

I had eaten akuri in Irani cafes in Mumbai and rediscovered it many years ago when my children were young. I was looking for an Indian egg recipe for Sunday brunches and came across the recipe in a book by Madhur Jaffrey. Before that I had attempted a brunch with more conventionally made egg bhujia but couldn't get the kids enthusiastic about that. Then we combined a big dish of somewhat runny akuri with a selection of European cheeses, smoked salmon and toast and it was an instant hit. Since then a Sunday brunch with my version of the akuri as the main dish has been a regular feature in our household. My daughter rates akuri as one of her favourite dishes and it is always a delight to cook the dish for the joy it brings without fail.

Egg is a favourite ingredient in Parsi cuisine. A standard trick is to put two or three fried eggs on top of a dry dish or a curry with a bit of seasoning – lo and behold you have a Parsi dish. This is a trick employed especially with vegetable dishes. Parsis don't seem to like vegetarian dishes and topping vegetables with eggs helps with the issue. A good example is **Bheeda Par Eeda**. The eggs are poured raw sunny side up on top of fried okra and then baked. Another example is **Salli Par Eedu**. Salli are matchstick shaped fried potato chips. This dish has fried eggs served on top of thin fried potato chips, either plain or in a tomato-based gravy. It doesn't sound much in description but comes out as a very satisfying breakfast dish.

A signature dish of Parsi cuisine is **Salli Boti**. It shows the Gujarati influence on Parsi food as the curry is a combination of sweet and sour tastes. The dish has mutton, preferably boneless, cooked in an onion and tomato-based curry with lots of chilli. It gets its sweet and sour taste from the addition of a small quantity of jaggery or sugar and vinegar to the curry at the final stage of cooking. It is served with a generous topping of salli, fried potato matchsticks. Like many other Parsi dishes, it is supposed to be eaten with pav or brown rice, both useful to soak up the curry.

The best known Parsi dish is probably **Chicken Dhansak** which is often found as a regional speciality on menus of generic Indian food restaurants. Dhansak is actually a generic label for a lentil and vegetables-based curry to which mutton or chicken is added. It is a fairly elaborate dish and requires a bit of effort to cook.

In the traditional version, the first step is to cook up to four different types of lentils, together with a number of vegetables such as pumpkin, brinjal and potatoes in boiling water. This lentil stew is blended into a thick gruel, probably to make the vegetables pieces invisible given the Parsi's dislike for them. Separately mutton or chicken pieces are cooked in a spice rich curry base of onions and tomatoes. A special and complex spice combination called dhansak masala, made of roasted cumin seeds, dried red chillies, cloves, cinnamon, cardamom, pepper, fenugreek, star anise, nutmeg, etc., is added. The meat is then mixed with the lentil and vegetable curry and the combination cooked further with stock or water. Jaggery, tamarind water and lime juice are added at the final stages to get the special dhansak taste, their proportions are dependent on the personal preferences of the chef. As I said earlier, it is not a simple dish to cook. I've only had this dish at restaurants where it is presented as one among many curries and may not enjoy the pride of place that it has in Parsi cuisine. I've read that at Parsi homes it is only eaten as part of a big Sunday lunch but not served on festive occasions as it is the dish used to end a mourning period after a funeral.

A dish which is of more recent Irani heritage is **Berry pulao**, created by one of the Irani restaurants in Mumbai called Britannia. It is a dish with many ingredients, and both looks and tastes extravagant. The distinguishing feature of this pulao is the topping of Iranian zereshk berries, also called barberries. This is supposed to be irreplaceable but other restaurants happily substitute it with cranberries. There are lots of crispy fried onions also as toppings. The meat in the pulao is served as chunky meat pieces with a spicy tomato sauce and there are also some kababs or, in the case of chicken, fried chicken balls. The rice is mostly cooked separately before the pulao is assembled and is infused with saffron.

A simpler dish to make in terms of ingredients is the **Patra Ni Machchi**, also written as Patrani Machchi, which is fish in banana leaves. The concept and technique is similar to the steamed fish wrapped in banana leaves that we have seen earlier in Bengal and Kerala. The Parsi paste is different. It is a green paste of coconut, coriander leaves, green chillies and garlic. When you open the banana leaves, the effect is similar to the bhapa maach or karimeen pollichathu. The green paste is not as appetising in appearance but any misgivings should be allayed once you dig in.

When we first set up home as a couple in Delhi, I decided that I'd do a bit of cooking. Till that time, I had been an enthusiastic observer in the kitchen but not a participant myself. I could make an omelette, boil rice, cook daal in a pressure cooker, make tea, etc. but that was pretty much it. My wife was very supportive – without her support that venture, like many others in my life, wouldn't have taken off since she had to eat what came out. Since we had a cook at that time, this was initially strictly a hobby. Like many novice cooks before me, I was loth to learn the basic dishes – roti, bhaat, daal, tarkari, etc. were too boring to learn.

Trying to find something interesting but not too difficult, I came across this dish called **Murghi Ma Kaju** (chicken with cashew nuts, Parsi style) in the recipe book that came with the Hawkins pressure cooker. It was perfect for me – a dish that no one in my immediate social circle had eaten before, so there would be nothing to compare it with, and with an exotic ring to it. The recipe requires a bit of grinding but is otherwise straightforward. The chicken is marinated in ginger garlic paste. You start by frying onions in oil, add some chilli and cumin seeds paste and then add the marinated chicken. The chicken is cooked with some water under pressure. Once the chicken is cooked, cashew nut paste and tomato purée – the recipe recommends ketchup! – are added at the final stage. The dish is a thick chicken curry with a strong taste of cashews and somewhat sweet. It was the star of my cooking quite a few times in those years. The funny thing is that I've never actually found this dish in an Irani café or a Parsi restaurant. I've been told that it is indeed a dish cooked in Parsi homes, so there is probably some truth in the recipe book's bold claim that this is 'chicken with cashew nuts, Parsi style'.

One of the best desserts in Parsi food is called **Lagan Nu Custard**. It is a Parsi version of crème brûlée, served as a dessert both at big home meals and at weddings. The latter version tends to be luxuriously garnished with sultanas, cashews, almonds and pistachios. The home and restaurant versions are somewhat more restrained, which allow you to enjoy the custard itself. The custard is a reasonably standard bake of boiled milk and eggs and is flavoured with vanilla, nutmeg and cardamom. It used to be made very sweet in the Irani cafes when I first tasted the dish in the 1980s, and the modern trend of sugar consciousness has only mildly moderated this dish.

I went on a short college trip to Mumbai in the summer of 1986. I've two unforgettable memories from that trip. The first was the football world cup in Mexico. I remember watching a few games late at night on TV at a friend's place where a number of us were staying. This was the world cup in which Argentina's Diego Maradona scored both the 'Hand of God' goal and the Goal of the Century in the quarter final match against England. It is one of my indelible memories, watching the game with a group of friends, seeing both the ridiculous and the sublime in one unforgettable game.

The second memory is of course food-related. It was the time of Ramadan when Muslims fast during the day. There is a road in Mumbai called Muhammad Ali Road, a designated 'khau gali' or food street, which has lots of food shops run mostly by Muslims. This street becomes the hub of post fast feasting, Iftar, during Ramadan. We went to this street one night. I had been to Iftar meals before, but that was the first time I had seen such a massive Iftar party at the street level. Since then I've been to Muhammad Ali Road a couple of times, the food is always very satisfying, but nothing beats the sheer energy and wonder of that first visit. It was crowded even then and I believe the crowds have become much larger in recent years. On our visit then, we were a group of about a dozen and managed to find seating spaces in a number of shops as we went about our tasting tour. That may be difficult now.

The foods available in Muhammad Ali Road during Iftar are not necessarily unique, most are found in other parts of the country during Iftar and otherwise. Some are given exotic names but are only mildly different variants of well-known dishes. This is especially true of the many different types of kababs and curries. Mutton seekh kabab and chicken tikka are widely available, in the standard form but also with many variations. Similarly, there are also many different types of non-vegetarian curries available.

One dish which is always found during Iftar on Muhammad Ali Road is called **Khichra** or **Khichda**. The name is a giveaway: this is the non-vegetarian version of khichri which, as you would recall, is rice and lentils cooked together. Khichra is similarly rice, wheat and lentils cooked together with chunks of meat added. The dish is probably derived both from the Indian khichri and the Middle Eastern Haleem, though the latter uses minced meat. The name khichra also reveals an interesting gender bias in food. In Hindi, words ending with the 'i' or 'ee' sounds are mostly feminine, those ending with 'a' or 'aa' masculine. By that standard, khichra, the non-vegetarian dish, is the masculine version of khichri, the vegetarian dish.

Another dish available on Muhammad Ali Road is **Nalli Nihari**. I've described nihari earlier in the chapter on Mughlai food. This is a spicy and rich dish which requires the meat to be cooked over low heat for a long time. The Muhammad Ali Road version is not very different in appearance and taste, though with the label of 'nalli' you should get only leg pieces in the curry. There are also shops selling mutton brain and liver dishes. In fact, one of the shops has a dish called 'barah' handi. Barah means twelve and this place serves dishes made from twelve different parts of the animal – don't ask! – all displayed in individual pots (handis).

You also get lots of vegetarian and sweet dishes in this food fest. There is one sweet which is quite unusual. It is called **Mawa Jalebi**, that is jalebi made from mawa or khoya, different from the standard jalebi made of maida. The mawa jalebi takes on a dark brown colour when fried and soaked in sugar syrup, so it looks very different from regular jalebi. It also feels quite different as it is not crunchy but soft on the bite.

Another sweet dish found in a number of shops is **Malpua** or **Pua**, described earlier in the Uttar Pradesh chapter. Variants of this dish are found in many states. The standard ones are poori-sized and made from a batter of maida, semolina, milk and yoghurt, which is spooned into a pan of hot oil, deep-fried and then soaked in sugar syrup. In a drier variant, the batter will have sugar added to it and the cooked malpua is then not soaked in sugar syrup. It is very often served with a generous portion of rabri, sweet condensed milk. It is quite customary to have malpua and rabri after a proper Iftar meal. But if you, like me, find malpua too heavy for dessert, there are a number of places which serve **Phirn**i, the Mughlai dessert which is like rice pudding. Had cold, it can be an ideal way to end a food journey in Muhammad Ali Road.

Mumbai also has a rich variety of fish and seafood, some local but many imported from the multiple sub-regional, community-based cuisines of the coastal areas of western India.

One of the best known fish dishes of Mumbai is the **Bombay Duck** or **Bombil fry**. This is a type of lizardfish found in the waters around Mumbai, though extensive fishing means it is no longer as easily available. The dish itself is reasonably straightforward and similar to the Kane rava fry found down the coast in Karnataka. Cleaned fresh fish is marinated in ginger garlic paste with some turmeric and red chillies, coated with rava (semolina) and rice powder mix and then either shallow or deep fried. The outer crust is crisp and golden and the fish inside is spicy.

The name of the fish is a little bit of a mystery. It seems that the word 'duck' is a mispronunciation by the British of the Hindi word for mail, 'daak'. How the fish came to be associated with mail is not clear. One story is that it was transported to Calcutta from Bombay on the mail train, the Bombay 'daak'. Credible, but the name seems to precede the days of railways in India. The other story is that its smell was thought to be similar to a stale room full of 'daak'. How wonderful that the intermingling of languages can lead to a fish being called duck.

On a business trip to Mumbai, I asked my colleagues to help me try some local seafood. We went for lunch to Mahesh Lunch Home. I was quite sceptical about it initially as the name isn't particularly inspiring. I subsequently found that this restaurant comes up in most listings of top seafood restaurants in Mumbai. Never judge a restaurant by its name, to paraphrase. It serves food primarily from coastal Karnataka, so my colleagues had missed my point about 'local' while getting 'seafood' right. We tried out a number of dishes including a Mangalorean fish curry, a crab cooked in butter, pepper and garlic (considered a speciality of the restaurant) and a Malabar prawn curry. I remember the curries were quite spicy and needed to be taken in small bites and slowly with rice or appam.

The other thing that I remember from Mahesh Lunch Home was that while there were a number of coastal specialities on the menu, there was nothing specific to Mumbai apart from Bombay duck fry. I've eaten fish curry in a number of restaurants in Mumbai, but rarely have I seen a fish curry listed as 'Mumbai fish curry' or even 'fish curry, Mumbai style'. The closest you get to a local fish dish is probably what you would find at the homes of the Koli, the indigenous fishing community of Mumbai. As a fishing community, they have a number of seafood dishes but they are not widely available. You do find dishes called **Fish Koliwada** and **Prawn Koliwada** in many restaurants but these are dry, fried dishes. In curries, you get a choice of a number of regional styles from outside Mumbai. The fish curries from the Konkan coast – regional cuisines include Mangalorean, Goan and Malvani (south Maharashtra) and a number of community-based cuisines – are generally made with lots of red chillies (expect a fiery red coloured curry) with a bit of sourness from kokam and mostly also have some coconut milk or grated coconut as an ingredient.

Most seafood restaurants also serve a variety of prawn and crab dishes. Prawn dishes, when cooked in regional styles, can be one of three types: prawns cooked in spicy curry; a dry, fried dish where the pawns are coated with either flour and spices or a spicy batter; and a masala dish where the prawns are cooked in a spicy, thick gravy. All types are likely to have lots of chilli. Crab dishes, on the other hand, are more commonly served grilled with either a thick masala gravy or a sauce. In many restaurants, you also get sea food cooked tandoori style, that is coated with a spicy paste and then cooked in a tandoor oven.

A good seafood restaurant in Mumbai will offer you many types of fish, prawn and crab dishes. The choice can sometimes be overwhelming – I've been to restaurants listing a couple of dozens of prawn dishes alone. It is sometimes best just to go with the restaurant's recommendations. The comforting thing is that it is rare to have a bad seafood meal in Mumbai restaurants.

Mumbai as a large metropolis is home to many migrant communities, especially from the various parts of Maharashtra and the west coast of India. Many of these communities have kept their cuisines alive in the city by not only cooking them at home but with restaurants and eateries dedicated to them. In the following chapters, I've described the foods of Maharashtra and Goa separately. But it is fair to say that, with some local help, you could experience quite a lot of these in Mumbai itself.

Khichra

Bombil fish or Bombay Duck

11
Goa

Konkan and Portuguese simmered together

Goa is the smallest state by area in India. It is situated on the western Konkan coast, squeezed between the big states of Maharashtra and Karnataka, with the Arabian Sea to its west. In culinary terms, it is unique among Indians states due to its long history as a Portuguese colony and the resultant fusion cuisine.

Prior to the conquest by the Portuguese, Goa was a small and relatively unknown part of the kingdoms of the Deccan. Its importance was mainly for its harbours which served as one of the import points for Arabian horses for the cavalry of the armies of the ruling kingdoms. Its modern history starts after Vasco da Gama, the Portuguese explorer, discovered the sea route from Europe to India round the Cape of Good Hope in his historic expedition in 1497 – 98 CE. The Portuguese were the first to take advantage of the new trade route, as bypassing the monopoly of the Arabian traders through the Red Sea was the main point of that expedition. This quickly converted to a battle for control and dominance of the Arabian Sea and Indian Ocean trade. The Portuguese, under a brilliant naval commander, Afonso (or Alfonso) de Albuquerque, were the clear winners and established a dominant position in the Indian Ocean trade for most of the sixteenth century. Goa, conquered by Albuquerque in 1510, was one of the first European colonies in India and became the administrative and naval capital for the Portuguese in Asia.

Goa remained a colony of Portugal for about 450 years till 1961 when it was annexed into India. 450 years is a long time and Goa has Portuguese imprint all over its religion, culture, language, food, architecture and everyday life. The Portuguese followed an active policy of religious proselytization and many of the local population converted to Catholic Christianity during their rule. It is estimated that during the mid-nineteenth century, Catholics made up about two thirds of the local population. Goa continued to be the epicentre of Catholic missionaries in Asia during the eighteenth and nineteenth centuries, even while the Portuguese power in the seas dwindled.

While Catholic religious practices were strictly enforced in Goa, in food and social behaviour a more syncretic approach prevailed. The local Catholics adopted the eating habits and practices of the Portuguese but also kept many of their local ingredients and cooking techniques. A distinct Goan Catholic cuisine has thus evolved, with many dishes inspired by Portuguese originals but with Indian ingredients. The population of Christians in Goa is now just about a quarter of the total, mostly due to emigration of Catholic Goans and immigration of Hindus from neighbouring regions. The traditional Goan Catholic cuisine however remains strongly entrenched and is also now widely available due to tourism.

Goa's beautiful beaches were always well known, so it was not an unknown tourist destination. After it was annexed into India, tourism received a big fillip. Goa initially gained global fame as a niche, hippy tourist destination in the 1960s. But once interest was kindled, there has been continuous and relentless growth in tourism, both foreign and domestic. Domestic tourism was further given a boost by Bollywood using Goa for many film shoots. Goa is now among the most popular holiday destinations for Indians and remains an established, if somewhat jaded, global tourist destination.

My first trip to Goa was in one of the 'discovery of India' holiday trips that my parents used to take us on. Goa was a long distance from Bihar. We had combined this with a stop in Bombay, itself a train journey of twenty-four hours plus. I think we spent three or four days in Bombay and then travelled on to Goa. Goa in the 1970s was already a prime tourist destination but not as overrun with tourists as it became in the next couple of decades.

One of the highlights of that holiday was a sea trip from Bombay to Goa, my first sea journey. This was twenty-four hours on a ferry, very basic and functional by the standards of today's cruise ships. You could book cabins with bunk beds, as we did, but most people travelled in communal passenger decks with no designated sleeping spaces. There used to be a party atmosphere on those communal decks. After the initial melee of finding space, most people settled down to enjoy the journey. I remember live music but am not sure if it was a band or some passengers with musical instruments. Food was plentiful. There were snacks and drinks vendors on board, a sit-down meal service and passengers, as in train journeys all over India, happily shared packed snacks. Many passed time playing card and board games while others entertained themselves, and the rest of us, with music and songs. In short, Goa started on the ship itself. I made this sea trip once more the other way around when I was in college. It was great fun both times, a little bit more the second time when I travelled on the communal deck with a group of friends. Unfortunately, these ferries were discontinued in the late 1980s and various attempts to start a similar service have not been successful.

It was on my second trip to Goa that I first tried **Pork Vindaloo**. When I was growing up, we did not eat beef or pork at home. We are Hindus and Hindus don't eat beef due to religious beliefs. Not eating pork was more difficult to understand. Pork is not eaten by Muslims due to their religious beliefs. In most of north India, Hindus and Muslims have lived together for centuries and I think both religions have tacitly (mostly) adopted the practice of not eating the meat abjured by the other. Thus, it was impossible to find beef or pork in the places that I grew up in.

Pork vindaloo is one of the best-known dishes of Goan cuisine. The name vindaloo is derived from the Portuguese dish 'carne de vinha d'alhos', which translates to meat in wine and garlic. Even though the dish has the Hindi word for potatoes 'aloo' in its name, it has no etymological connection with Hindi and should not have potatoes. This original Portuguese dish was meat (most commonly pork) marinated in wine and garlic. In Goan cuisine, the name became vindaloo and the wine was substituted with local palm vinegar (hence the understandable misconception that vindaloo means vinegar and aloo).

Pork chunks are marinated in vinegar and a masala powder made from mild red chillies (which give the gravy a red colour but not much heat), black pepper and other whole spices. The curry has a base of fried onions, garlic, ginger, green chillies and tomatoes to which a bit more of vinegar and tamarind water may be added. The marinated meat is cooked in this curry base over low heat till the meat is tender and the gravy thick. The cooking time is longish. The resultant dish has a rich, dark colour and a signature combination of sourness, tanginess and heat. Some chefs add a bit of jaggery for hints of sweetness as well. All in all, a complex dish deserving of its iconic status.

Unfortunately, pork vindaloo has gone through an adaptation in British curry houses which has to be deemed for the worse. Mild red chillies have been replaced with large quantities of strong red chillies. Vindaloo has thus simply become the synonym for the hottest dish in a series of increasingly hot curry dishes. The British curry house vindaloo can be of pork, lamb or chicken and is essentially meat cooked in a standard onion and tomato curry base with lots of red chillies and a little bit of white wine vinegar, the last an inadequate nod to the recipe of the original Goan dish. There is little subtlety in the dish and the large quantity of red chillies make it impossible to taste anything else. It has, however, in this avatar become a symbol of the pub and football popular culture of Britain. So, a Goan dish which originated in Portugal becomes a part of popular English culture through Indian restaurants mostly run by Bangladeshis. How is that for globalisation?

Another pork dish popular in Goan Christian homes is **Pork Sorpotel**. This is another Goan dish of Portuguese origin. A similar sounding dish is also found in Brazil, the 'other' well-known former Portuguese colony. The name of the dish is ostensibly derived from the Portuguese word 'sarapatel' which means confusion, a reference to the various cuts of meat which are used in the dish. Traditionally the dish was made with pork meat, pork offal and even some pork blood. Now the dish is mostly just made from pork meat though some liver pieces may be also be used. It is a dish widely cooked at home during festivals and special occasions, so there are many recipes. Generally, it is cooked in large quantities and eaten over many days. The use of vinegar in the curry makes the dish keep well. In fact, Goans believe that it tastes best on the third or fourth day after cooking, when the spices have completely infused into the meat and the curry has thickened.

Most Goans and people who have visited Goa would consider its seafood dishes as more emblematic of its cuisine than the pork dishes described above. Fish dishes are a part of both the main religious communities of the state. In fact, one of the pleasures of visiting Goa is to order a fish and seafood platter or thali at a beachside restaurant and be treated to half a dozen or more dishes at the same time. The thali is not a traditional Goan practice but a number of restaurants have caught on to the concept as a good way of demonstrating their culinary skills and selling all their wares. It works for the diners too, in a manner similar to a tasting menu where you trust the chef and the restaurant to put forward their best dishes. Trying out the platter in a few restaurants should ensure that you get to taste most of the main seafood dishes that I describe below.

The **Goan fish curry** does not have a nice-sounding, exotic name but is probably the most common dish that you will find in Goa. It is popular in both Hindu and Christian households and widely available in restaurants. The cooking technique is quite similar to methods found elsewhere on the Konkan coast and south Indian states. The key ingredient is a masala or spice combination which needs to be prepared separately. In the most popular fish curry dish, this masala is made by blending together mild red chillies, lots of fresh grated coconut, coriander seeds, cumin seeds, turmeric, garlic and tamarind paste. The masala is blended into a very smooth paste as the curry in this dish is supposed to be quite smooth. Any firm, white fish may be used though kingfish and pomfret are the most common. The curry is made by frying onions, tomatoes and green chillies with the specially prepared masala, and then giving it volume with water or better still coconut milk. Chunks of the fish, marinated simply in salt, lemon juice and turmeric, are added to the curry last and cooked in the hot curry. The dish is generally served with boiled rice for a simple and filling meal.

A less well-known fish curry is called **Ambot Tik fish curry**. 'Ambot' means sour and 'tik' means hot. The sourness in the dish comes from tamarind or vinegar or kokam or a combination. The fish should be relatively boneless: small shark and catfish are the preferred fish for this dish. Neither fish is easy to get, so this is not a dish that is easy to find, though you may get other fish in ambot tik masala. The cooking method is similar to the standard Goan fish curry with a special masala paste prepared separately. The ambot tik masala paste has mild red chillies, garlic, ginger, cumin seeds, peppercorn, cloves, cinnamon and tamarind or vinegar. Unlike the Goan fish curry, the ambot tik masala paste has only a little or no grated coconut to balance the taste of the souring agent and is hence sourer than the paste used in the Goan fish curry. The cooking method is otherwise similar to the fish curry, with the curry made by frying onions, tomatoes and green chillies with the special masala paste. The fish is separately marinated and is generally fried with the curry base before water is added to complete the dish.

A third type of fish curry is called **Fish Caldine** or **Caldinho**. This is a milder version of the standard Goan fish curry. The cooking method is the same but the special masala paste has no red chillies. The heat in the dish comes only from the whole green chillies fried with the onions and tomatoes and many cooks will use less or skip the green chillies totally. As a result, the curry is quite mild with the taste of the coconut dominating.

As is probably evident, the special masala used in the Goan fish curries is a combination of three key ingredients: red chillies, coconut and a souring agent (tamarind, vinegar, kokam). Changing the relative proportions of these ingredients creates the different types of fish curries. But this also offers scope for lots of individual creativity. If you try fish curries in different Goan restaurants, it should not come as a surprise if even the ones called by the same name taste somewhat different.

A couple of other Goan fish dishes are also worth describing. **Goan Rava fried fish** is similar to fried fish preparations found all along the Konkan coast. We have seen a version in Karnataka with kane fish. In Goa, kingfish, known as surmai locally, is most commonly used for this dish. The technique is to apply a thick masala paste to each fish piece, then coat the piece on both sides with rava (semolina) and shallow fry in a pan on high heat till the outer crust is crisp and golden. This is a dish often served as an appetiser or as a second fish dish along with a fish curry in a big meal.

A very interesting take on the standard fried fish is the **Fish Recheado**. The word recheado is supposed to mean 'stuffed'. This dish uses whole fish, typically pomfret and mackerel, which has been cleaned and split open. A spicy, fiery red masala is not only used to coat the fish but also stuffed inside the fish. The fish and the stuffing is kept aside or refrigerated for some time before cooking, to ensure that the masala infuses into the fish. Each fish may also be further coated with rava before being shallow fried. The masala is traditionally very hot and pungent with red chillies and toddy vinegar as the main ingredients. This is a signature fish dish of Goa and quite easily found in restaurants. Some restaurants may palm off a rava fried fish as a recheado, but it is a recheado only if the masala is stuffed inside the fish, not just coating the fish.

Prawn and crab dishes are also widely available. Goan prawn curry follows the same formula and ingredients as the Goan fish curry. The standard Goan prawn curry, in fact, has practically the same recipe as the fish curry, with the only difference being that the prawns need to be added somewhat earlier in the cooking process to ensure that they are fully cooked.

An unusual prawn dish is called **Prawn** or **Shrimp Balchao**. This is a dish supposedly created in the Portuguese territory of Macau. The dish is almost a prawn or shrimp pickle and can actually be stored for longish periods of time, as long as there is sufficient oil in it. As a result, you are far more likely to find the dish at homes rather than in restaurants. The balchao masala has a long list of ingredients, similar to the masalas used for the fish curries. Neither the masala paste nor the cooking process use any water, only vinegar, and that is the secret to its long life. The ingredients for the masala are a combination of mild and hot red chillies, cumin seeds, peppercorn, cloves, cinnamon, garlic, turmeric powder and vinegar. The shelled and deveined prawns are separately marinated in salt and turmeric and then fried till they are cooked. The balchao curry is made by frying onions, ginger and garlic with the special masala. The prawns are added to the mix and then the dish cooked till the gravy has thickened.

The two most popular crab dishes are Crab Xacuti (pronounced 'shakuti') and Crab Xec Xec (shek shek). There are two common varieties of crab used for these dishes: the blue sea crab and a freshwater variety called the mud crab which is also found in the backwaters of Kerala.

Xacuti (probably from the Portuguese word 'chacuti' which means dark brown) is the name for a specialist masala paste which forms the base for chicken, lamb, fish and seafood dishes. Chicken Xacuti is the best known and is described a little later.

Crab Xec Xec is a hot dish with a thick gravy, sometimes almost dry. The trick is again in preparing a special masala paste with some of the ingredients that we have seen in the fish curries: lots of red chillies, fresh grated coconut, onion, cumin seeds, coriander seeds, peppercorn, garlic, ginger and cloves. The ingredients are roasted separately and then ground together into a thick paste. The gravy base has fried onions and green chillies to which the masala paste, some tamarind and the crab, salted and cut into pieces, are added. The dish is cooked till the gravy becomes quite thick.

When we first moved to London, we stayed for a few years in a neighbourhood called Putney in the south west of the city. There is a restaurant called Ma Goa there. While some Goan dishes can often be found in many Indian restaurants, speciality Goan restaurants are not that common. We were of course delighted to have one so near to home. My wife and I have fond memories of Goan food, not least because we spent a part of our honeymoon there and discovered a shared love for seafood there. Ma Goa is still going strong. At that time, it had a menu of mostly Goan dishes, unlike now where the menu has a few Goan dishes with some popular north Indian dishes also thrown in. Fish curry (Fish caldine) with rice and a **Goan styled coconut chicken curry** (now called Nariyal Galina) were our favourites. The meals were always topped up with Bebinca, the traditional Goan dessert, which is still on the menu. During the time we lived there, Ma Goa also started offering takeaways. That transformed our at-home social engagements. Suddenly, our guests could be offered not just our home-made dishes or takeaway from a run of the mill Indian curry house but something very different and leagues ahead in taste. We had to sheepishly admit a few times that the coconut chicken curry which was the star of the meal was not from our kitchen but in fact ordered out.

There are a couple of chicken dishes in Goan food which complete the list of well known meat dishes from the state. The wonderfully named **Chicken Xacuti** is one. The dish has a deep red colour from the use of Kashmiri red chillies but unlike the Goan vindaloo, this dish is actually quite fiery as it has generous quantities of other red and green chillies and peppercorn as well. It is quite a complicated dish as there are a number of ingredients which go into making the special xacuti masala. One part of the masala has grated coconut as its main ingredient, with onions, ginger, garlic and green chillies. Another part has a number of spices roasted and ground into a paste. The spices include Kashmiri red chillies, cinnamon, cardamom, coriander seeds, peppercorn and a number uncommon spices such as star anise, poppy seeds, nutmeg, etc. The chicken is marinated with turmeric and salt. The dish is then prepared by frying onions and green chillies in oil and then adding the coconut paste, the spice paste and the marinated chicken with some water for the gravy. The whole mix is cooked till the meat is cooked and soft. A little bit of tamarind may be added at the finishing stage for a bit of tanginess. If you are looking for a Goan meat dish high on heat, xacuti is the one to try.

Another unique Goan dish is **Chicken Cafreal**, also known as **Galina Cafreal**. This is a relatively simple chicken dish with a greenish masala coating, the colour coming from the use of coriander leaves as the main ingredient in the marinade. Coriander leaves are often used as a garnish for curried dishes across the country. Cafreal is one of the few dishes in which it serves as a primary ingredient. The dish was introduced in Goa by the Portuguese and may have originated in Mozambique which was also a Portuguese colony. In the dish, the chicken is marinated in a paste made from lots of coriander leaves with ginger, garlic, green chillies and whole spices, including cumin seeds, coriander seeds and black pepper. After marinating for a few hours, the chicken is cooked in oil with the marinade and topped up with a dash of vinegar. On special occasions, even a bit of rum may be added. It is sometimes grilled in an oven rather than fried, and hence is also called the Goan tandoori chicken.

Unlike in most of south India, the cereal of choice with meals in Goa is not rice but bread made from wheat flour. Breadmaking was brought to Goa by the Portuguese. The **Goan pav** is now a part of foods across all of western India, also one part of the iconic vada pav and pav bhaji of Mumbai. It is a soft and buttery bun-like bread, made from leavened maida with butter, salt and sugar. The bread gets its softness from the dough which is made very soft. A light layering of egg during the baking gives the outer surface a very nice golden colour.

The other main type of bread is **Poi** or **Poee**, a leavened bread made primarily of atta (whole wheat flour), with a little bit of maida and wheat bran. The dough is rolled into thick individual pieces somewhat butterfly shaped before being baked. Poi bread is nicely browned and has a soft hollow inside, like a pitta bread. It is a great side dish to curries. It can also be eaten stuffed with meat: sausage in poi makes for a convenient meal on the go.

Plain, boiled rice is often served with the curries though more complex rice dishes are rare. Rice is also sometimes eaten as **Sanna**, a Goan rice cake similar in appearance to idli. The batter is made of ground rice mixed with grated coconut and fermented. Traditionally, coconut toddy was used as the fermenting agent though now yeast may be used for its greater convenience. Once fermented, the batter is poured into cups or moulds and steamed till the rice cakes are cooked. The lightly salted variety is a popular accompaniment to pork sorpotel and other curries. If sugar or jaggery is added to the rice batter, you get a sweet sanna which can be eaten as a snack on its own.

The most famous Goan sweet dish is **Bebinca** or **Bebik**, a traditional Goan cake. It is made from egg, coconut milk, wheat flour, sugar and ghee. The cake is multi-layered and can have as many as sixteen layers though about seven is more common. The cake batter is reasonably straight forward to prepare, essentially requiring all the ingredients to be mixed and whisked together. One half of the batter has caramel added to it such that the alternate layers are darker in the cake. After that, it is a time-consuming dish to cook, as each layer of the cake, about a quarter inch thick, is cooked sequentially in the oven with ghee used to separate the layers. When sliced and presented, it is customary to show off the layers by placing the cake sideways. It does not have the multiple tastes that you get from, for example, a tiramisu. I've sometimes wondered why the alternate layers are not flavoured somewhat differently, to give the dish a more complex taste. Perhaps because each layer has a subtle gradation of taste due to being cooked for different lengths of time. It makes for a great dessert by itself but also in combination with ice cream.

It is appropriate to end this chapter with a description of Goa's favourite tipple, **Feni**. This is a strong-smelling, alcoholic drink made most commonly from cashew fruit juice (cashew feni) or toddy from coconut palm (coconut feni). The word feni may be derived from the Sanskrit word for 'froth': a good quality feni produces a nice head of froth when poured into a glass. Feni has a high level of alcohol content and is usually had mixed with lemonade, soda or cola. It is a popular common man's drink and widely available. While Goans take pride in it, it is not a particularly smooth, subtle or great tasting drink. The intent is to give the drinker an alcoholic kick quickly and it does that well without any fuss. But it is an integral part of Goan social life and often the most affordable way to get a party going.

Pork Vindaloo

Fish Caldine

Crab Xec Xec

Bebinca

12
Maharashtra

Spices add life to variety of food

When I was living in the township in Barauni, a couple from Maharashtra, Mr. and Mrs. Deshmukh, lived in the house across the street. Their children were older, with one working and the other in university in Bombay at that time. With Mr. Deshmukh at work during the day, Mrs. Deshmukh used to be by herself. It must have been lonely and she had made friends with not only all the neighbouring adults but also the children. I'd often find her in her front yard when I got back from school and she would usually initiate a chat with a cheery 'how was school today?'. In the friendly environment of the township, it was not long before she was happily offering me and a couple of other children in the neighbourhood home-made snacks and sweets. I owe my first taste of Shrikhand or Sreekhand, a Maharashtrian sweet dish, to Mrs. Deshmukh. I also had my first taste of Maharashtrian meals at her place, a few times with my parents and many more times with other children.

Maharashtra is a large and prosperous state spanning west and central India. Surprisingly its cuisine is neither as evolved nor as well known as the cuisines of a number of other states of India. The reasons are geographical and cultural. Apart from the coastal areas, most of Maharashtra is in the Deccan plateau. The climate is tropical, but with low rainfall and high temperatures. The black soil of the region coupled with the climate makes agriculture suitable only for some types of crops. The region has always grown cash crops such as cotton and sugar cane but struggled with water-intensive food crops. The main cereal crops grown in this region have been the hardier millets such as jowar (sorghum), bajra (pearl millet) and ragi (finger millet). Rice is grown only in the narrower coastal regions between the Arabian sea and the Western Ghats. Wheat cultivation is more recent and only in areas with good irrigation.

In addition, the society has for centuries been dominated by Hindu brahmins, practising and propagating conservative and austere living. The city of Pune used to be the capital of the Maratha confederacy from late seventeenth century to early nineteenth century. One would have expected this to be an impetus for extravagance and enterprise in local cuisine, as seen in other parts of India. But the brahmins exercised control over the ruling classes in matters of day-to-day and household activities, including fairly strict rules on food. Even now the food of brahmins in the state is mostly vegetarian and required to follow even stricter rules during religious festivals, of which there are many during the year. The brahmins' eating habits have acted as a major influence on the cuisine of the entire state. As a result, much of the food is vegetarian, except in the coastal areas and a few sub-regions, and not particularly indulgent. The complexity in dishes comes mostly through the use of spices, often in special spice mixes created for specific dishes.

A description of the everyday food of the Marathi areas of the state gives a good idea of the nature of the cuisine. Flatbread made of millets is widely eaten especially in rural areas. A thick and coarse chapati type of bread made from these grains is called **Bhakri**. Jowar bhakri is the most common type. The dough is prepared by mixing jowar flour with hot water and then flattened by hand and cooked on a tawa. It is not uncommon for bhakri to be eaten just with pickle or chutney which was, and unfortunately still is, not a matter of choice but a reflection of poverty. It is not a great tasting or easy to eat flatbread, definitely a product of necessity rather than choice.

Pitla Bhakri is a staple food in rural areas of the state. It consists of **Pitla** or **Pithla** which is a curry made of besan, which as described earlier is the flour of chana daal or Bengal gram. The dish looks like daal but is less grainy. It can be made thick or thin, by varying the amount of water. The preparation is quite simple. Onions are fried in oil with some whole spices, garlic, ginger and chillies, then besan and water are added and the mix cooked till you get the desired consistency. The drier version of the dish is called **Jhunka** in some parts of the state. Pitla and jhunka are usually eaten with bhakri, made from either jowar or bajra. Pitla bhakri is widely available in small eateries and from roadside vendors across Maharashtra. It is also now becoming a fashionable, back-to-the-roots dish in restaurants serving traditional Maharashtrian food. In such restaurants, the bhakri is made tastier and softer with a bit of pampering from ghee or butter smeared on it. Having pitla bhakri is like having roti daal or bhaat daal, all comfort food and, if the daal or pitla is well-made, quite satisfying though probably not in anyone's list of top ten memorable meals.

A tastier flatbread is **Thalipeeth**, a savoury multi-grain roti. The dough is prepared from a mixed flour made from roasted grains of different types of cereals, including wheat, bajra and jowar, and even a few different types of lentils with some whole spices. Onions, coriander, perhaps even a couple of chopped leafy vegetables, and powdered spices are also added to the flour before it is kneaded. Portions of the dough are then flattened by hand and cooked over a tawa. The resultant dish is somewhat like a baked paratha. Like paratha, thalipeeth, served with butter or yogurt, makes for a complete meal and is quite popular for breakfast.

Another basic meal popular across homes, urban and rural, is **Varan Bhaat**. **Varan** is a plain daal made from toor daal. The daal is made by boiling the lentils in water with turmeric, salt and jaggery. If at all tempered, the tarka tends to be simple, such as cumin seeds, chilli, and asafoetida in hot ghee. In this form, varan daal is not very dissimilar to the arhar daal that used to be cooked at my home (and indeed millions of other Indian homes) on a daily basis, except for the use of jaggery which is more of a western India practice. When served more formally, the tarka can be a little more complex with mustard seeds, cumin seeds, asafoetida, curry leaves and green chillies in ghee. Varan daal is served with bhaat, that is boiled rice. It is easy to see why varan bhaat, served with chutney and pickles, is Maharashtrian comfort food: easy to cook and easy to eat. The plain variety is also a part of religious offerings, called naivedhyam in Marathi (the local language but the word is also used as a label for the people and the culture), that is food offered to deities on special religious occasions.

Rice is eaten not only as plain bhaat. A one pot meal of rice called **Masala Bhaat** is quite common. Rice is cooked with a few vegetables, with brinjal as a key ingredient, and a special spice mix used in Marathi cuisine called **Goda Masala**. Apart from the goda masala, the dish is pretty straightforward with the recipe somewhat like a vegetable pulao. Onions, tomatoes, chillies, ginger and garlic paste are fried with whole spices in oil. Then chopped vegetables and goda masala are added to the fried mix, followed by rice with water. The mix is cooked till the rice is soft and all the water absorbed. If it were not for the goda masala, this would be a somewhat bland vegetable pulao.

Goda masala is a special spice mix used in a number of Marathi dishes. The name translates to 'sweet masala' and is based on its sweet aroma. In taste, it is somewhat pungent but not very hot. There are two unusual spices used in this mix: dagad phool (rock flower) and nagkesar (cassia buds). Other ingredients include dry coconut, sesame seeds, bay leaves, dried red chillies, peppercorn, cumin seeds, coriander seeds, cinnamon and cloves. To prepare the goda masala, the spices are individually roasted, ground and then combined in the required proportions with turmeric, asafoetida and salt. It is sometimes called the Marathi garam masala. But as the list of ingredient spices shows, it is a much more complex spice combination and adds a characteristic taste and aroma to the dishes in which it is used, often as in the case of the masala bhaat transforming the dish from ordinary into something special.

A special type of daal which is often found in formal meals or Marathi thalis is called **Aamti**. This is another dish which uses goda masala. Any of the widely available lentils, toor or moong or chana daal, can be used. The daal is first cooked the standard way. A tarka is prepared separately by heating whole spices, chillies and bay leaves in ghee or oil to which the cooked daal is added. The daal is finally flavoured with goda masala, a souring agent (kokam or tamarind) and some jaggery. It is this last bit that makes the aamti different from other types of daal.

So far, there is not much in the dishes that I've described that makes Marathi cuisine stand out. The use of goda masala and other specialist spice combinations adds a little bit of differentiation to the dishes but not in a way to make them especially unique. That theme continues when you look at the vegetable dishes that accompany the cereals and lentils.

Vegetables are an important part of Marathi food. Cooked vegetables are generically referred to as **Bhaji**. Bhaji includes both dry and curried vegetables. A dry, fried vegetable dish is called **Pale Bhaji** and a curried vegetable dish is **Patal**

Bhaji. All kinds of vegetable dishes are covered under these broad labels. Okra, brinjal, various types of gourds, beans and leafy vegetables are all part of the cuisine. Many of the vegetable dishes are cooked using goda masala, so there is a Marathi theme to the tastes of all vegetable dishes.

A vegetarian curry made from legumes is called **Usal**. The main ingredient of this dish is sprouted legumes. Any of the popular legumes, green peas, chickpeas, brown chickpeas, kidney beans, moth beans, etc., may be used. Sprouted lentils can also be used. Most variants follow broadly similar ways of cooking the dish. The legumes are soaked in water for a day or two till they sprout. To make usal, the legumes are boiled in water with a bit of turmeric and salt. Separately, onions and tomatoes are fried in whole and powdered spices. The cooked legumes are then added to this mix with water and cooked together. Usal is very often paired with pav for a light meal, though it may also be served as one of the vegetables dishes in a full meal.

Some of the vegetables are also cooked with a masala stuffing. **Bharli Vangi** is a stuffed brinjal dish. Locally grown, small-sized brinjals are used for this dish. The stuffing is a paste made of coconut, onion, jaggery and goda masala. The stuffed vegetable is fried and then served in a gravy of the same masala used for the stuffing. Brinjal is a popular vegetable in many states, though in such dishes, the vegetable is often just the medium for the distinctive taste of the masala.

Vegetables are also served as yoghurt-based salad called **Koshimbir**. This dish is similar to but more elaborate than the north Indian raita. In a typical koshimbir, chopped onions, tomatoes, cucumbers, some chopped vegetables, peanuts, coriander, green chillies and seasoning are added to yoghurt in a bowl. The dish also has a tarka of cumin and mustard seeds in hot ghee. Like raita, it is served cold and acts as a balance to spicier dishes as a side dish in a meal.

If you go to specialist Marathi food restaurants, in Pune for example, and try a Marathi thali, you are likely to be served a large number of dishes: two or three vegetable dishes along with flatbreads (a selection of poori, thalipeeth, bhakri), aamti, rice (plain bhaat or masala bhaat or both), sweet dishes, koshimbir, papad, pickles and chutneys. A wide variety of chutneys is a feature of most Marathi meals. The meals tend to be quite satisfying and wholesome but you are unlikely to come out feeling in food heaven. Mostly it is to do with the absence of non-vegetarian dishes but it is also because of the similarity of the tastes of many of the dishes. For differences in tastes, you need to travel around this large state and discover some of the sub-regional cuisines.

Some of the sub-regional Marathi cuisines give meat, fish and seafood dishes more prominence. The mutton and chicken curries from Kolhapur, a city to the south east of Mumbai and north east of Goa, are considered a sub-regional speciality. For people of my generation, Kolhapur is best known for producing light and open-toed leather slippers, known all over India as Kolhapuri chappal. They are widely used in India, mainly because they keep the feet aired in the hot weather and are considered more stylish than other types of slippers made from rubber or plastic. The problem is that walking anywhere in these or any other type of slippers leaves your feet very dusty. It boils down to a compromise between keeping feet cool or clean.

I digress. Kolhapur is also known for its non-vegetarian curries with a generic label of **Rassa**, which is derived from the word 'ras' meaning juice or liquid. In usage, the word is similar to 'kari' in Tamil denoting a dish with a liquid gravy. There are different types of rassa dishes depending on the meat or fish used. Interestingly, these rassa dishes can be served as a meat curry or as a soup. The soup is made using only the meat stock with the meat itself then cooked and served as a separate dry dish.

There are two reasonably well known Kolhapuri rassa dishes. The red coloured curry is called **Tambda Rassa**. It makes for a rich and spicy mutton dish, with a curry base of onions, tomatoes and coconut with lots of spices. It gets its red colour from the use of a spice mix which has lots of red chillies and a long list of dry roasted and fried spices. The red chillies used are not mild and impart both colour and heat to the dish. This dish requires a very high level of tolerance to chillies. The other type of rassa dish is **Pandhara Rassa** which is a white and spicy curry, very different looking from the standard Indian non-vegetarian curry. There are no tomatoes in this dish. Coconut, as grated coconut paste and as coconut milk, provides the base and the colour to the curry. It is not a mild dish though. The heat in this dish comes from pepper, usually white pepper powder which is used in generous quantity.

Another sub-regional cuisine from Maharashtra with an independent identity is Malvani cuisine. It gets its name from a town called Malvan on the Konkan coast, north of Goa, though the cuisine is spread over the south west coastal region of Maharashtra, not just the town. There are quite a few Malvani restaurants in Mumbai. Most of these restaurants tend to be small and unpretentious eateries, often set up to cater to the immigrants from the region. The dishes are hence reasonably authentic. If you want to try some Malvani dishes in a more up-market setting, Karavalli in Bangalore, mentioned earlier, also serves a few typical dishes.

The cuisine in fact reflects its geographic location as a mix of Marathi, Konkan and Goan influences. As a coastal cuisine, seafood dishes dominate, though a chicken curry and poori dish called Kombdi Vade is one of the best known Malvani dishes in Mumbai. This is a cuisine which relies on local ingredients and produce. Most dishes have lots of coconut as the main ingredient in the curry or gravy, kokam is usually added for sourness and generous quantities of local red chillies are used for heat.

Malvani Fish Curry is a typical dish. It can be made with any of the easily available fish in the region; pomfret, king fish and mackerel are the most popular. The key ingredient is a signature paste made from fresh grated coconut, dried red chillies and a variable mix of other ingredients such as onions, ginger, garlic, cumin seeds, coriander seeds, etc. The colour can be quite fiery depending on the number of red chillies used. This masala is cooked in oil with garlic, onion and curry leaves. Marinated fish, which is cut into steaks, is then cooked in this masala paste before water is added to make the curry. Kokam pieces are added at the final stage of cooking. What you get is a hot curry somewhat balanced by the taste of coconut and kokam. Since very little onion and no tomato goes into the curry, the Malvani fish curry has quite a distinctive taste compared to better known Indian curries.

Another typical dish is **Kolambi fry** or fried prawns. The cooking technique is similar to dry, fried fish found in multiple coastal cuisines from Mumbai to Kerala. In this case, prawns are marinated, first in salt and lemon juice and then in ginger garlic paste, red chilli powder, turmeric and a special spice combination called **Malvani masala**. The marinated prawns are then coated in a flour of rice and rava (semolina) and shallow fried in oil, till the crust becomes golden. The same technique can be applied to different types of fish as well to get Malvani fish fry.

The Malvani masala used in this dish is a speciality spice combination of this cuisine and used in many dishes. It is a complex spice combination with more than a dozen spices, in defined proportions, roasted and powdered. A large quantity of byadgi red chillies, found extensively in the region, is usually a part of this special masala. In some recipes regular chillies are also included, so any dish with additional red chillies along with the Malvani masala is likely to be quite hot.

As mentioned earlier, one of the better known dishes from this region is called **Kombdi Vade**. This is a combination dish of two parts: a chicken curry called **Malvani Kombdi curry** and a poori-like dish called **Vade**. The Malvani kombdi curry has two special ingredients, the Malvani masala and a special coconut paste specially prepared for the dish. The coconut paste is made by roasting grated dry and fresh coconut with fried onions and ginger and garlic paste. The dish basically requires the marinated chicken to be fried with a small quantity of onions, some Malvani masala powder and the coconut paste. Once the frying is done, water is added to the mix to make the curry. The dish gets its taste from coconut and the large number of spices which go into the Malvani masala. It is a complex dish with the spices giving it a standout aroma and taste.

The vade used in this dish is also not straight-forward. The flour is mixture of rice flour, wheat flour and roasted urad and chana daal. Jowar flour may also be added. The various flours are mixed together, seasoned and may be lightly spiced. The dough is kneaded and then shaped into individual poori sized vade by hand. Traditionally, each vade is about 10 to 12 cm in diameter with a small hole in the middle. When deep-fried each vade puffs up like a doughnut-shaped balloon with a crisp brown or golden exterior. To eat the dish, you break the vade into small pieces and scoop up a bit of chicken and gravy into each piece.

Like most Indian cuisines, Maharashtrian food also has a number of fried, savoury snack dishes. I discovered these Marathi snacks not only on holiday and work trips to cities but also on multiple train journeys through the state. That is one fun part of long train journeys in India. As you pass through different states and regions, the food, especially the snacks, being sold by hawkers at the train stations keep changing according to local cuisines. A long train journey can provide opportunities for trying many different dishes.

It also helps that most passengers are quite open to sharing food on train journeys. On long train journeys, the sleeper classes have four or six sleeping berths in each cubicle and two on the side. If you are travelling alone, you are likely to have a number of strangers with whom you will spend long hours. During my college days, I used to travel only by train (air travel was prohibitively expensive and had limited connections) and have had many long journeys, including trips as long as 36 hours. It is inevitable that you get to know your fellow travellers on such journeys. Most travellers have some packed food at the start of the journey. If you are not too fussed about sharing food, you get to try a little bit of many different dishes. Between the food carried by your fellow travellers and sold by the hawkers on the stations, the journey can become a continuous multi-course feast of different types of foods.

Marathi cuisine is much more indulgent in snacks than it is in main dishes. A number of these snacks have the suffix **Vadi** in the name. The name is related to vada found in south India and badi found in north India. A good example is the **Aluchi Vadi**, a Maharashtrian speciality and a dish which is not found anywhere else in the country. The name is sometimes shortened to alu vadi, which can be confusing as aloo is potato in Hindi (but batata in Marathi). Aluchi vadi is a savoury snack made by rolling together multiple aluchi (colocasia) leaves smeared with a spicy batter of besan, coconut and tamarind. These rolls are steamed to cook the leaves. Then the rolls are cut into smaller pieces, cutting across the longitudinal axis of each roll to create individual pieces shaped like swirls, which are then shallow fried. Each piece comes out nicely crispy and spicy. **Kothimbir Vadi** is similarly made from lots of chopped coriander leaves mixed with besan and spices. **Suralichi** or **Surali Vadi**, which is called Khandvi in Gujarat, has yoghurt mixed with besan and spices and is described in the Gujarat chapter.

The first two vadi dishes described are crispy and spicy, not very different from a spicy pakora. Pakoras are also widely eaten in Maharashtra but are called bhaji, that is the same as cooked vegetables. The name of the vegetable as a prefix is normally the guide to whether the dish is a pakora or a dry, stir-fried vegetable, though this is not a fool-proof method. South Indian influence means that dishes named 'vada' are also widely available. Batata vada, mashed potatoes coated with besan and fried, is in fact almost a symbol of Maharashtrian and Mumbai food, as we have seen earlier.

One of the better known Maharashtrian snacks, outside Maharashtra that is, is **Poha** or **Pohe**. Poha (plural pohe) is dry, flattened rice. This dry rice enhanced with a few other ingredients is usually had as a light snack or for breakfast. The most common variant is **Kanda Poha** which is poha mixed with onions. It is a quick and easy dish to prepare. Onions are fried in oil with green chillies, curry leaves, turmeric powder and mustard seeds, then roasted peanuts and rinsed poha are added. The whole mix is cooked for a few minutes and then served warm. Other variants include **Batata Poha**, poha with potato, and **Dadpe Poha** which is poha with grated coconut. The poha dishes are usually served with garnishing, such as chopped coriander, grated coconut, crushed peanuts, sev, etc., to make them look and taste more interesting.

In Marathi homes, it is a well-established convention to serve poha to guests at teatime. It has also a key role in Marathi arranged marriages. It is the dish traditionally served to the groom's family when they visit a prospective bride's family. So strong is this tradition that arranged marriage is also colloquially called kanda poha in Marathi, as in 'they had a kanda poha marriage'.

Apart from poha, Maharashtra has contributed another speciality breakfast dish to the wider Indian cuisine. **Sabudana** is a carb rich food ingredient made from the tapioca starch extracted from the root vegetable of cassava plant. The word 'dana' roughly translates to a small, grain-sized food item. So sabudana refers to small pearl-like spheres made from the dried and processed starch extract. They are also sometimes called 'tapioca pearls'. They can be eaten as substitutes for cereals as they are rich in carbohydrate and are not considered grains. This is relevant during fasts observed during Hindu religious festivals when many devotees abstain from eating any grains.

Sabudana Khichri is a simple meal commonly prepared for breakfasts or during religious festivals in Maharashtra. Chunks of boiled potatoes are fried with cumin seeds, green chillies, curry leaves and peanuts and then sabudana is added to the mix. A few further minutes of cooking and the sabudana khichri is ready. Note that no lentils are used as that would be against the fasting convention. Potatoes are root vegetables, so they are acceptable. I am not sure I understand these fasting rules very well and sometimes they do give the impression of being made on the fly. When in doubt, there are always experts in every family that can be consulted. The rules, as a result, tend to vary from family to family, with each family insisting that their rules are the most authentic.

Many of the sweets that we find in north India are widely available in Maharashtra. Jalebi and laddu of different types are especially easy to get. Kheer and rabri, called **Basundi** in Maharashtra and Gujarat, are also quite common. But Maharashtra also contributes to the multitude of sweet dishes that are part of Indian cuisines with a couple of specialities.

I've mentioned **Shrikhand** earlier. It is a sweet yoghurt dish, where the base is thick yoghurt with all the whey removed. This is really the only tricky bit in this otherwise simple dish. Full-fat yoghurt needs to be wrapped in a thin muslin cloth and all the whey allowed to drip out over many hours. The remaining thick yoghurt can be flavoured in different ways to make shrikhand. The best variety is called Kesar Elaichi shrikhand, where sweetened yoghurt is gently flavoured with powdered green cardamom and saffron and served garnished with chopped almonds and pistachios. Another variant has mango pulp added for a wonderful Mango shrikhand.

A Maharashtrian sweet called **Modak** has become popular in the last few decades, mainly because of its use as an offering in the Ganesh Chaturthi festival. A cooked, sweet filling of coconut, jaggery and dried fruits is stuffed into rolled circular flats made from rice flour or maida dough. Each piece of dough is then folded into a ball in such a way that the outer surface has regularly spaced ridges which gives modak its distinctive look. The modak balls are either steamed or fried. Platefuls of modak are distributed during the festival and each modak is eaten like a laddu. It is possible to bite into each piece but that risks spilling some of the stuffing out, so it is safest to take the whole piece at one go. The ingredients for stuffing can be played around with, so there are a quite a few variants to the standard modak. A stuffing of mawa with coconut is quite expected, one with chocolate is less so. But both types can be found.

A somewhat more rustic sweet preparation is **Puran Poli**, which is also used as an offering in Ganesh Chaturthi. This is paratha with a sweet stuffing. The filling, or puran, is made from boiled chana dal and jaggery with a bit of flavouring such as cardamom powder, all cooked in ghee. The filling is then stuffed into balls of wheat dough, rolled and cooked as any other stuffed paratha on a tava.

It would be apt to end this chapter with a description of a ubiquitous Marathi and Konkan drink. Every full meal is always accompanied with a pinkish drink or soup called **Sol Karhi**. The colour is actually quite unappetising but the drink itself is cool and refreshing and is considered good for digestion. The main ingredients are kokam and coconut milk, with a bit of bite from green chillies. It can be had as a soup, as a curry with rice or as a digestif at the end of the meal, sometimes as all three in the same meal. It widely popular along the Konkan coast and can also be found in Goan and Malvani meals.

Usal Pav

Marathi Thali

Kanda Poha

Shrikhand

13
Gujarat
Snacks are also food

Gujarat and Maharashtra cuisines are similar. Gujarat is north of Maharashtra and, for most of the British rule, the two states were part of one administrative province called the Bombay Presidency. Apart from geographical contiguity, the two regions also have a long shared history, with a bilateral flow of people between the states. This has resulted in the intermingling of their foods, with many shared and similar dishes.

The people of Gujarat, Gujaratis, are probably the best known among Indians for trade and enterprise. This has partly been because Gujarat historically had the main ports for export of goods from north, west and central India to Arabia and Africa and from there to other parts of the west. In ancient times, Lothal was a big port city. Bharuch, Vallabhi and Khambat are some of the other cities mentioned in historic sources as important ports during various periods of Gujarat's history. Surat was the most important port on the west coast during the Mughal empire and remained so for a couple of centuries.

Trade meant that Gujaratis travelled for business to many of the places that India traded with, in east and south Africa and Arabia. Many settled there. Similarly, when the British took Indians as indentured labour to Africa and far flung islands, e.g. in the Caribbean, small numbers of Gujarati traders followed them. As a result, there have been pockets of Gujarati communities outside India for at least the last couple of centuries. More recently, a number of Gujaratis from East Africa were taken in as refugees by the UK in the 1970s. They are a significant part of the prominent British Indian ethnic group in the UK now. Many Gujaratis have also settled in the USA and Canada seeking economic opportunities in the last half century or so.

These expat Gujarati communities have had a critical role in the introduction and spread of Indian foods in many of these countries. As traders they have imported Indian food ingredients to allow the immigrant communities to continue to eat their own food at home. Also, by establishing Indian restaurants and shops, they have introduced the cuisine to the locals. This is one reason why Gujarati food has more prominence outside India than it has in India itself. I've had many more avenues for trying out Gujarati dishes while living abroad than I had in the years that I lived in India.

Gujarati food is mostly vegetarian. About sixty percent of the population of the state is vegetarian, one of the highest proportions of all states in India. It is said that the high incidence of vegetarianism is due to the influence of Jainism in the state. Jainism is an ancient religion and has 'ahimsa' (non-violence) to all living creatures as one of its tenets. In practice, this means vegetarianism of the type where no meat or fish is eaten. Practising Jains are small in number. Even in Gujarat, they account for only about one percent of the population. I doubt if the influence of Jains is the only reason for the extent of vegetarianism in the state. As in Maharashtra, the influence of Hindu brahmins and their customs is probably as important.

Gujarati food has a couple of other distinctive characteristics. Most main dishes are simultaneously salty, sweet and spicy. The sweetness especially makes Gujarati dishes stand out. For example, only a Gujarati daal will have hints of sweetness from added sugar or jaggery. In cooking technique, while frying is the most common way, as in other parts of the country, there are a number of Gujarati dishes which use steaming as a standalone cooking process. This is not something that you see very often in Indian cooking.

Snacks are more important in Gujarati cuisine than in any other state in India. Gujaratis not only snack in between meals but also eat snacks as appetisers and side dishes in main meals. Sometimes, a whole meal can be multiple snacks woven together with daal and flatbread.

There are two types of snacks in Gujarat. **Nashto** refers to fried snacks like sev, nimki, gathia, etc., each with small, savoury pieces, which can be stored, and are generally sold by sweet and snack shops. These dishes are typically eaten as snacks during teatime, mid-morning and early evening. **Farsan** are more filling snacks which are served not only at teatime but also as part of main meals. Within these two labels, there is a fantastic variety of snack foods in Gujarati cuisine. I will describe the popular ones that I've tried over the years at various places, many from Gujarati sweet and snack shops outside India.

A delightfully simple savoury snack is called **Nimki**, sometimes also called **Namak Pare**. Namak is the Hindi/Gujarati word for salt and the name 'nimki' just means salty. Similarly, namak pare means salty snack. The word nimki is sometimes also appended as a suffix to other snacks to denote a savoury taste. But when used as a standalone name, it usually refers to this particular snack. It is made from a dough of atta (plain flour) mixed with salt, and cumin and carom seeds for flavouring. The dough is rolled out like a thick roti and cut into small, diamond shaped pieces, about four or five cm in length. These pieces are then deep fried in oil so they become crispy and brittle. Once dried, they can be stored for a couple of weeks. This is a snack found in many states in India, eaten with tea and during festivals. It is likely to be one of the savoury snacks which you will be offered along with many sweets during festivals such as Diwali. Like potato crisps, they are quite irresistible and it can be difficult to stop at just a few. A sweet variant of this is called **Shakkar Pare** (sugar snack). It is simply plain flour pieces, nimki without the salt, soaked in sugar syrup after being fried.

Gathia is the name for strings of savoury fried besan, somewhat crispy but soft to the bite. It is a popular year-round snack, made from a soft dough of besan and baking soda, flavoured with carom seeds, asafoetida and black peppercorn. The trick in making this snack is to get the dough of the right consistency using both warm oil and water. The dough should be not as runny as the batter in pakora but also softer than what you would have for a flatbread. It should be soft enough to be squeezed out as strings but then must hold its shape when being deep-fried.

Gathia looks like **Sev**, which is also strings of savoury fried besan. But sev has a nice crunch to it. Sev can be eaten on its own but it is most often an ingredient in other dishes. Its crunchiness makes it a preferred ingredient for all kinds of chaat dishes, as we have already seen. It is also an ingredient in a speciality dry snack dish with the mysterious name **Mixture**. It is also known as Chewda in Gujarat, Madras Mixture in south India, Bombay Mix in the UK and Punjab Mix in the US. It is easily found in packaged form in stores all over and rarely prepared at homes. It is literally a mixture of a number of different dry snacks, each of which can be and is eaten on its own.

Of the many different types of dry snacks which go into Mixture, sev and gathia are both made from besan. Another dry snack made from besan is boondi or bundiya, small droplets of besan deep-fried in oil. It can be had as a savoury snack or dipped into sugar syrup for a sweet. Then, there are dry snacks of rice. We have already come across roasted flat rice, called poha in west India and chura in the north and east. Dry, puffed rice, called murhi or moora, is the key ingredient of the famous street foods bhel poori and jhaal murhi. The third type of dry snacks is made of lentils. The most common is called **Moong Daal Nimki**. This is split moong daal (yellow gram) washed, dried, deep fried and salted. Served in bowlfuls at teatime and with drinks, it is a surprisingly tasty and addictive snack. Similar in concept is the **Chana Daal Nimki**, which is the savoury snack of fried chana daal (Bengal gram). Only a little different is **Dal Moth**, which is made by deep frying whole masoor daal (red lentil with skin). Finally, there are dry snacks of nuts, most commonly peanuts and cashews, where the nuts are fried, salted and spiced. Not very different from salted nuts available in packs in supermarkets.

Peanuts are very popular all over India. India is the second largest producer and consumer of peanuts, after China. The plant is not native to India and is believed to have been first cultivated in South America in prehistoric times. I am not sure how and when it reached India but it is grown extensively, mainly for its oil, called groundnut oil. Gujarat is the biggest producer of peanuts in India and groundnut oil is the preferred medium of cooking in Gujarat and Maharashtra.

Roasted or fried peanuts are widely available as a cheap and healthy snack in India. In its most common form, shelled and roasted peanuts, in the red skin, are mixed with salt, chilli powder and some lime juice and sold in paper cones. In another form, peanuts, still in the pods, are roasted and sold by weight. A small paper pack containing salt or black rock salt is usually given as an accompaniment. This form used to be quite common on railway stations especially in smaller towns. Offering peanuts to fellow passengers was considered a great way to socialise and pass time on train journeys. So, groups of passengers would happily crack open the pods, snack on the nuts and chat, all the while dropping the pod shells on the floor of the train compartment. You can imagine the mess on the floors of the coaches at the end of the journey!

Mixture (Bombay Mix, Madras Mix, etc.) is just a mix of many of the dry snacks described above. There is no fixed recipe but a typical mix will have sev, poha, chana daal nimki, dal moth, peanuts, cashew nuts, mixed with salt, red chilli powder, etc. The idea is to get different types of crunchy tastes all mixed together. I used to think that this must be a snack created by or for the British in India. There a couple of arguments for such a case. It is often served with drinks at the bars of clubs and usually served in bowls to be spooned out, rather than eaten by hands. All signs of the British legacy. The name 'Mixture' itself is an English word. But there is an equally strong case that can be made for this snack to be of Gujarati origin. A shame then that none of its various names pay homage to Gujarat. This mixture also makes a good base for a chaat dish. Add a bit of boiled potatoes or boiled chickpeas, chopped onions, coriander leaves, chaat masala, chillies, top up with a couple of chutneys and you get a delightful **Mixture Chaat**.

Practically every snack that is a part of north Indian food is also a part of Gujarati cuisine in one form or the other. Besan (Bengal gram flour), as must be evident by now, is a much loved ingredient in a number of Gujarati snacks. Different types of **pakora**, called bhajiya or bhaji, are very widely available, with potato and onions being the most common vegetable ingredients. Most pakoras are made with the vegetable pieces coated in a spicy batter of besan and fried. **Samosa** is also widely available. The Gujarati samosa can be, like elsewhere, with a potato filling but you also find samosas with filling of cooked peas. Stuffed **kachori**, that is deep fried poori with a filling of spiced lentils, is as much a part of Gujarati food as it is of other parts of north India. There are also different types of **vada**, made by deep frying batter of different types of lentils.

One of the best known snacks or light dishes from Gujarat is **Dhokla**. It has become quite popular outside Gujarat and can be often found as one of the dishes offered by upscale hotels, along with other pan-Indian favourites – a good reflection of popularity among the more affluent.

Dhokla brings back a treasured memory from my childhood. In the townships that I grew up in, the women used to organise something called a Ladies'

Club. This would be the wives of the managers meeting on an evening every week to 'productively' socialise. Typically, this would turn into cultural exchanges where they would learn all kinds of things about their states and cultures from each other. This would of course include exchanging recipes for dishes and, in the spirit of 'showing is better than telling', many would cook the dishes and bring them to the club. Bear in mind that these were all mothers of growing children. Not surprisingly, those goodies would not all be eaten. I remember waiting for my mother to come back from the club on those evenings, knowing that there would be something nice in her bag. To the Ladies' Club I owe my first taste of many snack dishes from various parts of India, including dhokla.

The original variety of dhokla is made from a fermented batter of rice flour and besan. The batter is lightly spiced and seasoned and may have a bit of sugar. Once fermented, the batter is steamed in a closed pan and comes out quite light and fluffy. It is topped up with a tarka of mustard seeds, green chillies, etc. in hot oil and served in small pieces, shaped as cubes or cuboids. Its healthy reputation is based on the method of cooking, steaming rather than frying as is the norm with most Indian dishes. A variant, called **Khaman dhokla**, is made entirely of besan, with turmeric added to the batter for a more pronounced yellow colour compared to the rice flour-based version which is whitish. Dhokla is typically served with a couple of chutneys. It is a dish widely available as a breakfast option at small eateries but also favoured as a teatime and party snack. It is not uncommon to see large trays of cubed dhokla pieces with toothpicks stuck in them being served by waiters in weddings and other parties in cities all over India.

A lesser known Gujrati snack is called **Muthiya**. The name of this snack is derived from the Hindi/Gujarati word for fist, 'mutthi' because individual pieces of the dish are shaped by squeezing the dough in a closed fist. There are quite a few variants of muthiya, with the methi (fenugreek) variety one of the more common ones. The dough is made by mixing the ubiquitous and versatile besan with chopped fenugreek leaves, spices, seasoning and water. Small pieces of the dough are then shaped individually into cylindrical rolls by the aforementioned action of squeezing in a closed fist. Dozens are made at one go. These muthiya pieces can then be either steamed or shallow fried.

In Maharashtrian food, we find a snack called suralichi vadi. The same dish is called **Khandvi** in Gujarat. It is a snack of cylindrical rolls of steamed besan served with a garnish of chopped coconut, coriander leaves and fried mustard seeds. It is quite a tricky dish to prepare. The batter needs to be of a consistency that after steaming, it can be first spread on a pan and then it should set such that it can be rolled and cut. The batter is made of besan mixed with yoghurt, spices and water. Steamed besan tastes very different from fried besan; it is softer and a great conduit for the tastes of the other ingredients. This is a dish best bought from a snack shop though, as its cooking has very small margins for error.

A Gujarati snack (surprisingly not made from besan!) is **Handvo** which is a salty cake. It tastes much better than it sounds. The batter is a grand melange of rice, two or three different types of lentils, typically moong, toor and urad, a couple of grated vegetables and a few spices. The rice and lentil batter is traditionally fermented overnight but baking soda can help cut the time. The batter can then be baked in an oven or steamed in a cooker. When cooked, it looks very much like a cake. It is served in cake-like slices but eaten with a green chilly chutney.

Besan is again the main ingredient in a street food available during religious festivals called **Fafda**. These are very thin strips of besan dough deep fried in oil. The dough is made of besan and water, spiced with salt, pepper, turmeric and carom seeds. Deep frying makes this crispy like a papad and it can be eaten on its own with chutney or with a thin karhi for a light meal.

So far, I've only described the snacks that form a part of Gujarati cuisine. Much as it seems that Gujaratis eat only snacks, they do eat regular meals as well.

My first stay in Gujarat was in the largest city, Ahmedabad, while doing a summer internship in college. Initially, I stayed in the hostel of a local college, with food provided by the hostel. Hostel food borrows from the local cuisine but is also adapted to the tastes of the students, especially in colleges which have students from all over India. The hostel food, hence, offered only glimpses of Gujarati food.

After a few weeks, the hostel shut down for maintenance and I had to find accommodation in another boarding house, a working men's hostel, quite different from a college hostel. The accommodation was quite basic with multiple beds in dormitories. Every morning when we left for work, we had to tie our bags with a chain to the bed and put a lock on it. This was because the hostel administration explicitly refused to guarantee against theft! Most of us didn't have any valuables but even clothes and toiletries were at risk if left loose. Not one of the best places that I've stayed in. But one plus point was that the hostel had a dining hall serving basic meals at a good value. A combination of the food in the boarding house and nearby local eateries was my introduction to regular Gujarati food.

Regular food in Gujarat is often called 'daal – bhaat – rotli – shaak', that is lentils, rice, flatbread and vegetables. Within these generic dishes, there are a number of different types, many similar to found in other parts of the country, but quite a few specific to Gujarati cuisine.

Flatbreads are mostly made of wheat and millets flour and are collectively called **roti** or **rotli** or **rotio**. The word roti without prefix or suffix normally means a flatbread made of wheat flour and the especially thin ones are called **Phulka**. It is quite an evocative name: 'phul' means 'to expand' describing the last step in the making of this roti when it is placed directly over the flame and expands like a balloon. But also in the name is the word 'hulka' or 'halka' which means light, a very apt description of this roti. To me, food with such brilliant and precise names bring joy even before I eat them. A few well and freshly made phulkas can transform a meal, as I discovered in the men's hostel in Ahmedabad.

For flatbreads made from other flours, the names of the rotis are more mundane, simply including the name of the flour it is made from as a prefix. So, we have Bajri no rotio (roti of pearl millet), Makai no rotio (roti of corn) and Juvar no rotio (roti of sorghum). Like in Maharashtra, we also have a type of flatbread called bhakri, which in Gujarat is a thick roti of wheat flour.

A Gujarati flatbread speciality is called **Thepla**. This is similar to thalipeeth found in Maharashtra and belongs to the broad family of different types of parathas found all over the country. The basic idea is to include vegetables and spices in the dough such that you get a flatbread which can be a meal in itself. Like thalipeeth, thepla is made from a mix of wheat and millets flour with besan, though a mix of only wheat flour and besan is also acceptable. Methi (fenugreek) leaves is the other main ingredient. A few of the standard spices are also added. Once the dough is prepared, each thepla is rolled out and cooked on a tawa like a paratha. While the fenugreek variety is the most common, other varieties include spinach, radish and amaranth. Like most stuffed parathas, theplas are eaten for breakfast or a light meal with yoghurt and pickles.

Once cooked and dried, theplas keep well and, as a result, are a Gujarati favourite for journeys. I first ate thepla on a train journey from Delhi to Mumbai many years ago when a Gujarati gentleman shared his packed food with me. He had a dozen or so theplas packed in a standard tiffin box with some pickles. His wife must have expected him to share, otherwise the quantity seems excessive for one individual. Whatever the back story, once we had started talking, he was happy to share his food with me. I remember I had nothing to offer in return and could only buy him tea from a railway station vendor as my contribution to our shared meal.

Another flatbread speciality from Gujarat is called **Khakhra**. This is made very crisp, almost like a papad, and is eaten as a snack rather than as roti. The dough can be made from just plain wheat flour with some seasoning, though a masala variant has besan and a number of spices. The key technique in making khakhra is to roll out the dough very thin, otherwise it will become a roti. When being roasted on a tawa, khakhra needs to be continuously pressed such that it gets properly cooked to crispiness on both sides. It looks and feels like papad and may be served as an alternative.

In regular meals, rice is eaten as just bhaat, that is rice boiled in water. In special meals or when a multi-course thali is being served, different types of rice dishes may be served. Vegetable pulao is a part of the cuisine. The Gujarati variant is called **Masala Bhaat**, as in Maharashtra, and is similarly made with vegetables such as carrots, peas and cauliflower.

A slightly unusual Gujarati rice dish is called **Biranj**. It is sweet but eaten as part of a main meal. The name is derived from the Persian word for rice, birinj. The connection with another word of Persian origin, biryani, is obvious. For the biranj dish, long grain rice is first fried with a small quantity of chana daal in ghee and whole spices and then cooked in water. The quantity of water is key as too much water will make this into a khichri-like mush. With the right amount of water, the rice and chana grains cook together but remain separate. Saffron, sugar and many different types of roasted dried fruits, cashew nuts, raisins, pistachios, almonds, etc. are added to the dish. The saffron gives the dish a nice yellow colour and its aroma, as always, signals extravagance. When served in a thali, biranj can be eaten either in between a couple of spicy dishes, as a change of taste, or towards the end as a sweet dish.

Daal is a necessary part of every Gujarati meal. Daal can be made of any of the lentils that are available in the country, though toor and moong daal are more popular. A typical Gujarati daal is lentils boiled in water with turmeric powder, seasoning, jaggery and a souring agent, kokam or tamarind. The last two ingredients give the Gujarati daal its distinctive 'khatti-meethi' (sour and sweet) taste. I've eaten this type of daal many times and the sweetness always comes as a surprise. It takes getting used to. Like everywhere else, daal is always tempered with whole spices roasted in hot ghee: this chhonk is called vaghar in Gujarat.

The rice and daal combination of **Khichri** is the definition of comfort food in Gujarat. The plain variety is made, as in other parts of the country, with equal quantities of short grain rice and whole moong daal boiled in water with turmeric, asafoetida and salt. The water quantity needs to be accurate such that the khichri comes out as a wet solid mass, not dry and not runny. A bit of hot ghee on top and the dish is ready to eat. Though moong daal is the preferred lentil, other lentils can also be used. Gujarati households also enhance the basic recipe, most commonly by adding vegetables, to make a more complete one pot meal. Two or three vegetables, for example potatoes, peas and cauliflower, are sometimes cooked with the khichri to get a **Tarkari Khichri**. This dish used to be a favourite of the cooks at that men's hostel in Ahmedabad I stayed in. You can see why – it is easy to cook in large quantities, nutritionally wholesome and tasty enough to be generally accepted, if not popularly demanded.

In north India, there is a saying: *'Khichri ke chaar yaar, dahi, papad, ghee aur achaar'* (Khichri has four friends: yoghurt, papad, ghee and pickle). These accompaniments are always available in an Indian kitchen, so a meal with khichri is really easy to put together. In Guajarati homes, it is customary to eat khichri with a curry called **Karhi**. We have come across this dish earlier in other states. In Bihar and east Uttar Pradesh, it is the curry in the two-part dish called karhi badi. The Gujarati karhi is the same concept but cooked somewhat differently. Unlike the karhi found in north and east India, which is yellow in colour, the Gujarati karhi is almost white and thinner. The basic mix is the same, yoghurt and besan, but with a larger quantity of water added. The mix is cooked in a pot with hot ghee and spices, with little or no turmeric. Since it is a Gujarati dish, it also has a small quantity of sugar added. The resultant dish is quite watery. It is usually served just as it is, that is without pakora or badi added to it and serves as a side dish in most meals.

Vegetable dishes in Gujarat are called **Shaak** or **Bhaji**. The former is similar to the label Saag used in other parts of the country for dishes made of leafy vegetables especially spinach. In Gujarat, the nomenclature of many vegetable dishes has the vegetable name in Gujarati paired with the suffix shaak. Thus, we have bateta nu shaak (potato), bhinda nu shaak (okra), dudhi ganthia nu shaak (lauki/bottle gourd), karela nu shaak (bitter gourd), ringan nu shaak (brinjal), kobi bateta nu shaak (cabbage and potato), palak nu shaak (spinach), etc. The names don't tell much about the dish apart from the main ingredients. These dishes can be dry or curried, spicy and, in the case of curried dishes, with a hint of sweetness.

For example, **Bateta nu Shaak** is a simple dry fried potato dish which also has a curried version called raswala bateta nu shaak. In the dry version, potatoes are fried in oil with a few whole and powdered spices and finished with a bit of sugar or jaggery and lemon juice. In the curried version, water and chopped tomatoes are added for the curry. Onions and garlic are not normally used in these dishes, in adherence to Jain traditions of cooking. Sugar or jaggery is not always added to vegetable dishes and curried dishes are more likely to be sweetened than dry ones.

Stuffed vegetables are called **Bharela**. For example, **Bharela Karela** is stuffed bitter gourd. The name has a nice ring to it, but the dish will only appeal if you like karela. These dishes are similar to the stuffed vegetables found in Maharashtra, such as the bharli vangi or stuffed brinjal, described in the previous chapter.

A much more elaborate vegetable dish is **Undhiyu** or **Oondhiya**. The name is derived from the Gujarati word 'undhu' which means inverted or upside down. The dish used to be traditionally cooked in earthenware pots sealed and placed upside down in fire pits in the ground. It is a stew of many vegetables: the main ones are brinjal, unripe banana, potato, beans, peas and purple yam. The vegetables are stuffed or coated with a coconut and spice mix masala, specially prepared for the dish. The snack muthiya, described earlier, is also added as an ingredient. Undhiyu is considered a special dish and is served often at Gujarati weddings and special occasions.

Most Gujarati meals are served in a thali, that is a large plate, with the curries and vegetables served in individual bowls arranged along the inside circumference of the round plate, the rice and rotis towards the bottom of the plate with a few chutneys and pickles also placed on the plate. The Gujarati thali is probably the reason why the concept of a thali meal has become well-known in Indian restaurants abroad, travelling along with the Gujarati diaspora.

Gujarati cuisine includes many of the sweets that are found in other north Indian cuisines, such as jalebi, laddu, barfi, rasgulla, gulab jamun, halwa, etc. Shrikhand and basundi are considered as much a part of Gujarati food as Marathi food. Gujaratis don't like shrikhand being called just a Marathi dish. You do get very good quality shrikhand in Gujarat, especially during the summer when you get **Aam Shrikhand**, yoghurt flavoured with pulp from local mangoes.

Another familiar Gujarati sweet is **Ghughra**, called gujia or pirakia elsewhere. This is a readily identifiable sweet because of its semi-circular shape and crinkled edge. The Gujarati version is made with a sweet stuffing of mawa or khoya and lots of chopped dry fruits and nuts inside an outer deep-fried casing of maida. This is a popular festival food, making an appearance in all the important festivals.

The kheer equivalent is called **Doodhpak** or **Doodh Pak** in Gujarat and is also one of the dishes made during religious festivals. It is not very different from rice-based kheer dishes made elsewhere in the country, though the Gujarati version uses less rice in proportion to the milk for a more watery kheer.

To end the description of Gujarati food, we have a signature sweet dish made of besan (I did call this the favourite Gujarati ingredient!). The dish is called **Mohanthal**. The name signifies its special place in the celebration of Janmashtami, the festival to celebrate the birth of Krishna who is also known as Mohan. The dish belongs to the same family as besan barfi and Mysore pak, all have besan roasted in ghee as the key ingredient. In Mohanthal, a little bit of milk and ghee is added to the besan flour which is cooked in more ghee. A sugar syrup is added to the cooked besan with saffron and cardamom powder for flavouring. The mixture is poured into a pan, garnished with chopped nuts and allowed to set. Once set and cold, it is cut into barfi sized pieces.

Mixture

Dhokla

Thepla

Gujarati Thali

14
Rajasthan

Highest percentage of vegetarians and the best known dish is 'Red Meat'

Rajasthan is the largest state by area in India. It has a unique geography among Indian states in the form of the Thar Desert, also known as the Great Indian Desert, which covers about two thirds of the state's area. Running from the north east to the south west of the state is the Aravalli range, a long line of not very tall hills. The western side of this range is desert and scrubland. The smaller eastern side of the range is more fertile with forests and cultivated land. The climate is hot and dry. Agriculture is adapted to the harsh conditions and produces mostly hardy grains such as millets, oilseeds and cash crops. The difficulty in growing vegetables and fruits has had a clear impact on the cuisine of the state. In addition, water is a precious resource and this has led to practices of minimising water usage in cooking. Since the state produces lots of milk (it is the second largest producer of milk in the country), milk and milk products are used extensively as ingredients in cooking.

Rajasthan is the state with the highest levels of vegetarianism in the country. More than two thirds of the population is estimated to be vegetarian. They practice a form of lacto-vegetarianism, with no meat, fish or eggs in the diet. Vegetarianism combined with the absence of locally grown vegetables creates problems. The local cuisine has overcome the deficiencies of the land with ingenuity, utilising cereals, lentils, spices and milk products in creative ways. For example, besan (Bengal gram flour) is a very popular ingredient for dishes, as popular as in the neighbouring state of Gujarat. We shall see this in a plethora of dishes which use besan as a substitute for vegetables.

I remember my first trip to Rajasthan vividly. This was a wonderful motorcycle trip with a group of friends from Delhi to Jaipur. I was in college in Delhi at that time and in possession of a brand new, sleek, red motorcycle. There was a bit of economic change and some unusual parental indulgence behind that acquisition.

The economic change first. It is not well-known that when Rajiv Gandhi became the Prime Minister of India in 1984, he initiated some limited reforms in the Indian economy. These were not as wide ranging as the reforms introduced in the 1990s by the government under P V Narasimha Rao but started the process of opening up India's economy. One of the visible signs of the reforms were on the roads, with the introduction of a new car, the Maruti Suzuki, and many new motorcycles. Two wheelers, in the form of staid scooters, were till then the most popular form of mechanised personal vehicles, but they were of poor quality and not great to drive. Due to the reforms, a few new motorcycles were introduced within a short span of time, each a joint venture between an Indian company and Japanese motorcycle manufacturer: TVS with Suzuki, Hero with Honda and Escorts with Yamaha. The local market leader in scooters, Bajaj, followed a little later with Kawasaki. These bikes, small in size, but far superior than existing two wheelers in build quality, looks and handling took the market by storm. The bikes were very similar in specs and looks with little to choose between them. But in a few years, Hero Honda was the clear market leader, based on a brilliant advertising campaign focussing on its fuel efficiency: 'Fill it, shut it, forget it'.

I had bought one of the earliest of these bikes to come to market. There was a bit of unusual parental indulgence behind that purchase. My elder brother and I overlapped for a year in our college. Our parents had sent us some money to buy an electronic gadget for home, a Japanese VCR if I remember right. We had not been able to find one (the woes of a closed economy) and the money was lying in our account. I am not sure how we managed to get permission for the motorcycle. My parents were typical middle-class parents of that generation, for whom thrift was second nature and things like motorcycles extraordinary extravagance for college students. Then there was also the perceived risk associated with boys on motorcycles. I think since these motorcycles were not as yet widely available and known, we were able to oversell their safety. At the end of it, we were still a VCR short at home but proud owners of a new bike.

So that's how that first trip to Rajasthan came about. Three of us with brand new bikes got together and roped three more of our friends and set out for Jaipur for a few days' trip. Delhi to Jaipur is not far, about 280 kms (175 miles). We did this trip with a few side stops, lots of sightseeing and even more of eating. One of the group was a Jaipur resident, so we had both a place to stay in Jaipur and local knowledge.

That was the first time I tried the signature Rajasthani dish, **Daal Bati Churma**. In fact it is more a meal than a dish with three dishes-in-one: Daal and bati make the main meal and churma is the sweet dish that follows. **Bati** has the same name as a dish in UP and is also made of wheat flour but does not have a stuffing like the UP bati or the Bihari litti. In this case, a stiff dough is made of wheat flour with a little bit of rava (semolina), salt and ghee. Small sized balls are shaped by hand. The balls are then roasted, in a tandoor or directly over coal fire, till the outside is brown and crusty. The batis are then soaked, literally dunked, into a bowl of warm ghee before being served. A more (relatively speaking) healthy way is to crumble the bati and mix in a bit of ghee. Either way the dish is not complete without ghee.

Daal, in this case, is a mixed daal sometimes using as many as five lentils. Any or all of moong, masoor, chana, urad and toor can be used. The tarka has whole spices, standard spice powders, green chillies, etc. all fried in ghee. Onions and tomatoes may also be used. When five lentils are used to make the daal, it is called Panchmel daal or Panchratan daal; panch, as we have seen earlier, means five. This daal is quite similar to the daal panchratan or mili juli daal we have come across earlier in the Uttar Pradesh chapter.

The traditional way to serve daal bati is with a few batis in a plate and the daal in a bowl. You crush the batis with your hands and spoon daal over, just as you would for rice and daal. However, when served as a part of a thali in restaurant meal, daal bati is very often served in a bowl with the bati crushed and the daal already mixed in. This is the way most outsiders experience daal bati. Hence, the reason that we think of it as a single dish rather than a combination.

Churma is a sweet dish made from dry bati, that is bati before it is dunked into ghee. A few roasted batis are ground into a coarse powder. The coarse powder is then further roasted in ghee with cardamoms, almonds and powdered sugar or jaggery. It is usually served as a coarse mix but can also be served as a laddu. **Churma Laddu** is made by shaping churma by hand into a ball and then lightly coating with poppy seeds. This is a festive sweet dish, associated in Rajasthan with Ganesh Chaturthi, the festival celebrating Ganesh, the elephant headed god, whose favourite sweet is supposed to be laddu. In Maharashtra, modak, a laddu like sweet dish, is considered Ganesh's favourite sweet. It is nice that our gods change their favourite sweet according to the tastes of the devotees in each state!

Apart from daal bati churma, a Rajasthani thali will always include a number of vegetarian dishes. A number of Rajasthani vegetarian dishes use a preparation called **Gatte** (singular gatta) as the main ingredient. Gatte are fried besan pieces which are made from a dough of besan mixed with yoghurt and spices. The dough is shaped into thin cylindrical, sausage-like shapes and these are boiled in water first. They are then cut into small discs and fried till they are browned on the outside. These fried besan pieces are called gatte. They can be eaten on their own as a side dish or snack but are more commonly added as an ingredient to main dishes.

The most common dish of gatte in a thali or a meal is **Gatte ki Sabji**. The curry in gatte ki sabji is a smooth gravy with onions and yoghurt giving it body. (In the Jain version, there will be no onions and the curry will be either only of yoghurt or yoghurt with tomato). The gravy is then spiced with the standard powdered spices and cooked till it is thick and consistent. The turmeric added to the yoghurt gives the curry a nice yellow colour. The gatte pieces are added at the last stage. It is a simple dish where the gatte provide the dish substance in the absence of meat and vegetables and the taste comes from the spices used in the curry. It is very widely eaten in the state, found at homes and in restaurants and eateries of all types. The dish can be eaten with rice or roti.

Shahi Gatte, also called **Govind Gatte**, is a richer, in cost and ingredients, version of gatte ki sabji. Before the gatte rolls are boiled, they are stuffed with paneer (cottage cheese) or mawa (thickened milk) or both. Otherwise the cooking process is the same as the plain gatte ki sabji. The title shahi in this case seems to indicate some connection with royal kitchens. It is more likely just an adjective applied to differentiate it from the plain gatte ki sabji. Shahi gatte, in keeping with its elevated status, is eaten with naan or paratha not just plain roti, for a more indulgent meal.

Gatte are also used the main ingredient in a couple of rice dishes. Rice dishes are not that common in Rajasthani food, so these are special occasion dishes. **Gatte ka Pulao** is definitely a special and festive occasion dish, with gatte substituting for meat. Compared to the pulao found in other north Indian states, this should be considered one of the simpler varieties. A variant of this dish is **Gatte ki Khichri**. Rice and a lentil, such as moong daal, are boiled together to make a somewhat dry, thick and plain khichri. This khichri is then cooked in spices with the cooked gatte for the full dish.

Gatte ki sabji is related to karhi badi that is found in other states. There are a couple of differences. Gatte, unlike badi, have yoghurt as a key ingredient for softness and is boiled to keep its softness when cooked; the secondary deep frying is only done to brown the surface. Second, the curry of gatte ki sabji has no besan, unlike the karhi of karhi badi. There is a dish in Rajasthan called **Karhi Pakora** which is also of the same family of dishes. Rajasthani karhi is the same construction as the karhi found in other parts of north India, but usually cooked without any onions or garlic in conformance with Jain traditions. A liquid mix of besan and yoghurt with turmeric powder and salt is added to a range of whole spices fried in oil. The mix is then cooked together to get karhi. It is a really simple dish to make and is often served as a side dish in a full meal or thali. If you add fried pakoras, made by deep frying dollops of a batter of spiced besan, to karhi you get karhi pakora.

Gatte are so widely used mainly because there are not many vegetables which are native to Rajasthan. One dish, known probably because it is unusual rather than for any real culinary distinctiveness, is **Ker Sangri ki Sabji**, made of ker or kair berries and sangri beans which grow in the scrublands of the state. The dish is made as a dry, masala dish. The berries and the beans need to be soaked for a few hours to soften them before they are boiled. The boiled vegetables are fried with whole and powdered spices, including red chillies, and a little bit of yoghurt till the masala coats the vegetables. So, a typical vegetable masala dish with atypical vegetables.

The most common meal in rural Rajasthan is **Bajre ki Roti**, a roti made of bajra (pearl millet), eaten with a simple chutney called **Lahsoon ki Chutney** or garlic chutney. As we have seen in other parts of the country, such simple meals are not a matter of choice but mostly due to poverty. Rotis made of millets are more difficult to make, coarser and not as good to taste than those made of atta (wheat flour). They have been popular traditionally because of being more easily available and cheaper. A modern twist is that they are now considered healthier than wheat flour rotis because they are gluten free, high on fibre and have good nutrients. The chutney is made by grinding together garlic with red chillies and seasoning. It is a chutney that is often served in more elaborate meals as well and is quite a tasty if sharp accompaniment.

Most of the flatbreads found in north India, such as roti, poori and paratha, are also widely eaten in the urban and rural areas of Rajasthan. A type of roti called **Missi Roti** is popular all over north India including Rajasthan. This roti is made of a mixed flour of besan and atta. Proportions are up to personal preferences; an equal proportion is probably the most common. The flour is spiced with whole spice seeds, red chilli, asafoetida, turmeric and also has chopped onions, green chillies, ginger, coriander, etc. The rotis are cooked over a tawa usually with a little bit of oil or ghee. They are eaten with daal, pickles, etc. for a full meal.

Besan is also used to make another flatbread called **Chilla** or **Cheela**, a dish found in many states but which may be of Rajasthani origin. This dish is often described as 'dosa made from besan'. Besan is mixed with spices as in the missi roti but more quantity of water is added to get a pouring consistency. Chopped onions, tomatoes, green chillies, ginger and coriander are also usually added to the batter. The batter is then cooked by spreading a thin layer on a pan greased with oil, just as for dosa. Chilla is a breakfast dish, eaten with yoghurt or chutney. Like masala dosa, chilla can also be stuffed with a spicy potato or paneer preparation to get a masala variant. Most fans of dosa will chafe at the comparison but it is quite justified. I know that I mistook a plain chilla for a type of dosa the first time I ate it, before being gently corrected by my host.

Many of the above dishes are often served together in a full meal or thali. While there is no fixed list of dishes in a thali, a Rajasthani vegetarian thali may typically include the following dishes: gatte ki sabji, karhi, ker sangri ki sabji, daal, boondi raita, roti, papad, lahsoon chutney and pickles. The dishes are served in small bowls, so the meal while rich in variety is not necessarily large. I've eaten

Rajasthani thalis both in restaurants and at homes and never found the quantity of food to be overwhelming.

Rajasthani thali is sometimes also called 'Marwari thali'. The two are similar but not the same. The Marwari thali is associated with a community of people from Rajasthan collectively referred to as 'Marwari', a community known in India for its business and trading acumen.

The name of the community is derived from the region of Marwar, the name of one of the larger old Rajput kingdoms, now no longer in existence, in the south west of the state in and around Jodhpur. But the Marwari name has traditionally been applied to the business and merchant community from not just Marwar but also other districts in Rajasthan. People of the bania or trader castes from these regions were initially merchants and moneylenders in the region, along the trade route from Delhi to Gujarat. During the Mughal period, many of them migrated to the main trading centres of the empire especially in north, central and east India. Small communities of Marwaris settled in key cities such as Delhi, Agra, Surat, Kanpur, Banaras, Patna, Murshidabad, Dhaka (now in Bangladesh), etc. and became critical to the economy of the empire. By the time of the later Mughals in the eighteenth century, they were the most prominent merchant and moneylending community in north India. One family of Marwaris was even bestowed the title of Jagat Seth ('banker of the world') by the Mughal emperor and was one of the main financiers of the economy for many decades.

As the British East India Company gained power in the east of the country, the Marwaris became their intermediaries in local trade. They continued to flourish as the British rule was established in India. In the twentieth century, many of the bigger Marwari families became industrialists; the Birla family are the most famous of these. Marwari families continue to be prominent in Indian business today.

The Marwari are not a homogeneous group. Within the community are Jains and Hindus, even some Muslims. They are known to be socially conservative and the Jain and Hindu parts of the communities practice lacto-vegetarianism. Some Jains also have further restrictions on eating root vegetables including potatoes, onions, garlic, etc. In matters of food, Marwaris have been remarkably loyal to the cuisine of their origin. A Marwari meal hence bears a lot of similarity to a vegetarian Rajasthani meal, irrespective of where in India they are. In Rajasthan itself, a Marwari meal will be different from the usual Rajasthani meal mainly in the absence of root vegetables. The dishes otherwise are likely to be the same.

Papad is a must-have accompaniment to a Rajasthani thali. Papad, also called poppadum and a variety of other names all over India, is a pan-Indian dish and has already been mentioned several times in this book. They are crisp, brittle and almost always circular shaped. They are made of a lentil flour, usually urad, mixed with salt and oil, rolled out into a very thin, flat circle and then dried, traditionally in the sun. The flour may also be flavoured with chilli, black pepper, asafoetida, cumin seeds, etc. Once dried, they can be stored for a long time. Before eating, each dried papad is either deep fried in oil or roasted directly over fire or in an oven. While they can be made from scratch at home, packaged dried papads have been available for decades and are the easiest way to have papad. In most Indian meals, papads are served with the main meal and tend to be an accompaniment, to be crushed into small bits and mixed in with rice and daal or a curried dish for an added feel of savoury crunch.

One creative use of papad can be seen in Rajasthan in a dish called **Papad ki Sabji**, or a vegetable dish of papad. This may be the only dish where papad is used as an ingredient as far as I know. The curry is made by frying onions or tomatoes in oil with the standard spices and then thickened with yoghurt. Roasted or fried papad pieces are added to the curry and cooked along with the curry. They lose their crispiness when cooked in the curry. The result is a somewhat strange but quite tasty dish. This is another example of ingenuity in vegetarian dishes in Rajasthan. It is a dish extensively prepared at homes in the hot summer months when vegetable availability is especially low.

There are other dishes that may also be served in a typical thali. A full meal is sometimes started with a sweet dish called **Lapsi**. This is a Gujarati dish also found in Rajasthan. It is made by roasting daliya (broken wheat) in ghee and then boiling in water. Once cooked, sugar and chopped nuts are added. This is a dish used as a prasad or food offering on religious occasions, so sometimes a festive meal starts off with a small quantity of this prasad as a first course.

Boondi Raita is a special type of raita. Boondi are small drops of plain besan batter deep fried in oil. These added to yoghurt with a few spices gives us boondi raita. This is a simple dish, made even simpler by the fact that boondi is easily available as a packaged product in grocery stores, so preparing this dish requires no cooking. Boondi is quite versatile. Dunked into sugar syrup, it makes for a sweet called bundiya, described in earlier chapters. In a plan or salted form, it can also be added to chaat or vegetable dishes for a bit of texture and crunchiness.

The main sweet dish in a thali is typically a laddu and/or a halwa. An unusual type of halwa served with a Rajasthani thali is **Moong Daal Halwa**. Lentils don't seem an obvious candidate for a dessert, so there is bit of magic required for this dish. That magic comes from using lots of ghee to roast the ground moong daal. The ghee needs to be absorbed by the daal paste. Once the ghee is absorbed, a solution of milk and sugar is added to the roasted daal. The mashed daal provides body to the halwa and is basically a conduit for the taste of ghee, milk and sugar.

Most of the above dishes are fairly easy to make. While this is true for most Rajasthani vegetarian dishes, one delicacy called **Dahi ke Kabab** is more complicated. I first came across this dish in a couple of upscale restaurants in Jaipur, but it may not be a Rajasthani speciality as I've since found it in other states. It is often called the vegetarian galauti kabab as it has a similar soft, melt in the mouth texture. The key ingredients are hung curd and roasted besan. The hung curd requires quite a bit of preparation time. Fresh yoghurt needs to have the whey completely taken out, requiring the yoghurt to be strained for six to eight hours. If this is not done properly, the kababs will be difficult to shape. Roasted besan gives the kabab body. There is a fine balance in the quantity of besan used as the kababs become harder and don't taste as good with more besan. Lots of other ingredients go into the kabab dough. The kababs are shaped by hand into patties which are pan fried with a lot of care. If well-made, they come out really soft and deserving of the 'vegetarian galauti kabab' label.

Rajasthani food includes many of the non-vegetarian dishes that are found in other states of north India. This is due to both geographical proximity and cultural exchanges. There is no real boundary or separation between Rajasthan and its neighbouring states. The dishes of the north must have been historically known and eaten in Rajasthan by the non-vegetarians in the population. The best known non-vegetarian eating social class in Rajasthan are the Rajputs. The term means 'sons of kings' and was first used in around the eleventh century to denote the rulers and the ruling class of a number of kingdoms in north and north west India, including Rajasthan. The term is the label for 'a large multi-component cluster of castes, kin bodies, and local groups, sharing social status and ideology of genealogical descent'. From a food perspective, they eat meat and are credited with creating many of the non-vegetarian dishes of Rajasthani cuisine.

The Rajputs established a number of kingdoms in what is now Rajasthan. The region was in fact known as Rajputana, the land of Rajputs, in the past. The Rajput rulers of the various kingdoms that constitute the state of Rajasthan have been aligned with the empires of north India since the times of Emperor Akbar in the sixteenth century CE. It would be reasonable to expect that the secrets of the Mughal kitchens would have been known to the Rajput royal kitchens as well. However, there are not many examples of Mughlai dishes being refined or modified in Rajput kitchens. There is no 'Rajput biryani' or 'Jaipuri kabab'. The typical Rajasthani meat dishes seem to have emerged from local ingredients and practices, notably the tradition of hunting among Rajput kings and nobles.

Lal Maas or **Maans** is the best known non-vegetarian dish from Rajasthan, a fiery red meat curry originating from Rajput cuisine. The name translates simply to 'red meat'. It used to be and can be still made from any game meat, such as wild boar, venison, etc. though goat meat is most commonly used now. Red chillies are used in large quantity in this dish. They were used in the olden days not only for taste but also to help to mask the odour of the game meat. The chillies traditionally used are a Rajasthani variety called Mathania which gives a strong red colour to the dish (hence the name).

There are a few different ways to make lal maas. The common elements across the different ways to cook are the limited use of spices except large quantities of red chillies; slow cooking to make the meat tender and imbued with the chillies; and use of yoghurt to somewhat balance the heat of the dish. In the traditional way of making the dish, a special powder called kachri powder, made from a cucumber-like vegetable found in Rajasthan, is also added. It helps to soften the meat and adds a mild sour taste to the dish.

One method of cooking starts off with onions fried in ghee with a few whole spices to which ginger garlic paste, the meat and red chilli paste are added. The meat is first fried and then cooked in water till it is tender. Yoghurt is added at an intermediate or final stage. The chilli paste gives the dish its fiery colour and heat, though it is not uncommon to increase the heat with the addition of a bit more of red chilli powder. Mustard oil is the preferred cooking medium. There are very few spices used in this method of cooking which is unusual for an Indian dish. It was probably because this method of cooking was used in hunting camps where the mobile kitchens were lightly equipped.

Lal maas may be derived from a hunting dish called **Jungli Maans**. This dish is as simple as it gets. It is game meat or lamb cooked in a generous quantity of ghee with whole red chillies and salt. Water is added to get a bit of a gravy on the dish, otherwise it can be cooked dry. It is one of the simplest meat dishes, in terms of ingredients, that you will find in India.

Safed Maas, also called **Mohan Maas**, means white meat, clearly named in relation and contrast to lal maas. It is a more luxurious dish in terms of ingredients and is probably a dish from the Rajput royal kitchens. The curry is white or cream in colour as it gets its body from yoghurt, cream and milk. The dish can be made without chillies for a mild and atypical meat dish. Even if a few red chillies are added, this is still a much milder dish than lal maas. The initial process is fairly standard requiring whole spices to be roasted in ghee and then onions and ginger garlic paste to be fried. Since the gravy needs to be smooth the onion may be puréed rather than sliced. Mutton is separately boiled or fried to an almost cooked state and then added to the onion mix with yoghurt, cream and milk. The dish may also have a paste of nuts, including cashews, almonds, etc. added to it. Sometimes even khoya is added. Lal maas and safed maas are often served one after the other in an elaborate meal or a banquet, to give the diner an experience of a nice contrast of colour and tastes.

There aren't many speciality chicken dishes from Rajasthan. Many of the dishes described earlier in the chapters on Delhi/Punjab and Mughlai food are eaten in Rajasthan, often with minor adaptations in ingredients and process. For example, a type of chicken tikka called **Murgh ke Sule** is often part of elaborate, non-vegetarian meals. Small pieces of boneless chicken are marinated in yoghurt, ginger garlic paste and spices, including red chilli, black pepper and kachri powder. The chicken pieces are then skewered and roasted. The dish, like chicken tikka, is served with raw onion and a green chutney and can also be served as an appetiser or as a party snack.

Like Gujarat, Rajasthan also has a number of snacks. A snack from Rajasthan known all over the country is **Bikaneri Bhujia**. It is a sev like snack, originating from Bikaner in north west Rajasthan. Sev, as described earlier, are small strings of deep fried besan, used in many chaats. Bikaneri bhujia is made from the flour of a lentil called Moth or Moth daal which grows locally. The cooking process is similar to that of sev: the batter is pressed through a special type of sieve to get strings dropping into hot oil to be deep fried. Bikaneri bhujia is a deeper colour and crunchier than sev. It is also supposed to have a much longer shelf life. It is eaten as a snack and may also be sprinkled on dishes for added crunchiness.

Bikaneri bhujia was popularised nationally by a snack manufacturer called Haldiram's. This company started as a sweet and snack shop in the Bhujia Bazaar of Bikaner in 1937. This is a bazaar where practically every shop seems to make large quantities of the local bhujia every day, leading a local wit to comment that 'this is a city where one half of the population is occupied with making bhujia and the other half with eating it'. Haldiram's has since grown into a large company manufacturing and selling a variety of packaged food products, though Bikaneri bhujia remains one of its flagship products.

A friend, Manoj, who is from Bikaner, used to wax eloquent about Bikaneri bhujia when we were studying together in Calcutta. The south Indians in our group of friends had never heard of Bikaneri bhujia. To make converts of us all, Manoj brought bhujia from Bikaner to the hostel a few times. I remember this more because of his impassioned advocacy of the bhujia rather than its taste. He may have been on to something. The Bikaneri bhujia was given a Geographical Indication in 2010 to prevent snack manufacturers from calling any old sev 'Bikaneri bhujia'. The making of bhujia is a big cottage industry in and around Bikaner and the GI is probably less for culinary distinctiveness and more for economic protection.

I've described kachori earlier in the Uttar Pradesh chapter. Kachoris are very popular in Rajasthan, both for breakfast and as snacks. Kachoris are not complicated in terms of ingredients but require a bit of time and effort. As a result, they are popular as street food and mostly eaten outside homes at small eateries and snack shops. A type of kachori, called **Pyaaj ki Kachori** (onion kachori) is a Rajasthani speciality. Contrary to its name, its stuffing has a good quantity of not only onions but also potatoes. The kachori itself is similar to what is found in other north Indian states. **Mawa Kachori**, another type of kachori, is a sweet dish made on special occasions and festivals. This is a kachori made of maida, stuffed with sweetened mawa or khoya and nuts, deep fried and further dipped in a sugar syrup.

Rajasthanis, like people all over India, are fond of sweets. Sweets described in earlier chapters, such as gulab jamun, jalebi, laddu, different types of barfi, rasmalai, rabri, halwa, kheer, etc., can easily be found in sweet shops in Rajasthan.

There are not many sweets which are found only in Rajasthan. One such traditional sweet, associated with religious festivals, is **Ghewar**. It is made of maida mixed with ghee, milk and water to a pouring consistency. When cooked, it comes out as a disc the size of a roti but much thicker, with a hole in the centre and is usually served with a topping of rabri or malai (cream). It is one of the more complicated sweets to make, made at homes only during festivals but available in sweet shops more routinely. The complicated part is deep frying the batter to get a golden brown, lacy disc with a hole in the centre. This is achieved by pouring the batter into circular moulds for shape. The moulds don't have a bottom and float in hot oil. The batter is poured into thin strings. As the strings cook, they are gently pushed against the walls of the mould to create a disc with a hole in the centre. Once cooked, each disc is dunked in flavoured sugar syrup and then topped with rabri or cream. The sweet is generally eaten as stand-alone dish.

Daal Bati

Gatte Ki Sabji

Lal Maas

Bikaneri Bhujia

15
Best of the Rest
Some well known, others not so much

I've so far described the prominent regional cuisines of India. There are pockets of distinctive food found in other states as well. My experience of these foods is more limited, but for the sake of completeness I've described a personal selection of dishes from other states, some well known, others not so much.

Kashmir

Ideally, Kashmir should have a full chapter on its cuisine. But I've never been to Kashmir and only eaten Kashmiri dishes occasionally. My most direct experience of traditional Kashmiri food has been in Delhi in a somewhat unusual way. We know someone from Kashmir who has a business selling Kashmiri carpets and handicrafts. A few times, after he has managed to get us to buy a carpet or a handicraft of value, he throws in a home-cooked Kashmiri dinner as part of the deal. So, I've had the chance to try many of the dishes that I've described below. But it is a small sample of all the delights that make up Kashmiri cuisine.

Kashmir is part of Jammu & Kashmir, till recently the northern most state of the country. In a recent controversial decision, the central government split the state into two Union Territories (a Union Territory is directly administered by the central government): Jammu & Kashmir and Ladakh. Kashmir is the northern part of the former, a large valley between the Himalaya and Pir Panjal mountain ranges. It is a beautiful place with a mild and pleasant climate for most of the year and a few cold months in winter. It has millennia-long traditions of eating meat and using whole spices in curries to provide warmth. Apart from the plains of north India, the major influences have been from Central Asia and Persia. While Kashmiri food is often grouped together with Mughlai cuisine, it has actually evolved independently and is reasonably different.

One of the remarkable features of Kashmiri food is the celebratory or special occasion feast called **Wazwan**. This is a multi-course feast and in its most elaborate form can consist of thirty-six (!) courses. Most of the dishes are meat based. Not for the faint hearted or those with small appetites. Even a smaller wazwan would have no less than fifteen courses. There are set rules about how the meal is eaten and a defined sequence of courses. Diners are seated in groups of four and each group eats out of a shared large plate. The plate is initially served with a large mound of rice, marked out into quarters by seekh kababs, and a few courses. The rest of the courses then follow. I've eaten some individual dishes but never a full wazwan. Having seen the full list of dishes, I wonder how anyone could work through all those dishes in one meal. The trick seems to be to have only a little of each dish. As many of the dishes are quite delicious, this can be difficult.

Kashmiri food has lots of meat. Mutton (goat meat), lamb (sheep meat) and chicken are the most popular. There are many different types of curried dishes with yoghurt used extensively in curries. In a marked difference from Mughlai food, dishes tend to be made with more of whole spices and less of the myriad powdered spices of north Indian and Mughlai food. Dry ginger powder and ground fennel seeds are a couple of unusual spices used in many dishes.

Kashmiri red chilli, a type of chilli which carries the name of the region, is used extensively for colour. These chillies are quite mild, so the dishes are not hot. Kashmiri chilli is used in curries all over India. Most of the output of Kashmir itself is locally consumed, so the Kashmiri chilli generally used is actually grown elsewhere, with Karnataka being one of the main producers. Just as well that the Kashmiri red chilli does not have a Geographical Indication. That would create problems for curries all over the country.

One of the best known Kashmiri dishes is **Rogan Josh**, which is always part of a wazwan meal and described earlier in the Mughlai chapter. The Kashmiri version is not the fiery curry that you get in many Indian restaurants outside India but a beautifully flavoured, red coloured mutton curry.

A well-known Kashmiri dish, which is also always part of a wazwan meal, is **Gushtaba** or **Goshtaba**. This dish is usually the last meat dish of the meal and is followed by desserts. It is a complicated and time-consuming dish to cook. The meat is in the form of gently spiced meat balls in a curry mainly of yoghurt. The meat is traditionally pounded with a wooden mallet till it becomes completely soft and pulpy. This process takes time and effort. The meat can be directly spiced with ginger powder, ground fennel seeds, black pepper, etc. before being shaped into balls. The curry is separately cooked by whisking yoghurt with milk and water to a thin liquid. The liquid is boiled with ghee or mustard oil and a few whole spices. The meat balls are then added to the curry and the whole mix simmered till the balls are cooked and soft. Alternatively, the meat balls may be separately boiled in water with whole spices and then added with the stock to the yoghurt-based curry at an intermediate stage. The curry is pale coloured. Gushtaba is quite a mild dish with a wonderful aroma. It can be eaten as a main dish outside a wazwan and is best eaten with rice.

A complementary dish to gushtaba, and also included in a wazwan, is **Rista** or **Riste**. It is similar to gushtaba but with a red curry and spicier. The meat balls are prepared in the same way as gushtaba, though to differentiate, the rista balls are slightly smaller. When preparing for a wazwan, the meat balls for both the dishes are prepared at the same time. If prepared independently, the rista meat balls may have red chilli powder added for a bit of heat. Traditionally, the curry is a thin curry made by cooking chilli paste with asafoetida and water, coloured red with a solution of local flower called moval (cockscomb). Sometimes fried onion paste may be added to give the curry a bit more body. Simmering the meat balls in the curry makes them absorb some of the chilli and the colour, so this dish is visually and in taste quite different from gushtaba though similar in construction.

Mutton Yakhni is yet another dish with a mild, yoghurt-based curry. This is a simpler dish than gushtaba and rista. The mutton is first separately sautéed and boiled with whole spices. Yoghurt is added to this meat and stock and the whole mix simmered till the meat softens and the curry has the desired consistency. Traditionally, yakhni does not have any chilli, though a bit of chilli does it no harm.

A special Kashmiri dish which is not usually part of wazwan is **Gucchi Pulao**. **Gucchi** is the name for a special type of mushroom, morel mushroom, which grows naturally in the foothills of the Himalayas. These mushrooms are not cultivable and hence have to be foraged. Being rare, they are very expensive. They don't look like regular button mushrooms and have heads shaped like twisted, cellular structures. They have a strong, savoury taste and are used as the star ingredient in a number of dishes. Gucchi pulao is considered one of the better ways of eating gucchi as the spices can be kept to a minimum to let the taste of the mushroom come through, with the rice giving the dish volume. The cooking process is like a vegetable pulao where sliced gucchi pieces are fried in ghee with a few whole spices, rice is added and then the mix cooked in water.

There is a vegetarian dish from Kashmir which has been adopted and adapted in many other states. This is **Kashmiri Aloo Dum**, or **Dum Olav** as it is locally called. I've described a couple of variants of this dish earlier in the chapters on Bengal and Uttar Pradesh. All Indian cookbooks have some version of this dish included. In the Kashmiri dish, the curry is made of yoghurt with a masala paste of Kashmiri red chillies, ginger powder, ground fennel seeds, etc. The potatoes are separately boiled or fried and then added to the gravy and cooked, such that a thick, smooth gravy coats the potatoes. I've described this dish quite simply, but it looks and tastes fantastic. The dish is one of the best examples of how the humble potato can be transformed through great cooking.

Kashmir can get quite cold. Hot tea drinks are hence quite popular, on their own and with meals. A special tea called **Kahwa** is served at the end of meals. This is a green tea, flavoured with spices, such as cardamom, cloves, cinnamon and saffron, and served with chopped nuts. Milk is normally not added to this tea though a bit of honey may be added for sweetness. Apart from kahwa, a salty tea called **Noon Chai** is the hot beverage of choice in Kashmir. A bit of baking soda added to the drink gives it a pink colour. It is made by boiling tea leaves first with water, salt and baking soda and then with milk. Salty tea can be a shock to the taste buds the first time. It helps that the drink looks nothing like tea, so if you pretend you are drinking some exotic salty pink beverage, all should be fine.

Madhya Pradesh

Madhya Pradesh (MP) is the second largest state by area in India and is in the centre of the country. It is named accordingly: Madhya Pradesh translates to 'central province'. It is bordered by Uttar Pradesh in the north, Chhattisgarh in the east (Chhattisgarh used to be a part of MP till 2000), Maharashtra to the south, Gujarat and Rajasthan to its west. The foods of all these states have influenced the food of MP, with the strongest influence being from UP and Rajasthan. The western part of MP has been populated since ancient times and has a long history. It is reasonable to assume that the food of this part of the state has influenced the foods of its neighbouring regions as much as been influenced by them.

I've only been to the state for a couple of times for holidays, though I've passed through it a number of times on train journeys. One abiding memory is of wonderful hospitality from the local staff of the Taj group hotel at Khajuraho. The MP tourism agency extols the hospitality of its people, as you would expect such an agency to do. But we had the rare experience of something actually out of the ordinary. We were holidaying in Khajuraho, the town with the famous old temples with racy sculptures, on our first anniversary. I had booked a dinner at the restaurant of the Taj hotel and informed them about its celebratory nature. The staff were extra solicitous and we had a wonderful candle-lit dinner. The restaurant did the gracious thing of bringing out a complimentary celebration cake for us. We paid by signing for the bill and left quite happy and satisfied. So far, very good but nothing out of the ordinary. The extraordinary part was that the restaurant never presented the bill to my credit card. Without making a fuss about it or even telling us overtly, they made the whole dinner complimentary. I've been a fan of the Taj hotel group ever since but I am sure that the hospitality of the local staff had as much of a role.

The capital of MP is Bhopal. The city is unfortunately better known for one of the world's worst industrial disasters. In 1984, toxic gases leaked from a pesticides factory in the city owned by the multinational Union Carbide. More than 600,000 people were exposed. The death toll over the years has been in many thousands, with the health of hundreds of thousands impacted even decades after the gas leak.

Bhopal is also known for its food. In the weakening of the Mughal empire in the eighteenth century, one of the Mughal soldiers established a small kingdom in Bhopal. It somehow survived through the chaos of that century and continued as one of the princely states during the British rule. Mughlai food was hence the dominant cuisine of the upper classes here, with a couple of specialities credited to the city. One interesting historic fact. During most of the nineteenth century, the kingdom was ruled by queens rather than kings. Under four successive Begums (queens) ruling from 1837 to 1926, Bhopal saw modernisation with much attention given to public works, arts and culture.

There are a couple of Mughlai dishes associated with Bhopal. One of them is **Bhopali Gosht Korma**, the name making the origin indisputable. This dish is different from the mild Mughlai korma dish described earlier. The main difference is the use of a variety of whole spices in a special masala paste, including a couple of non-standard ones such as mace and nutmeg. Mutton is boiled separately with seasoning and then cooked in fried onions, ginger garlic paste, chilli powder, etc. To this mix, the special masala paste and yoghurt are added. The curry of the dish is not very hot (it is after all a korma dish) but has a stronger spiciness due to the whole spices used.

Chicken Rizzala or **Green Chicken Korma** is also believed to be a Bhopal speciality. The green colour of the gravy in this dish comes from using lots of coriander leaves along with mint leaves. There are a couple of ways of making this dish. A modern technique requires fried onions, coriander leaves, mint leaves and green chillies to be puréed. Chicken pieces are fried with spices and then the green paste is added for the gravy. Alternatively, the whole gravy is cooked first with onions, yoghurt, coriander leaves and spices till you have a green mush. The chicken is then added to the mush and cooked till done. By the time the chicken is cooked, the green mush becomes a thick gravy. The use of coriander to give body to the gravy is unusual in Indian cooking. Coriander leaves are normally used only for flavouring. One other dish which uses coriander leaves in the gravy is chicken cafreal, found in Goa and described in that chapter. The two dishes taste quite different though as the rizzala has a Mughlai spicy taste compared to the vinegary taste of the cafreal.

Yet another green coloured dish is **Palak Poori**, found in a number of northern states and quite popular in MP especially during festivals. This is not a complicated dish. A paste of spinach leaves, green chillies and ginger is mixed into wheat flour to make the dough. Once the dough is prepared, then the process is the same as a normal poori, that is individual pooris are rolled out and deep fried in oil till they puff out nicely. The palak pooris have a distinct tinge of green and are easy to identify. They can be eaten with any of the dishes that pooris are eaten with but also just with chutney and pickles.

Kachori, with a stuffing of lentils, is as popular in MP as it is UP and Rajasthan. In most of MP a variety called **Khasta Kachori**, meaning crispy kachori, is among the most popular street foods. The flour for this type of kachori can be of maida or atta or a mix. The stuffing is a mix of urad daal and moong daal, fried in whole and powdered spices.

An unusual street food found in Indore, a city famous for its street food, is called **Bhutte ka Kees**, made of corn. This is best described as a savoury corn halwa. Grated corn is added to fried cumin seeds, asafoetida, ginger and chillies. After frying the mix, milk is added till the corn is cooked and a halwa-like mush remains. It is served with grated coconut and may even have a bit of sugar sprinkled. It is meant to be eaten as a snack, though depending on the size of the serving, it could even be a light meal.

A wonderful sweet dish from MP is **Mawa Bati**. It looks like gulab jamun and also has mawa or khoya as the main ingredient. The main difference from gulab jamun is that the mawa bati is cooked crisp on the outside. The dough is made of the same type of special mawa used for gulab jamun, mixed with maida, milk powder, etc. The dough balls are deep fried in ghee till they are a dark brown and crisp on the outside. They are then soaked in sugar syrup. Think of this dish as a crispy gulab jamun and similarly quite sweet.

Odisha

Odisha (which used to be spelt Orissa till 2011) is an eastern state with a long coast with the Bay of Bengal. It shares borders with West Bengal, Jharkhand, Chhattisgarh and Andhra Pradesh.

Odisha has a long tradition of culinary excellence based on local ingredients. It is believed that many Odia (the people of Odisha) cooks plied their skills in the rich households of Bengal in the last few centuries and many of the best known Bengali dishes may be Odia in origin. This is similar to the story of French cuisine being developed by Italian cooks brought by Catherine de' Medici, who became queen of France by marriage in the sixteenth century. In the case of Odisha, it has led to skittishness on origins of dishes, including the roshogolla controversy described earlier in the Bengal chapter. For simplicity, I've restricted my description to some of the common dishes found in the state today irrespective of origins.

Like the Kashmiri wazwan, many of Odisha's popular vegetarian dishes can be found in or take inspiration from one grand meal. This is the **Chhappan Bhog** ('Meal of fifty-six dishes') which makes up the Mahaprasad (great religious food offering) of the famous Jagannath Temple in Puri, a town in Odisha. The main deity of the temple is Jagannath, another name for Krishna. There are a couple of religious beliefs that explain the existence and importance of the Mahaprasad in this temple. The first is the belief that, of the four 'dhams' or main religious sites of Hinduism associated with Vishnu (Krishna is an avatar of Vishnu), he bathes at Rameswaram (in Tamil Nadu), dresses at Dwarka (in Gujarat), eats at Puri (in Odisha) and meditates at Badrinath (in Uttarakhand). Because he eats in Puri, the ritual of offering food to the deity becomes especially grand here, hence the Mahaprasad. The fifty-six dishes practice is associated with a particular feat of Krishna. He protected his village from the wrath of the rain god by lifting a mountain (on one finger no less!), under which the villagers sheltered for seven days. In doing so, he had to fast for the duration. The chhappan bhog is essentially thanking him and giving him back the fifty-six dishes (seven days, eight dishes daily) that he missed during his fast.

As an aside, the deities of Jagannath Temple are carried out in a chariot in an annual procession around the town accompanied by thousands of devotees. The word 'juggernaut' was derived from this Jagannath Temple procession.

The dishes prepared for the Mahaprasad are sold, after being offered to the deities, in a dedicated marketplace in the temple. They provide a good representation of the vegetarian dishes that are part of Odisha cuisine. The dishes include preparations of rice, lentils, vegetables, milk, sweet dishes, pancakes and snacks. I've been to Puri a couple of times and am reasonably sure that I've had a few dishes from the Mahaprasad. Unfortunately, I don't remember specific dishes in any detail. I don't think that is a damning statement on the dishes as both my trips were when I was quite young. The descriptions below are mostly based on research and other people's experiences.

Plain rice is called **Anna** in Odia, similar to annam in Andhra Pradesh, both words are derived from the Sanskrit word for food. Simple rice preparations include anna, ghee anna, khechudi (same as khichri), etc. One of the notable rice dishes is cooked rice mixed with water and salt called **Pakhala**. While pakhala dishes in the Mahaprasad are made from rice cooked on the day, this is a dish often made at homes from leftover rice. **Dahi Pakhala**, cooked rice mixed with yoghurt, salt and water, is the most popular variant. Onions and green chillies may be used as garnishing to alleviate the blandness. A couple of other varieties are **Ada Pakhala**, cooked rice with ginger and water, and **Mitha Pakhala**, cooked rice with sugar and water. **Basi (stale) Pakhala** is cooked rice in water and fermented overnight. All these variants are eaten at breakfast or lunch and act as coolants during summer months.

Dalma is a special type of dal. The way it is written, it can sound like 'mother of daal' but that is probably just coincidence. It is a lentil and vegetable stew made of toor daal and a selection of vegetables, from brinjal, pumpkin, yam, bottle gourd, papaya, raw banana etc. The daal stew is flavoured with a spice combination special to Odisha food called **Panch** or **Pancho Phutana**. This is a mix of five whole spices (similar but not the same as the Bengali panch phoran): mustard, cumin, fenugreek, fennel and nigella seeds roasted in mustard oil.

The vegetable dishes can be of a few different types. Most are similar to vegetables dishes found in the northern and eastern states. Green, leafy vegetables are widely eaten and are collectively labelled **Saaga** (or saag). The name of the vegetable is put as a prefix. Thus, **Kosala saaga** is made of amaranth leaves, **Palanga saaga** of spinach, etc. These dishes are simply vegetable leaves pan fried in mustard oil with a few spices and cooked till the leaves become a mush. In some cases, saaga is given a bit of crunch with fried 'badi', fried droplets made of lentil batter. Other types of vegetable dishes are made with a thin curry of onions fried in spices and coconut milk. These are generically called **Rossa** (similar to rasa). For example, a vegetable curry made of potatoes and pointed gourd is called **Aloo Potol Rossa**.

Odisha's cuisine stands out for its sweets. A number of sweet dishes are collectively labelled **Pitha**. They are cake or pancake-like dishes, mostly made during religious festivals. A few of them are also part of the Mahaprasad. One of the more popular ones is **Poda Pitha**. It is quite a difficult dish to cook and get right. It is made from a batter of fermented rice paste and skinless black gram. Grated coconut, jaggery, ginger, cashew nuts, raisins and baking powder are mixed into the batter. The batter was traditionally baked in a closed container over a charcoal fire. It may now be baked over low heat in a cooker or in an oven. The batter needs to cook thorough with the outer surface brown and crusty and the inside soft. It is not always easy to get right. Once cooked, it is served cut into cake-like slices.

Chhena is the favoured ingredient in a number of milk-based sweets. The Odisha **Rasagola**, like the Bengali roshogolla and the north Indian rasgulla, is made of chhena shaped into small, spongy balls and cooked in sugar syrup. The Geographical Indication to the Odisha variant has been given on the grounds of its somewhat different size and texture. But as I've said earlier, that may be a clever bureaucratic fudge to try and kill off a pointless controversy.

A dish made of chhena and indeed originating from Odisha is called **Rasabali**. Chhena, mixed with sugar and a little flour, is shaped into balls or patties and then deep fried in oil till the outer surface becomes charred brown. The balls are then soaked in sweetened and flavoured milk. Each serving is a couple of the fried chhena balls or patties floating in the sweet milk. The dish is similar to rasmalai (which is rasgulla served in sweet, thickened milk or rabri) and as delightful.

Another unique preparation of chhena from Odisha is called **Chhena Poda**. It is supposed to be Lord Jagannath's favourite sweet and is very popular in the state. It is quite easily found in sweet shops, but also made at homes as it is a relatively simple dish to make. The dough is made of chhena mixed with sugar or jaggery, cardamom powder and chopped cashew nuts and raisins, with a little bit of rice flour or semolina. The dough is baked in a dish lined with sal leaves. The baking gives the top surface a brown colour and a cake-like appearance. It is served in slices and eaten as a snack or with meals.

Apart from the vegetarian chhappan bhog dishes, the cuisine of Odisha includes many meat and fish dishes. For a state with a long coastline, freshwater fish are surprisingly preferred over the saltwater variety. Rohu and Katla are the preferred varieties. The most common fish dish is **Machha Jhol**, a fish curry with a thin curry, with onions fried in mustard oil with spices, including ground mustard seeds for a distinctive taste. Comparisons with the more famous Bengali machher jhol are inevitable. A variant is **Dahi Machha**, a curried fish dish with a yoghurt-based curry. Prawns, called chingudi locally, are the most common seafood, generally sourced from prawn farms in the state and in Andhra Pradesh to its south. Prawn dishes can be prepared as a jhol (thin curry) or dry fried along with some vegetables.

Assam and the North East States

The North East states comprise Assam, Sikkim, Meghalaya, Arunachal Pradesh, Nagaland, Manipur, Tripura and Mizoram. In the past, they used to be called the 'seven sisters', before the kingdom of Sikkim became a part of India in 1975. The eight states are collectively called the North East now, somehow the seven sisters label never converted to the eight sisters in popular idiom. Assam is the largest by population in this group, the rest are among the smallest states by population in India. With the exception of Assam, the other states are culturally quite different from the rest of the country. The people belong to many different tribes who have lived in these hilly states for centuries and have been relatively less influenced by the culture and habits of the people in the plains to their west in the sub-continent.

The food of the region is often grouped together as North Eastern food for convenience. There are some similarities across the region. The most obvious one, when you look at the food through the lens of Indian food, is the absence or limited use of the spices usually associated with Indian cuisine. There is very little use of the 'standard' spices of Indian cooking such as cumin, coriander, turmeric, cloves, cinnamon, cardamom, black pepper, etc. in the foods of the region. Chillies, however, are used extensively, sometimes as the only flavouring ingredient – one good example where 'hot' and 'spicy' are not synonymous. The preferred methods of cooking are boiling, roasting and stir-frying; extensive frying or deep frying is not as popular in the region as in the other parts of the country.

These are the similarities across the region, otherwise the food is not really the same across the eight states. The culture and food of Assam especially has elements of both Bengali and North East influences. My parents lived in Guwahati, the capital of Assam, for a few years during my undergraduate years and I ended up spending a number of holidays there. The impression I formed then was that the food is both similar and different to the food found in the Gangetic plain. In culinary terms, it tends towards simplicity and functionality, probably the reason why it is not mentioned often among the delights of the foods of India. That is also the reason why Assamese food does not feature much in restaurants outside the state.

Rice is the main grain in Assam, as in Bengal and Bangladesh. Most meals are eaten with boiled rice providing body to the meal. This is helped by the fact that rice grows easily in the state and many varieties of rice are grown locally. Due to an abundance of rivers and ponds, fish is the second most important food of Assamese cuisine. Fish is called Mas in the local language, which sounds like machh of Bengali but also like maans, the word for meat, in Hindi. **Masor Tenga**, a sour fish dish, is the signature dish of the state. A typical Assamese meal of rice, daal, vegetables and fish curry does not look very different from what you will find in Bengal though the dishes are cooked somewhat differently.

Meat dishes are of chicken, duck, pigeon and sometimes pork. Mutton and lamb are not that widely eaten due to lack of easy availability. Meat dishes are traditionally cooked as a broth, using ginger, garlic, curry leaves, lemon juice and fermented bamboo shoot. In the ingredients used, there is some similarities with the way meat is cooked in South East Asia.

Among other interesting features of the cuisine is the practice of eating insects. While not common in the urban areas, it is quite widespread among a number of the tribal communities. Red ant eggs are in fact considered a delicacy.

Assamese food uses more spices than the foods of the other North East states, but still less than the other parts of India. Chillies and locally grown herbs are extensively used. Assam is famous for producing **Bhoot Jolokia**, the 'ghost chilli', which is one of the hottest varieties of chilli and may have started the race for creating hotter and hotter hybrid chillies. It is not extensively used in regular cooking due to its heat but may be used in in chutneys and sometimes in pork and fish dishes.

One unique type of Assamese dish is **Khar**, the generic name for a range of dishes. A khar dish is typically served at the beginning of a meal. These dishes get their name from an alkaline liquid, also called khar or kola (banana) khar, which is made by mixing and filtering water added to ashes of dried, burnt banana skin. Used in small quantities, it is supposed to be a good stomach cleanser. In larger quantities it may even be used as a detergent to wash clothes! This liquid is added to a variety of dishes made of vegetables or fish. A traditional vegetarian khar is **Posola Khar**. The main ingredient is posola, the edible part of banana stems, cooked in mustard oil with ginger, garlic, chillies and a little bit of the kola khar liquid. Khar can be similarly added to dishes where the main ingredient is lentils or fish.

Complementary to the alkaline taste of khar is the sour taste of Tenga. The most common tenga dish is Masor Tenga, a lightly spiced sour fish curry. The sourness of the dish is usually from tomatoes but lemon or other souring agents may also be used. Any of the abundant local freshwater fish may be used for the masor tenga dish. The cooking process is straightforward. Fish pieces are first fried in oil with mustard seeds and then kept aside. In the most common variant, the curry is made by frying tomatoes in the same oil with turmeric, chillies and seasoning and then adding water for the curry. The fried fish pieces are added back to the curry at the final stage. The dish tastes sourer and is hotter than the Bengali machher jhol to which it is often compared.

Most Assamese meals are accompanied by a side dish of a mashed vegetable called **Pitika**. This is similar to the bharta or chokha dishes seen elsewhere in the country. Boiled or roasted vegetable is mashed and mixed with raw onions, green chillies, ginger, coriander leaves and mustard oil. Raw mustard oil gives this dish a distinctive, pungent taste. The most common pitika dish is made from mashed potatoes and is simply called **Aloo Pitika**.

One of the most unusual dishes found in Assamese food is made from silkworm pupae, locally called **Polu**. The pupae are boiled and then fried in mustard oil with ginger, garlic, chillies and salt. The dish is considered a snack and may be served with drinks. It is not normally a dish served with meals though some restaurants now do so, probably because of its exotic nature.

Most sweets found in Assam are also found in other eastern states. Bengali sweets such as roshogolla, shondesh, rasmalai, etc. are widely available in urban areas. **Pitha** is the name of a local range of sweet and savoury snacks made from rice. Variants of these are found in other eastern states as well. In Assam, they are mostly made during religious festivals and special occasions. There is a number of different types of pitha. Most are made from a specific type of sticky rice called bora rice. **Til Pitha** is a rice roll stuffed with til (sesame seeds) roasted, ground and mixed with melted jaggery. Another variant is **Ghila Pitha** in which coarse rice flour is mixed with melted jaggery, shaped into small patties and fried.

Assam is of course best known worldwide for its tea. **Assam tea** is a black tea, known for its strong taste and colour. The state is among the largest producers of tea in the world; Assam tea is available practically anywhere you get tea. A lot of the produce is consumed within India itself as this strong tea is especially preferred for the milky tea had all over the country.

While it is generally accepted that tea cultivation was introduced in India by the British to create an alternative production source to China, there is evidence that the specific variety of the Assam tea plant used to grow wild in Assam and was known to local tribes. Large scale cultivation started only in the early nineteenth century. The climate and soil of Assam was very suitable for tea cultivation and there has been no looking back. Tea has changed the agricultural economy of the state and it is now the most important part of the state's economy. In this case, the Geographical Indication for Assam Tea seems to be entirely justified.

In the rest of the North East states, foods vary by tribes. The tribes tend to have their own ways of cooking and specific, favoured dishes. One common feature is the need for preservation of food, through drying and fermentation or, in the case of meat, by salting and smoking. Pork is by far the most popular meat in these states. Each state has its own popular pork dish: a type of pork pulao in Meghalaya, pork stew with wild yam leaves in Nagaland, pork and bamboo shoot curry in Tripura, etc. Chicken, fish and beef are also eaten in all the states. No mention of North East food is complete without mentioning that dog meat is eaten in Nagaland: not widely, but enough for it to be well known. Meat dishes are mostly simply made, with the meat boiled with a vegetable or leaves and flavoured with ginger, garlic and chillies. Nothing that will particularly excite a gourmet.

Fish is eaten both fresh and fermented. Fish is often combined with vegetables or fruits or leaves. For example, in Manipur a salad made of papaya, chickpeas and fermented fish is quite popular. In Tripura, a fish paste made of fish fermented with salt and mustard oil, with a strong odour, is added to a number of dishes. Fish may also be combined with vegetables in a stew or soup for a simple, hearty and nutritious dish, if not really touching the high notes of culinary excellence. Most of the vegetables eaten in these states are found locally and foraging is unusually common in the more remote areas. Bamboo shoots and yams are regular food, eaten in combination with meat and fish or with other vegetables and fruits.

North East food is slowly getting known in other parts of the country. While there are not many specialist restaurants, a few adventurous ones have started listing North Eastern dishes in their menus. How popular these dishes prove to be in the rest of the country is yet to be seen. The limited use of spices may mean that the dishes may end up appealing only to a niche.

Gushtaba and Aloo Dum

Stuffed Kachori

Pakhala

Tea, India's favourite beverage

Final Word: The Future

Indian food continues to evolve. The latest trend is of fusion foods which combine elements of various regional Indian cuisines and other world cuisines in innovative ways. Many avant-garde chefs have been at the forefront of this trend. It is impossible to name all the fine chefs who have made their mark in the last couple of decades, but I'd like to mention a few. Manish Mehrotra helms the Indian Accent in Delhi, which has been rated the best restaurant in the country for the last few years. Similarly, Gaggan Anand, who has trained under Ferran Adria of El Bulli fame, has brough molecular gastronomy to Indian food through his acclaimed restaurant Gaggan's in Bangkok, Thailand (recently closed – the chef has opened a new restaurant called Gaggan Anand in the same city). Before them, Atul Kochhar took Indian cuisine upmarket in the UK with finely-crafted and presented dishes, in his Michelin-starred restaurant Benares in London. Most of these restaurants are expensive and their star dishes are not, as yet, part of mainstream Indian food. But this is the way cuisines evolve and hopefully some of the best dishes will be copied in due course and become more widely available.

One innovation which has taken roots is gol gappa filled with quirky drinks. The spicy water in the gol gappa has always been experimented with, tamarind and mint being the traditional favourites as described earlier. A restaurant in Delhi, Punjabi by Nature, introduced **Vodka Gol Gappa** in the early 2000s. The spiced liquid in this gol gappa is a dash of vodka mixed with water and various spices. The dish was a roaring success and has led to the creation of a number of unusual gol gappa variants. Not only can the liquid be spiked with different types of alcohol, the stuffing, traditionally boiled potatoes or chickpeas, can be also changed, for example to minced meat. Gol gappa 'shots', alcoholic and non-alcoholic, have become an accepted pre-dinner ritual in many restaurants and bars in the big cities. I was served six different types of gol gappa shots as the first item in a tasting menu in the Indian Accent not too long ago.

A simpler modification is the filling in a dosa, adapted to local tastes. While masala dosa means a filling of spicy potatoes everywhere, you can also have a filling of paneer, cheese, egg, chicken, lamb, pork, mixed vegetables, sweet potatoes, tofu, etc. I've even seen fillings of sweet and sour chicken for a **Chinese dosa** and baked beans, cheese and salsa sauce for a **Mexican dosa**! A non-vegetarian dosa, with a spicy, minced lamb filling, actually works remarkably well for a hearty lunch but is not as widely available because most dosa restaurants tend to be 'vegetarian only'. These variants are good for a change of taste, but for purists like me the traditional masala dosa remains unbeatable.

Indian cuisine has also adopted and adapted the pizza. Pizza is widely available in the cities in India. The adaptations are, as expected, in the toppings but also with the base itself. The toppings are essentially Indian dishes replacing the conventional Italian or American toppings. Thus, paneer tikka and chicken tikka are among the most widely available pizza variants in India. A vegetarian speciality is capsicum (peppers) with onions. More interesting are pizza-like dishes made by putting pizza toppings on traditional Indian flatbreads. So, a round naan with a traditional pizza topping such as pepperoni and cheese creates a hybrid dish called **Pepperoni Naanza**. Uttapam, called the Indian pizza as you will recall, is of course very suitable for conversion to Indian-style pizza. You only need to change the topping to a traditional pizza topping and, voila, you have an **Uttapam Pizza**.

As the cuisines of India evolve, there will be many new dishes added. Some will evolve from existing local dishes, others will be adaptations of dishes from abroad. Many of these new dishes will not be identified with any specific region but will have a pan Indian footprint. This is nothing new. The foods of India, as I've described in this book, have followed this tradition for centuries. New dishes get created as cooks of Indian food, in India and abroad, modify existing dishes or incorporate new ingredients and cooking techniques to their repertoire. Long may this tradition continue.

References

I've used a large number of sources for the descriptions of the dishes in this book. Some of my sources were home cooks but I've also used a number of publicly available sources such as cook books and web sites. I found some that I referred to many times. I've listed these below for the benefit of readers who would like to try cooking some of the dishes mentioned in this book. This is not intended to be an endorsement of the recipes in these books and web sites as I've not personally tried them out. As long as you are prepared to tweak the recipes to your personal tastes and cooking style, they should be useful.

Cookbooks
Camellia Panjabi – *50 Great Curries of India*
Madhur Jaffrey – *An Invitation to Indian Cooking; Illustrated Indian Cooking*
Premila Lal – *Indian Recipes*
Maunika Gowardhan – *Indian Kitchen*

Books on Indian Food
K.T. Achaya – *A Historical Dictionary of Indian Food*
Lizzie Collingham – *Curry: A Tale of Cooks and Conquerors*
Colleen Taylor Sen – *Feasts and Fasts: A History of Food in India*
Krishna Gopal Dubey – *The Indian Cuisine*

Cooking Websites and Videos
NDTV food – food.ndtv.com
Nisha Madhulika on YouTube and nishamadhulika.com
Chef Ranveer Brar on YouTube
The Bombay Chef (Varun Inamdar) on YouTube
Sanjeev Kapoor on YouTube and sanjeevkapoor.com

Tarladalal.com
Maunikagowardhan.co.uk
Vegrecipesofindia.com
Indianhealthyrecipes.com

Photo Copyrights

Front Cover	Front Cover	Odua Images/ Shutterstock
Back Cover	Chillies	K Pereverzeva/ Shutterstock
Table of Contents	Indian Thali	Indian Food Images/ Shutterstock
Introduction	Map of India	Awesome_art_Creation/ Shutterstock
1. Bengal	Machher Jhol with Bhaat	S Mahapatra
1. Bengal	Kosha Mangsho	S Mahapatra
1. Bengal	Jhaal Murhi Vendor	The Teaching Doc/ Shutterstock
1. Bengal	Roshogolla	Sudarshan negi/ Shutterstock
2. Bihar	Daal with Bhaat	Indianstyle/ Shutterstock
2. Bihar	Roti or Chapati or Phulka	neo_crimson/ Shutterstock
2. Bihar	Litti Chokha	Mukesh Kumar/ Shutterstock
2. Bihar	Poori Aloo	SMDSS / Shutterstock
2. Bihar	Jalebi	SMDSS / Shutterstock
2. Bihar	Thekua	Avijit Bouri / Shutterstock
3. Punjab and Delhi	Tandoori Chicken	StockImageFactory.com/ Shutterstock
3. Punjab and Delhi	Murgh Makhani or Butter Chicken	India Picture/ Shutterstock
3. Punjab and Delhi	Matar Paneer	Sam Thomas A / Shutterstock
3. Punjab and Delhi	Aloo Paratha	Indian Food Images/ Shutterstock

3. Punjab and Delhi	Chhole Bhature	India Picture/ Shutterstock
3. Punjab and Delhi	Samosa	Indianstyle/ Shutterstock
3. Punjab and Delhi	Pakora	StockImageFactory.com/ Shutterstock
3. Punjab and Delhi	Motichoor Laddu	Deepak Bishnoi/ Shutterstock
4. Mughlai	Biryani	Sam Thomas A / Shutterstock
4. Mughlai	Shami Kabab	Fanfo/ Shutterstock
4. Mughlai	Seekh Kabab	highviews/ Shutterstock
4. Mughlai	Nihari	Fanfo/ Shutterstock
4. Mughlai	Chicken Korma	Paul_Brighton / Shutterstock
4. Mughlai	Naan	DronG/ Shutterstock
4. Mughlai	Gulab Jamun	successo images/ Shutterstock
4. Mughlai	Kulfi	StockImageFactory.com/ Shutterstock
5. Uttar Pradesh	Kachori	Creative-I / Shutterstock
5. Uttar Pradesh	Jeera Aloo	Indian Food Images/ Shutterstock
5. Uttar Pradesh	Papri Chaat	Indianstyle/ Shutterstock
5. Uttar Pradesh	Dahi Poori	Soumitra Pendse/ Shutterstock
6. Tamil Nadu	Dosa with Chutney and Sambar	C K Sajan
6. Tamil Nadu	Idli	C K Sajan
6. Tamil Nadu	Tamil Meal on a Banana Leaf	C K Sajan
6. Tamil Nadu	Chicken Chettinad	C K Sajan
6. Tamil Nadu	Payasam	C K Sajan
6. Tamil Nadu	Filter Coffee served in Dabra	C K Sajan

7. Kerala	Meen Moilee	Santhosh Varghese/ Shutterstock
7. Kerala	Karimeen Pollichathu	Santhosh Varghese/ Shutterstock
7. Kerala	Appam	Sam Thomas A / Shutterstock
7. Kerala	Puttu with meat curry	Santhosh Varghese/ Shutterstock
8. Karnataka	Set Dosa	Santhosh Varghese/ Shutterstock
8. Karnataka	Bisi Bele Bhaat	Sam Thomas A / Shutterstock
8. Karnataka	Ghee Roast Chicken	Wandering Pickle/ Shutterstock
8. Karnataka	Mysore Pak	Sam Thomas A / Shutterstock
9. Andhra Pradesh & Telangana	Pesarattu	Deeksha Amrutha/ Shutterstock
9. Andhra Pradesh & Telangana	Different Types of Chutneys	Prabhas Roy/ Shutterstock
10. Mumbai	Bhel Poori	Soumitra Pendse/ Shutterstock
10. Mumbai	Paani Poori	Soumitra Pendse/ Shutterstock
10. Mumbai	Vada Pav	Indianstyle/ Shutterstock
10. Mumbai	Akuri	ManaswiPatil/ Shutterstock
10. Mumbai	Khichra or Haleem	Fanfo/ Shutterstock
10. Mumbai	Bombil or Bombay Duck	yuda chen/ Shutterstock
11. Goa	Vindaloo	Paul_Brighton / Shutterstock
11. Goa	Caldine	PI/ Shutterstock
11. Goa	Crab Xec Xec	Sankalp Malik/ Shutterstock
11. Goa	Bebinca or Bebik	exebiche/ Shutterstock

12. Maharashtra	Usal Pav	StockImageFactory.com/ Shutterstock
12. Maharashtra	Marathi Thali	StockImageFactory.com/ Shutterstock
12. Maharashtra	Kanda Poha	Azra H/ Shutterstock
12. Maharashtra	Shrikhand	Indian Food Images/ Shutterstock
13. Gujarat	Mixture	StockImageFactory.com/ Shutterstock
13. Gujarat	Dhokla	Indianstyle/ Shutterstock
13. Gujarat	Thepla	Indianstyle/ Shutterstock
13. Gujarat	Gujarati Thali	52 grapes/ Shutterstock
14. Rajasthan	Daal Bati	Indian Creations/ Shutterstock
14. Rajasthan	Gatte ki Sabji	Indian Creations/ Shutterstock
14. Rajasthan	Lal Maas	A S Food studio/ Shutterstock
14. Rajasthan	Bikaneri Bhujia	Indian Creations/ Shutterstock
15. Best of the Rest	Goshtaba and Aloo Dum	Prabhas Roy/ Shutterstock
15. Best of the Rest	Stuffed Kachori	StockImageFactory.com/ Shutterstock
15. Best of the Rest	Pakhala	Fanfo/ Shutterstock
15. Best of the Rest	Tea, India's favourite beverage	Kondoruk/ Shutterstock
All Chapters	Namaste	Manju Mandavya/ Shutterstock

Index of Dishes

Dish	Page	Chapter
A		
Akki Rotti	155	8. Karnataka
Akuri, Ekuri	185	10. Mumbai
Allapuzha Meen Kari, Alleppey fish curry	130	7. Kerala
Aloo Bhujia	19	2. Bihar
Aloo Dum	91	5. Uttar Pradesh
Aloo Potol Rossa	256	15. Best of the Rest
Aloo Tarkari	90	5. Uttar Pradesh
Aloo Tikki	97	5. Uttar Pradesh
Aloo Tikki Bun or Bun Tikki	97	5. Uttar Pradesh
Aloor Dum	7	1. Bengal
Ambot Tik Curry	197	11. Goa
Anda (Egg) Bhujia	13	1. Bengal
Anna	255	15. Best of the Rest
Annam	166	9. Andhra Pradesh & Telangana
Appam	119, 136	6. Tamil Nadu, 7. Kerala
Arisi, Arici	116	6. Tamil Nadu
Assam Tea	260	15. Best of the Rest
Avakaya, Avakai	165	9. Andhra Pradesh & Telangana
Aviyal, Avial	141	7. Kerala
B		
Badami Thandai	103	5. Uttar Pradesh
Baingan	18	2. Bihar

Baingan ki Lonje	91	5. Uttar Pradesh
Bajre ki Roti	237	14. Rajasthan
Balchao	199	11. Goa
Bangude Puli Munchi	154	8. Karnataka
Barf ka Gola (also Chuski)	180	10. Mumbai
Barfi	56	3. Punjab and Delhi
Basundi	215	12. Maharashtra
Batata Poha	214	12. Maharashtra
Batata Vada	178	10. Mumbai
Bateta nu Shaak	229	13. Gujarat
Bati	88, 235	5. Uttar Pradesh, 14. Rajasthan
Bati Chokha	88	5. Uttar Pradesh
Bebinca, Bebik	202	11. Goa
Bedai or Bedmi Poori	87	5. Uttar Pradesh
Bengali Fish Fry	2	1. Bengal
Berry Pulao	186	10. Mumbai
Bhaat	3	1. Bengal
Bhaji	229	13. Gujarat
Bhajiya, Bhaji (also Pakora)	223	13. Gujarat
Bhakri	206	12. Maharashtra
Bhang	103	5. Uttar Pradesh
Bhapa Maach	3	1. Bengal
Bharela Karela	229	13. Gujarat
Bharli Vangi	209	12. Maharashtra
Bhature	51	3. Punjab and Delhi
Bheeda Par Eeda	185	10. Mumbai
Bhel Poori (also Chaat – Bhel Poori)	176	10. Mumbai
Bhindi ka Salan	92	5. Uttar Pradesh
Bhindi, Bhindi Bhujia	17	2. Bihar
Bhoot Jolokia	259	15. Best of the Rest
Bhopali Gosht Korma	253	15. Best of the Rest
Bhutte ka Kees	254	15. Best of the Rest

Bikaneri Bhujia	244	14. Rajasthan
Biranj	227	13. Gujarat
Biryani	61	4. Mughlai
Biryani – Awadhi or Lakhnavi	63	4. Mughlai
Biryani – Degi	63	4. Mughlai
Biryani – Hyderabadi or Kachchi	63	4. Mughlai
Biryani – Kolkata	64	4. Mughlai
Bisi Bele Bhaat or Bhath	150	8. Karnataka
Bombay Duck (also Bombil Fry)	190	10. Mumbai
Bombay Sandwich	179	10. Mumbai
Bombil Fry (also Bombay Duck)	190	10. Mumbai
Boondi Raita	240	14. Rajasthan
Bun Maska	184	10. Mumbai
Bundiya	32	2. Bihar
Butter Chicken (also Murgh Makhani)	39	3. Punjab and Delhi
Byadgi Chilli	152	8. Karnataka

C

Cafreal	201	11. Goa
Caldine, Caldinho – Fish	198	11. Goa
Chaat	94, 175	5. Uttar Pradesh, 10. Mumbai
Chaat – Aloo Tikki	97	5. Uttar Pradesh
Chaat – Bhel Poori	176	10. Mumbai
Chaat – Papri	95	5. Uttar Pradesh
Chaat – Samosa	96	5. Uttar Pradesh
Chaat – Sev	96	5. Uttar Pradesh
Chaat – Sev Poori	176	10. Mumbai
Chaat Masala	94	5. Uttar Pradesh
Champaran Mutton Curry	22	2. Bihar
Chana Daal Nimki	222	13. Gujarat
Charu	167	9. Andhra Pradesh & Telangana
Chemmeen Asadh	135	7. Kerala

Chemmeen Kari	135	7. Kerala
Chemmeen Moilee	135	7. Kerala
Chemmeen Varuthatu	136	7. Kerala
Chepala Pulusu	169	9. Andhra Pradesh & Telangana
Chettinad Chicken Curry	122	6. Tamil Nadu
Chewda (also Mixture)	222	13. Gujarat
Chhappan Bhog	255	15. Best of the Rest
Chhena Poda	257	15. Best of the Rest
Chhole	51	3. Punjab and Delhi
Chhole Bhature	51	3. Punjab and Delhi
Chhole Tikki	98	5. Uttar Pradesh
Chicken 65	123	6. Tamil Nadu
Chicken Curry	23	2. Bihar
Chicken Manchurian	12	1. Bengal
Chicken Tikka	38	3. Punjab and Delhi
Chicken Tikka Masala	39	3. Punjab and Delhi
Chicken Xacuti	200	11. Goa
Chigli Chutney	155	8. Karnataka
Chilla, Cheela	238	14. Rajasthan
Chokha	25	2. Bihar
Choru	116	6. Tamil Nadu
Chow Chow Bhat or Bhath	152	8. Karnataka
Churma	235	14. Rajasthan
Chuski (also Barf ka Gola)	180	10. Mumbai
Chutney – Hari	95	5. Uttar Pradesh
Chutney – Imli	94	5. Uttar Pradesh
Crab Masala	136	7. Kerala
Curd Rice	117	6. Tamil Nadu

D

Daal	5, 19	1. Bengal, 2. Bihar
Daal – Aamti	208	12. Maharashtra
Daal – Awadhi or Lakhnavi	88	5. Uttar Pradesh

Daal – Chholar	5	1. Bengal
Daal – Kali Masoor ki	88	5. Uttar Pradesh
Daal – Mili Juli	89	5. Uttar Pradesh
Daal – Panchmel, Panchratan	235	14. Rajasthan
Daal – Tarka	40	3. Punjab and Delhi
Daal – Varan	207	12. Maharashtra
Daal Lazeez	89	5. Uttar Pradesh
Daal Makhani	40	3. Punjab and Delhi
Daal Panchratan	89	5. Uttar Pradesh
Daal Bati Churma	235	14. Rajasthan
Daddojanam	166	9. Andhra Pradesh & Telangana
Dadpe Poha	214	12. Maharashtra
Dahi ke Kabab	241	14. Rajasthan
Dahi Machha	257	15. Best of the Rest
Dahi Poori	96	5. Uttar Pradesh
Dahi Vada	98	5. Uttar Pradesh
Dalma	256	15. Best of the Rest
Dhansak	186	10. Mumbai
Dhokla	223	13. Gujarat
Dibba Rotti	163	9. Andhra Pradesh & Telangana
Do Pyaza	77	4. Mughlai
Doodhpak, Doodh Pak	230	13. Gujarat
Dosa, Dosai, Dose	107, 147	6. Tamil Nadu, 8. Karnataka
Dosa – Chinese	264	15. Best of the Rest
Dosa – Davangere Benne	149	8. Karnataka
Dosa – Masala	108	6. Tamil Nadu
Dosa – Mexican	264	15. Best of the Rest
Dosa – Mysore Masala	148	8. Karnataka
Dosa – Neer	148	8. Karnataka
Dosa – Paper	109	6. Tamil Nadu
Dosa – Podi	109	6. Tamil Nadu
Dosa – Rava	109	6. Tamil Nadu
Dosa – Set	148	8. Karnataka

Dum Aloo, Dum Olav	251	15. Best of the Rest
Dum Pukht	62	4. Mughlai

E

Erachi Ularthiyathu	139	7. Kerala

F

Fafda	225	13. Gujarat
Farsan	221	13. Gujarat
Feni	202	11. Goa
Filter Coffee	124	6. Tamil Nadu
Fish Curry	23	2. Bihar
Fish Mappas	130	7. Kerala

G

Gajrela, Gajar ka Halwa	55	3. Punjab and Delhi
Ganne ka Ras	101	5. Uttar Pradesh
Gathia	221	13. Gujarat
Gatte ka Pulao	237	14. Rajasthan
Gatte ki Khichri	237	14. Rajasthan
Gatte ki Sabji	236	14. Rajasthan
Ghee Roast Chicken	153	8. Karnataka
Ghewar	245	14. Rajasthan
Ghughra (also Gujia, Pirakia)	230	13. Gujarat
Gil-e-Firdaus	82	4. Mughlai
Goan Fish Curry	197	11. Goa
Goan Rava Fried Fish	198	11. Goa
Gobhi	18	2. Bihar
Gobi Manchurian	12	1. Bengal
Gobindobhog Rice	3	1. Bengal
Goda Masala	208	12. Maharashtra
Gol Gappa – Vodka	264	15. Best of the Rest
Gol Gappa (also Puchka, Paani Poori)	96	5. Uttar Pradesh

Gongura Maans, Mamsam	168	9. Andhra Pradesh & Telangana
Gucchi Pulao	251	15. Best of the Rest
Gughni Chura	28	2. Bihar
Gulab Jamun	81	4. Mughlai
Gulkand	46	3. Punjab and Delhi
Gunpowder	162	9. Andhra Pradesh & Telangana
Guntur Red Chilli	161	9. Andhra Pradesh & Telangana
Gushtaba, Goshtaba	250	15. Best of the Rest

H

Haleem	76	4. Mughlai
Halwa	54	3. Punjab and Delhi
Handvo	225	13. Gujarat

I

Idiappam, Idiyappam	137	7. Kerala
Idli	110	6. Tamil Nadu
Iguru	167	9. Andhra Pradesh & Telangana
Ishtu – Kozhi	138	7. Kerala
Ishtu – Mutton	139	7. Kerala

J

Jal Jeera	102	5. Uttar Pradesh
Jalebi	31	2. Bihar
Jeera Aloo	91	5. Uttar Pradesh
Jhaal Murhi	7	1. Bengal
Jhunka	207	12. Maharashtra
Jungli Maans	243	14. Rajasthan

K

Kabab, Kebab	67	4. Mughlai
Kabab – Barrah	71	4. Mughlai
Kabab – Galauti or Gilawat	68	4. Mughlai

Kabab – Hariyali	72	4. Mughlai
Kabab – Kakori	69	4. Mughlai
Kabab – Murgh Lahsooni	71	4. Mughlai
Kabab – Reshmi	71	4. Mughlai
Kabab – Seekh	68	4. Mughlai
Kabab – Shami	67	4. Mughlai
Kabab – Shikampuri	70	4. Mughlai
Kachori	86	5. Uttar Pradesh
Kachori – Aloo	87	5. Uttar Pradesh
Kachori – Banarasi	86	5. Uttar Pradesh
Kachori – Khasta	254	15. Best of the Rest
Kadala Kari	137	7. Kerala
Kaddu	18	2. Bihar
Kahwa	251	15. Best of the Rest
Kala Khatta Gola	181	10. Mumbai
Kanda Poha	214	12. Maharashtra
Kandi Podi (also Gunpowder)	162	9. Andhra Pradesh & Telangana
Kane Rava Fry	153	8. Karnataka
Kappa	136	7. Kerala
Kappa Meen Kari	136	7. Kerala
Karela	17	2. Bihar
Karhi	24, 89, 228	2. Bihar, 5. Uttar Pradesh, 13. Gujarat
Karhi Badi	24	2. Bihar
Karhi Pakora	237	14. Rajasthan
Karimeen Pollichathu	131	7. Kerala
Kathi Roll	9	1. Bengal
Keema	26	2. Bihar
Keema Matar	26	2. Bihar
Keema Pav	179	10. Mumbai
Ker Sangri ki Sabji	237	14. Rajasthan
Kerala Matta Rice	141	7. Kerala
Kerala Meen Kari	130	7. Kerala

Kesari Bhat or Bhath	152	8. Karnataka
Khaja	32	2. Bihar
Khakhra	227	13. Gujarat
Khaman Dhokla	224	13. Gujarat
Khameeri Roti	79	4. Mughlai
Khandvi	224	13. Gujarat
Khar	259	15. Best of the Rest
Khara Bhat or Bhath	151	8. Karnataka
Kheer	54	3. Punjab and Delhi
Khichra, Khichda	189	10. Mumbai
Khichri, Khichdi	65, 228	4. Mughlai, 13. Gujarat
Khubani Ka Meetha	82	4. Mughlai
Kichadi	141	7. Kerala
Kodi Kura	167	9. Andhra Pradesh & Telangana
Kodi Kura – Konaseema	167	9. Andhra Pradesh & Telangana
Kofta	92	5. Uttar Pradesh
Kofta – Malai	93	5. Uttar Pradesh
Kofta – Nargisi	93	5. Uttar Pradesh
Kohra	18	2. Bihar
Kolambi Fry	211	12. Maharashtra
Koli Saaru	154	8. Karnataka
Koliwada – Fish, Prawn	191	10. Mumbai
Kombdi Vade	212	12. Maharashtra
Kori Gassi	152	8. Karnataka
Kori Rotti	153	8. Karnataka
Korma	76	4. Mughlai
Korma – Navratan	76	4. Mughlai
Kosha Mangsho	6	1. Bengal
Koshimbir	209	12. Maharashtra
Kulcha	79	4. Mughlai
Kulfi	81	4. Mughlai
Kura, Koora	167	9. Andhra Pradesh & Telangana

Kurumulaku Kozhi (also Pepper Chicken)	140	7. Kerala
Kuzhambu, Kozhambu, Kulambu	120	6. Tamil Nadu
Kuzhambu – Chettinad Kozhi Varutha (also Chettinad Chicken Curry)	122	6. Tamil Nadu
Kuzhambu – Keerai	121	6. Tamil Nadu
Kuzhambu – Kozhi Milagu	121	6. Tamil Nadu
Kuzhambu – Kozhi Varutha	121	6. Tamil Nadu
Kuzhambu – Vendakkai Puli	121	6. Tamil Nadu

L

Laal Maas or Maans	242	14. Rajasthan
Lachcha Paratha	80	4. Mughlai
Laddu	55	3. Punjab and Delhi
Laddu – Churma	236	14. Rajasthan
Laddu – Motichoor	55	3. Punjab and Delhi
Laddu – Til	55	
Lagan Nu Custard	188	10. Mumbai
Lahsoon ki Chutney	237	14. Rajasthan
Lai, Ramdana	32	2. Bihar
Lapsi	240	14. Rajasthan
Lassi	56	3. Punjab and Delhi
Lauki	18	2. Bihar
Lemon Rice	116	6. Tamil Nadu
Lentil Rice	117	6. Tamil Nadu
Litti	25	2. Bihar
Litti Chokha	25	2. Bihar
Litti Keema	26	2. Bihar
Luchi, Loochi	7	1. Bengal
Lukhmi	52	3. Punjab and Delhi

M

Machha Jhol	257	15. Best of the Rest

Machher Jhol	2	1. Bengal
Madras Fish Curry	123	6. Tamil Nadu
Madras Prawn Curry	123	6. Tamil Nadu
Makki di Roti	47	3. Punjab and Delhi
Malabar Parotta	138	7. Kerala
Malpua, Pua	100, 189	5. Uttar Pradesh, 10. Mumbai
Malvani Fish Curry	211	12. Maharashtra
Malvani Kombdi	212	12. Maharashtra
Malvani Masala	211	12. Maharashtra
Masala Bhaat	207, 227	12. Maharashtra, 13. Gujarat
Masala Noodles	12	1. Bengal
Masor Tenga	259	15. Best of the Rest
Matar ka Nimona	92	5. Uttar Pradesh
Matar Paneer	42	3. Punjab and Delhi
Mathania Chilli	242	14. Rajasthan
Mawa Bati	254	15. Best of the Rest
Mawa Jalebi	189	10. Mumbai
Mawa Kachori	245	14. Rajasthan
Meen Kari	136	7. Kerala
Meen Manga Kuzhambu	124	6. Tamil Nadu
Meen Moilee, Molly	129	7. Kerala
Meen Pollichathu	131	7. Kerala
Minapattu, Minapa Attu	163	9. Andhra Pradesh & Telangana
Misal Pav	179	10. Mumbai
Mishti Doi	6	1. Bengal
Missi Roti	238	14. Rajasthan
Mixture (also Chewda, Madras Mix, Bombay Mix)	222	13. Gujarat
Mochar Ghonto	5	1. Bengal
Modak	215	12. Maharashtra
Mohanthal	230	13. Gujarat
Moong Daal Halwa	241	14. Rajasthan
Moong Daal Nimki	222	13. Gujarat

Murabba	99	5. Uttar Pradesh
Murgh ke Sule	243	14. Rajasthan
Murgh Makhani (also Butter Chicken)	39	3. Punjab and Delhi
Murgh Masallam	77	4. Mughlai
Murghi Ma Kaju	187	10. Mumbai
Mushroom Masala	48	3. Punjab and Delhi
Muthiya	224	13. Gujarat
Mutton Curry	22	2. Bihar
Mutton Yakhni	250	15. Best of the Rest
Mysore Bonda	156	8. Karnataka
Mysore Pak	157	8. Karnataka

N

Naan	79	4. Mughlai
Nadan Kozhi Kari	139	7. Kerala
Nalli Nihari	189	10. Mumbai
Nashto	221	13. Gujarat
Nenua, Torai	18	2. Bihar
Nihari, Gosht Nihari	75	4. Mughlai
Nimbu Paani	102	5. Uttar Pradesh
Nimki, Namak Pare	221	13. Gujarat
Noon Chai	251	15. Best of the Rest

P

Paan	46, 101	3. Punjab and Delhi, 5. Uttar Pradesh
Paani Poori (also Gol Gappa, Puchka)	177	10. Mumbai
Pachadi	164	9. Andhra Pradesh & Telangana
Pachadi – Allam	164	9. Andhra Pradesh & Telangana
Pachadi – Gongura	165	9. Andhra Pradesh & Telangana
Pachadi – Tamati	164	9. Andhra Pradesh & Telangana

Pakhala	256	15. Best of the Rest
Pakora	52	3. Punjab and Delhi
Palak Paneer	19	2. Bihar
Palak Poori	253	15. Best of the Rest
Pale Bhaji	208	12. Maharashtra
Panch Phoron	2	1. Bengal
Pancho Phutana	256	15. Best of the Rest
Pandhara Rassa	210	12. Maharashtra
Pandi Curry	155	8. Karnataka
Papad, Poppadum	20, 240	2. Bihar, 14. Rajasthan
Papad ki Sabji	240	14. Rajasthan
Paper Sweet	171	9. Andhra Pradesh & Telangana
Pappu	166	9. Andhra Pradesh & Telangana
Pappu – Gongura	166	9. Andhra Pradesh & Telangana
Pappu – Mudda	166	9. Andhra Pradesh & Telangana
Pappu Charu	167	9. Andhra Pradesh & Telangana
Paratha, Parantha	42	3. Punjab and Delhi
Paratha – Aloo	43	3. Punjab and Delhi
Paratha – Anda (egg)	44	3. Punjab and Delhi
Paratha – Mooli	44	3. Punjab and Delhi
Parwal	17	2. Bihar
Parwal ki Mithai	17	2. Bihar
Patal Bhaji	208	12. Maharashtra
Pathiri	137	7. Kerala
Patra Ni Machchi	187	10. Mumbai
Pav	201	11. Goa
Pav Bhaji	177	10. Mumbai
Payasam	124, 142	6. Tamil Nadu, 7. Kerala
Payasam – Elaneer	124	6. Tamil Nadu
Payasam – Gothambu	143	7. Kerala
Payasam – Pal, Pal Ada	142	7. Kerala
Peanuts	222	13. Gujarat
Peda, Mathura ka Peda	99	5. Uttar Pradesh

Pepper Chicken	140	7. Kerala
Pepperoni Naanza	265	15. Best of the Rest
Pesarattu, Pesara Attu	162	9. Andhra Pradesh & Telangana
Pesarattu – MLA	163	9. Andhra Pradesh & Telangana
Petha, Agra ka Petha	99	5. Uttar Pradesh
Phirni	81	4. Mughlai
Phulka (also Roti, Chapati)	226	13. Gujarat
Pirakia, Perakia, Gujia	33	2. Bihar
Pitha	256, 260	15. Best of the Rest
Pitika	260	15. Best of the Rest
Pitika – Aloo	260	15. Best of the Rest
Pitla Bhakri	206	12. Maharashtra
Pitla, Pithla	206	12. Maharashtra
Poha, Pohe	214	12. Maharashtra
Poi, Poiee	201	11. Goa
Pollichathu	131	7. Kerala
Polu	260	15. Best of the Rest
Pongal	118	6. Tamil Nadu
Pongal – Khara	118	6. Tamil Nadu
Pongal – Sakkarai	119	6. Tamil Nadu
Poori	27	2. Bihar
Poori Aloo	27	2. Bihar
Poornam Booleru, Poornalu	171	9. Andhra Pradesh & Telangana
Pootharekulu (also Paper Sweet)	171	9. Andhra Pradesh & Telangana
Poriyal	120	6. Tamil Nadu
Posola Khar	259	15. Best of the Rest
Puchka (also Gol Gappa, Paani Poori)	8	1. Bengal
Pulao	65	4. Mughlai
Pulao – Vegetable or Veg	65	4. Mughlai
Pulihora	166	9. Andhra Pradesh & Telangana
Pulusu	167	9. Andhra Pradesh & Telangana
Punugulu	163	9. Andhra Pradesh & Telangana

Puran Poli	215	12. Maharashtra
Puttu	137	7. Kerala
Puttu Kadala Kari	137	7. Kerala
Pyaaj ki Kachori	244	14. Rajasthan

R

Rabri	54	3. Punjab and Delhi
Ragda Pattice	178	10. Mumbai
Raita	40	3. Punjab and Delhi
Rajma	41	3. Punjab and Delhi
Rasabali	257	15. Best of the Rest
Rasagola – Odisha	257	15. Best of the Rest
Rasam	119	6. Tamil Nadu
Rasmalai	11	1. Bengal
Rayalseema Natu Kodi Pulusu	168	9. Andhra Pradesh & Telangana
Recheado	198	11. Goa
Rewari	100	5. Uttar Pradesh
Rista, Riste	250	15. Best of the Rest
Rizzala	253	15. Best of the Rest
Rogan Josh	78	4. Mughlai
Rogan Josh	249	15. Best of the Rest
Roomali Roti	79	4. Mughlai
Roshogolla, Rasgulla	10	1. Bengal
Rossa	256	15. Best of the Rest
Roti – Tandoori	37	3. Punjab and Delhi
Roti, Chapati (also Phulka)	20	2. Bihar
Royyala Iguru	169	9. Andhra Pradesh & Telangana
Royyala Vepudu	169	9. Andhra Pradesh & Telangana

S

Saag – Palak	18	2. Bihar
Saag Aloo	19	2. Bihar
Saaga	256	15. Best of the Rest

Saagu	149	8. Karnataka
Saaru	154	8. Karnataka
Sabudana Khichri	214	12. Maharashtra
Sadham, Sadam, Satham	116	6. Tamil Nadu
Sadham – Elumichai (also Lemon Rice)	116	6. Tamil Nadu
Sadham – Paruppu (also Lentil Rice)	117	6. Tamil Nadu
Sadham – Thayir (also Curd Rice)	117	6. Tamil Nadu
Sadhya, Sadya	140	7. Kerala
Safed Maas, Mohan Maas	243	14. Rajasthan
Salli Boti	186	10. Mumbai
Salli Par Eedu	185	10. Mumbai
Sambar	111	6. Tamil Nadu
Sambar – Keralan	141	7. Kerala
Sambar – Udupi	149	8. Karnataka
Samosa	51	3. Punjab and Delhi
Sanna	201	11. Goa
Sappadu	116	6. Tamil Nadu
Sarson da Saag	47	3. Punjab and Delhi
Sattu	25	2. Bihar
Sev	32, 221	2. Bihar, 13. Gujarat
Sev Bundiya	32	2. Bihar
Sev Poori (also Chaat – Sev Poori)	176	10. Mumbai
Shaak	229	13. Gujarat
Shahi Gatte, Govind Gatte	236	14. Rajasthan
Shahi Tukra	82	4. Mughlai
Shak	5	1. Bengal
Shakkar Pare	221	13. Gujarat
Sharbat	102	5. Uttar Pradesh
Sharbat – Rooh Afza	103	5. Uttar Pradesh
Sheermal	80	4. Mughlai

Shikanji	102	5. Uttar Pradesh
Shondesh, Sandesh	11	1. Bengal
Shrikhand	215	12. Maharashtra
Shukto	4	1. Bengal
Sol Karhi or Kadhi	216	12. Maharashtra
Sona Masoori, Sona Masuri	166	9. Andhra Pradesh & Telangana
Sorpotel	196	11. Goa

T

Tahiri or Tehri	89	5. Uttar Pradesh
Tambda Rassa	210	12. Maharashtra
Tandoori Murgh, Tandoori Chicken	38	3. Punjab and Delhi
Tarkari	16	2. Bihar
Tarkari Khichri	228	13. Gujarat
Thalipeeth	207	12. Maharashtra
Thandai	103	5. Uttar Pradesh
Thekua	32	2. Bihar
Thepla	226	13. Gujarat
Thoran	142	7. Kerala
Tikka	70	4. Mughlai
Tikka – Achari Murgh (Chicken)	70	4. Mughlai
Tikka – Murgh Malai	70	4. Mughlai
Tikka – Murgh Zafrani	71	4. Mughlai
Tikka – Paneer	71	4. Mughlai
Tilori, Tilauri	20	2. Bihar
Tirupati Laddu	170	9. Andhra Pradesh & Telangana
Torkari	5	1. Bengal

U

Ulava Charu	167	9. Andhra Pradesh & Telangana
Undhiyu, Oondhiya	229	13. Gujarat
Upma, Uppittu	151	8. Karnataka

Uppudu Pindi, Uppindi	164	9. Andhra Pradesh & Telangana
Uragaya, Ooragaya	165	9. Andhra Pradesh & Telangana
Uragaya – Nimmakaya	165	9. Andhra Pradesh & Telangana
Usal	209	12. Maharashtra
Uttapam	111	6. Tamil Nadu
Uttapam Pizza	265	15. Best of the Rest

V

Vada, Vadai	111	6. Tamil Nadu
Vada – Masala	111	6. Tamil Nadu
Vada – Medu	111	6. Tamil Nadu
Vada Pav	178	10. Mumbai
Vadi	213	12. Maharashtra
Vadi – Aluchi	213	12. Maharashtra
Vadi – Kothimbir	213	12. Maharashtra
Vadi – Suralichi, Surali	213	12. Maharashtra
Varan Bhaat	207	12. Maharashtra
Varuval	123	6. Tamil Nadu
Varuval – Kozhi	123	6. Tamil Nadu
Varuval – Meen	123	6. Tamil Nadu
Vepudu	167	9. Andhra Pradesh & Telangana
Vindaloo	195	11. Goa
Virundhu	116	6. Tamil Nadu

W

Wazwan	249	15. Best of the Rest

X

Xacuti – Chicken, Crab	199	11. Goa
Xec Xec – Crab	199	11. Goa

About the Author
Shalabh Prasad

Shalabh is a business executive with a passion for food. He was born in Begusarai in the state of Bihar in India and spent most of his early years in the eastern states of Bihar, Bengal and Assam. These years were spent in public sector townships which were unusually a microcosm of the states of India. His love for the foods of India was probably seeded at that time. Since then he has travelled widely in India during his college and working years, developing and indulging his curiosity and passion for food. He moved to the UK in the late 1990s. His work takes him back to India frequently and his love for all kinds of Indian food is only mildly tempered by the exigencies of age.

Shalabh has previously authored *India: A Beginner's History*. He writes as Shalabh Prasad using his family surname but is known in his personal life as Shalabh Kumar. He lives in Surrey, UK.

www.ingramcontent.com/pod-product-compliance
Lightning Source LLC
Chambersburg PA
CBHW060044230426
43661CB00004B/653